INSIDE LIVES

Tavistock Clinic Series
Margot Waddell (Series Editor)
Published and distributed by Karnac

Orders
Tel: +44 (0)20 8969 4454; Fax: +44 (0)20 8969 5585
Email: shop@karnacbooks.com
www.karnacbooks.com

INSIDE LIVES

PSYCHOANALYSIS AND THE
GROWTH OF THE PERSONALITY

Margot Waddell

KARNAC

LONDON   NEW YORK

First published in 1998 by Gerald Duckworth & Co Ltd

Revised edition published in 2002 by
H. Karnac (Books) Ltd.
6 Pembroke Buildings, London NW10 6RE

Reprinted 2003, 2005

British Library Cataloguing in Publication Data

A C.I.P. for this book is available from the British Library

ISBN 1 85575 937 3

Edited, designed, and produced by The Studio Publishing Services Ltd,
Exeter EX4 8JN

Printed in Great Britain   **1005918336**

www.karnacbooks.com

CONTENTS

For
My parents, James and Dorothy
and my children, Nicholas and Anna

Acknowledgements

This being the kind of book that it is, it seems appropriate to reverse the customary order of acknowledgements and thanks. My first and deepest debt of gratitude is thus to my parents and to my children and step-children, for being their wise, forbearing, encouraging and challenging selves: to James and Dorothy, to Nicholas and Anna, and to David, Sarah and Emma. Next my thanks are to my intellectual mentors and my analytic teachers, from all of whom I have learned so much: initially to the memory of Martha Harris, from whom, on arrival at the Tavistock, I first heard about something called "personality development"; and to Donald Meltzer who enabled me to think about it; more recently, to Michael Feldman, Hanna Segal and Leslie Sohn. I am particularly grateful to the many students, colleagues and patients who, over the years, and often unbeknownst to themselves, have contributed so richly to the thinking that has gone into this book. A work such as this draws on the thought and experience of a great number of people. It is hard to say a sufficient "thank you" to friends and colleagues who, at different stages of the "development" of the manuscript, have been so untiringly helpful and enthusiastic. Some have read parts of the text, others, with quite extraordinary generosity, have laboured through the whole thing, meticulously, critically and with enormous interest and support. Whatever significant omissions or questionable commissions remain are, in the end, only my responsibility. So, my thanks are to: Ines Cavill, Pip Garvey, Jeremy Mulford, Priscilla Roth, Margaret Rustin, Alison Swan-Parente, Diana Thomas, Gianna Williams; above all, to Rachel Davenhill and Rozsika Parker for the early drafts, and, in the finishing strait, to David Wiggins. Of these last, in each case the sensitivity of insight, the belief in the project and the rigorous commitment to clarity, intelligibility and simplicity have helped me immeasurably.

The book would, literally, not have been "written" but for the technological brilliance, willingness, warmth and involvement of Sandra Masterson who, under pressure, put up with endless drafts and re-drafts, and with changes of heart and of mind. More formally, but no less sincerely, my thanks are to the resources of the Tavistock Clinic, most especially to Michèle and Marcos de Lima, to Eleanor Morgan, to Nick Temple and to my own place there, the Adolescent Department. Finally, my thanks are due to Duckworth, the original Series Publisher, and to Karnac for bringing out a second and extended edition, greatly improved by Nicola Bion's generous and painstaking help with revision.

Series editors' preface

Since it was founded in 1920, the Tavistock Clinic has developed a wide range of therapeutic approaches to mental health which have been strongly influenced by psychoanalysis. It has also adopted systemic family therapy as a theoretical model and a clinical approach to family problems. The Clinic is the largest training institution in Britain for mental health, providing post-graduate and qualifying courses in social work, psychology, psychiatry, child, adolescent and adult psychotherapy, as well as in nursing and primary care. It trains about 1,400 students each year in over 45 courses.

The Clinic's philosophy is aimed at promoting therapeutic methods in mental health. Its work is founded on the clinical expertise which is the basis of its consultancy work and research. This series aims to make available the clinical, theoretical and research work that is most influential at the Tavistock Clinic. It sets out new approaches in the understanding and treatment of psychological disturbance in children, adolescents and adults, both as individuals and in families.

Inside Lives belongs at the heart of the thinking and working of the Tavistock Clinic. Its aim is to bring psychoanalytic theory to life, to make it accessible to a much wider range of readers, both lay and professional, than would normally be familiar with this kind of approach. In the simplest of terms it tells the most complex of stories: the story of the internal development of a person from infancy to old age. In so doing, it reflects and encompasses the generational structure of the Clinic as a whole, tracing the interacting influences—between infant, child, adolescent and adult—on the nature and quality of emotional growth and development.

Nicholas Temple and Margot Waddell
Series Editors

Foreword to the second edition

Since *Inside Lives* was first published, I have been asked a number of times about the "last years", about the time of life when mental and physical depradations have taken a person into that twilight life which no dawn follows. My own interest and concern has turned increasingly to these final days and to the predicament of the very old—especially in relation to confusion and dementia. Only scarce resources and very partial understanding are accorded to those who suffer abjectly diminished capacities when mental deterioration arrests, scrambles or reverses the developmental pathways which we have traced in these pages.

So, I decided to take the opportunity of a second edition to conclude the book with a further chapter—"The Last Years". This Chapter brings things full circle. For it focuses on precisely those aspects of psychoanalytic understanding and observational thought which have shaped the thinking of the rest of the book. Throughout, I have been drawing on early infant and child development and exploring those capacities which foster emotional growth in babies and young children. It is these same capacities which are also so relevant and consoling in extreme old age.

In the past two years I have had the privilege of being able to draw on some sensitive and detailed observations carried out within a single family. This has encouraged me to explore the ways in which psychoanalytic knowledge of early development may contribute very immediately to understanding enfeebled states of mind and to find meaning in some of those opaque and bizarre ways of communicating which may be all that remain to somebody who is reaching the end of their life.

Author's note

Because some of the work described in this book goes back over many years, it has not, in every case been possible to acknowledge, or adequately to thank all those involved—those to whom I am both indebted and profoundly grateful. All names and details have been changed to ensure confidentiality.

A historical note

In March 1896 Freud first applied the term "Psychical Analysis" to the treatment he was offering to his disturbed patients. Within the next decade he was to publish two works which between them encompassed a new vision of human experience and, some would argue, reshaped the consciousness of the Western World: *The Interpretation of Dreams* and *The Three Essays on Sexuality*. What the following ninety-two years have made clear is that, despite many misconceptions, psychoanalysis is a living, developing field of study. Drawing on Freud's genius, it continues to evolve new models in the light of clinical experience and defies tidy definition or conceptualization.

Freud constantly doubted, modified and re-worked his own theories. Latterly his interests began to extend to problems of the composition of the self, but the main metaphor remained that of unearthing buried cities; the main model was a medical one, that of curing symptoms; the main therapeutic method was reconstructive, the detailed establishing of past trauma as the "cause" of present difficulties.

The emphasis on the personality as a whole characterized the work with children which began in the 1920s and was to have so dramatic an impact on the theory and practice of psychoanalysis generally. The field was dominated by two Viennese women, Melanie Klein and Anna Freud. Both were concerned with developmental models and with deficits in experience, and both shared a more forward than backward looking emphasis. Yet while Anna Freud's position remained close to her father's, Klein's, by contrast, despite her locating it within the Freudian tradition, resulted in what amounted to a fundamental re-framing of psychoanalytic thought.

Klein was one of the first psychoanalysts to work directly with children, indeed with very young children. Her own analyst, Karl Abraham, memorably told her that the future of psychoanalysis lay in this area of the work. With her ideas, and those of her colleagues, certain basic psychoanalytic concepts, for example, of penis envy and of castration anxiety, lost their centrality, to be replaced by an extraordinarily rich and complex picture of the inner life of the young child, and even of the baby. In this picture it was the nature and quality of emotional relationships which took precedence, rather than ones based on the quantitative intensity of biologically driven forces.

Klein and others, notably W. R. D. Fairbairn and D. W. Winnicott, traced a crucial developmental shift from anxiety about self-survival to concern for others, emotional responsibility and a desire to repair. With the linking of development to ethical concerns and matters of value, psychoanalysis gradually became less instinct-bound and more interested in emotional life and in meaning. This interest in the formative effect of early relationships became known as an "object relations" approach, a term which, albeit clumsy, stresses the primary significance of the nature and quality of relationship between self and other.

It was with these ideas about the role of infantile anxiety and environmental failure, later detectable in the symbolic arena of speech and play, that the ground was laid for the psychoanalytic understanding and treatment of psychotic processes (regarded by Freud as not amenable to psychoanalysis) and, more recently, of autistic and borderline states. Again clinical experience yielded new insights. The origins of these severe learning and developmental difficulties began to be located in disturbances of thought, of which the emotional determinants were sought in the earliest unconscious exchanges, and in the quality of care in the infant's primary relationship with his mother.

It was Wilfred Bion, working in the fifties, sixties and seventies, whose work concentrated attention on the relationship between the way in which a person uses his or her mind and that person's capacity for emotional development. He, and those influenced by him, both elaborated and refined Klein's thinking and also took it forward in innovative and sometimes very different ways. Thus the term "post-Kleinian" refers to a number of psychoanalysts and psychotherapists who have drawn on, and are drawing on, a Kleinian framework in terms either of developing within it, or of setting forth from it on their own paths.

These changing theoretical emphases are reflected in the psychoanalytic method. Analysts and therapists have become not so much detached experts as involved participants, reflecting on their own conscious and unconscious responses which then constitute less an interference (as Freud had believed) than an indispensable part of the working method. Internal conflicts now tend to be formulated in terms of the predominance of different aspects of the self, and of a person's struggles to become free of the deadening grip of narrow self-interest; to be more open to the truthfulness of intimate relationships; to have a mind of one's own and a respect for that of others.

"Call the world if you Please 'The vale of Soul-making'"
Keats, *Letters of John Keats*, 1987

Introduction

I n these pages I have set out to tell a story. In many ways it is a simple one. It is told from my own point of view; it is rooted in one particular psychoanalytic tradition, that of Kleinian and post-Kleinian thought, and it is embedded in work which I have been doing for the last twenty-five years. But in another sense, it is the most complex of all stories: that of how a person grows up, or, perhaps, of one way of thinking about how a person grows up. The story is not told in orthodox developmental terms, nor yet as a comprehensive view of how, expositionally, psychoanalytic theory would explain such matters. It is, rather, an attempt to trace the unfolding of the inside story, of the inner life of a person, the ways in which he or she may become more, or become less, capable of having their own experience.

A forward-looking emphasis on development, rather than a backward-looking one to possible sources of symptoms, character-ized Klein's work from early on. Drawing on her pioneering play-technique with children, she elaborated on Freud's work, stressing the pervasive force of infantile impulses in adult life and the richness and complexity of the life of the mind, continuously active even when outside conscious awareness. She called this activity "unconscious phantasy". She suggested that human development was less a matter of evolutionary progress from one psycho–sexual stage to the next, as Freud had suggested, than of different states of mind, each typified by particular defences, anxieties and qualities of relationship.

Klein, in particular, was interested in the kind of factors which enable a child to acquire a zest for life, to develop valued and secure relationships, a healthy curiosity and a strong imaginative capacity. She listened to what young children were talking about and paid close attention to what they expressed in their play. She followed their thoughts, fantasies and ideas, not only about their daily concerns but especially about inside matters—about what was going on in their own bodies and in those of their mothers. As a consequence, she presented an extraordinarily vivid and diverse picture of the inner life of the young child, and, by inference, of the baby too. The mind became a kind of internal theatre, a theatre for generating the meaning of external experiences, one in which was enacted the stuff of fairy tales. Klein became convinced that a person was shaped from the first less by biological drives than by relationships, ones which originated in the first exchanges between mother and infant.

My interest is also in the ordinary, creative development of a person. So often it is some of the more troubled aspects of growing up which not only need attention themselves, but which illuminate the day-to-day processes. My hope is that the many aspects of the many lives I have had the privilege to draw on, whether directly or through the work of colleagues, will both offer some insight into the theoretical concepts which underlie this way of thinking and will convey what it is like to think psychoanalytically as well as parentally. These latter are by no means the same thing, but the extraordinarily difficult process of growing up on the inside as well as on the outside does have certain features in common with the psychoanalytic process—features which will be traced in the following pages. In each case there may be shared goals: those of self-knowledge and a capacity to have as integrated a sense of self as may be possible.

Throughout, the emphasis is less on the observable details of any particular interaction than on the possible meaning of that interaction in the inner world of the person concerned. The notion of an inner world is one which psychoanalysts take for granted, but it is important to try to be clear about what we mean when we talk about it, for it has so central a place in a book such as this. The psychoanalyst Joan Rivière, describing the Kleinian view, put the matter very clearly:

> When we speak of the inner world this does not, of course, denote anything like a replica of the external world contained within us. The inner world is exclusively one of *personal* relations, in which nothing is external, in the sense that everything happening in it refers to the self, to the individual in whom it is a part. It is formed solely on the basis of the individual's own desires towards other persons and of his reactions to them as the objects of his desires. This inner life originates at least at birth, and our relation to our inner world has its own development from birth onward, just as that to the external world has ... Thus, our loving and hating of others relates as much (and more crudely) to that aspect inside us as to those outside us. [1952, p. 162]

Such complex psychoanalytic ideas need to be made more accessible. The attempt to do so has proved a much greater challenge than I anticipated. Much remains to be understood. Indeed, it could be argued that psychoanalysis itself is only in the foothills of exploring what Freud somewhere described as "that most marvellous and mysterious of all instruments, the human mind". These ideas are not drawn on here to explain human nature, but rather to describe some of its qualities and characteristics. Philosophers and writers have engaged with these same issues throughout the ages. It is partly for this reason that I have so often found myself drawing on poetry, drama and fiction for a different, and more resonant, language in which to express such matters. But beyond this, to look to literature is to emphasize how important to personal growth are imagination and understanding, how closely related is the capacity to think to the capacity to form symbols and to derive meaning from experience. Psychoanalytic approaches can all too easily stray from description into explanation. Wordsworth well recognized such a danger:

> But who shall parcel out
> His intellect by geometric rules ...
> Who that shall point as with a wand, and say
> This portion of the river of my mind
> Came from yon fountain? [*Prelude*, ll, pp. 243–249]

In this book the concern is with the way in which psychoanalysis can illuminate not so much the developmental milestones but the growth of individual consciousness, so elusive a thing as development, the moral and emotional growth of the self, the character. In describing these processes in relation to the experience of individual babies, children, adolescents and adults, my hope is that some light will also fall upon the theories themselves.

The fact that there seems to be an underlying drive towards development in every person, as in every patient, discourages the view that adverse circumstances at one stage or age are necessarily determinant. The defensive measures which someone may need to adopt for psychic survival at one point in his life may imprison him within that regressive or self-protective mode. Or else they may come to be part of a holding operation, in which case they can be relaxed in the light of later, more positive experiences. Development, that is, runs unevenly.

The capacity to develop, to experience one's life in such a way that one can learn from it as well as about it, is rooted in an enormous range of interlocking factors for which psychoanalytic theory provides certain central concepts and descriptive mechanisms. A working and re-working of these concepts in relation to someone's lived experience, at different ages and in different states of mind, will offer the basic elements of the developmental picture presented here, a picture which will convey how a person's sense-of-the-world, and his view-of-himself-in-the-world, gradually acquire meaning and definition.

Ben Nicholson (1984) described his notion of what teaching art is all about: "It is really a question of discovering the real artistry in a person (everyone has it but often deeply buried) and then liberating this—it is, I suppose, enabling someone (or indeed oneself) to become more fully alive" (p. 6). His words well convey my own interest in writing this book, and, in fact, my interest in psychoanalysis itself.[1]

Note

1. I have Martina Thomson to thank for this quotation from her book *On Art and Therapy: An Exploration* (1997, p. 6).

CHAPTER ONE

States of mind

"Time present and time past
Are both perhaps present in time future,
And time future contained in time past"

T. S. Eliot

Notions of growth and development imply a linear progression, one most straightforwardly described in the chronological passage of time from birth to death. There is, however, something in this developmental aspect of human nature which simple chronology cannot lay hold of. It is what some psychoanalysts call "states of mind".

There is no easy psychological definition for what Eliot intimates in the poem above, and yet the lines convey something that is crucial to the endeavour of understanding what is meant by the notion of "states of mind". Any one state of mind in the present, however fleeting, is founded in the past, and at the same time it encompasses a possible future. Much rests on its nature and quality. Does it nurture the seeds of developmental possibility? Does it further confine potential growth within a static or frozen "mind-set"? Does it put development back on a reverse course, binding the personality to a past self from which it is difficult again to depart? Such states may be ephemeral or they may be entrenched. They may be ones which lend encouragement to moving on, or offer temptation to look back.

Each single state of mind, however temporary, has an impact on the personality as a whole. The degree of impact varies according to the interplay between the particular developmental stage concerned and, within that stage, the attitude of mind which is dominant at any one time.

It is certainly possible to describe the physical, and even to some extent the emotional and behavioural characteristics of any particular developmental phase or stage, but each person's experience also has its own complex specificity. His "present" is imbued with the lights and shadows of his own past, and of his parents' past. It looks forward to his own future, to his parents' future, even to his potential children's future.[1]

The theories of Klein and Bion have made it possible to think about the nature and meaning of human behaviour as it is affected by the changing predominance of different mental states and by the impact of those states on the developmental shifts appropriate to specific ages: for example infancy, latency, adolescence, adulthood. These mental states or attitudes Klein designated "positions", by which she intended something like the perspective from which someone might view himself and his relationships with the world. Such are the paranoid–schizoid position and the depressive position.[2] The theory of "positions" from which life and relationships are experienced constituted a significant shift within psychoanalytic understanding, a shift away from an emphasis on the explaining and curing of discrete symptoms and towards one in which the developmental possibilities are traced in the person as a whole, in their relation with prevailing mental states.

The term "paranoid–schizoid" describes the earlier position, that of the very young infant. It encompasses both the nature of the predominant anxiety, that is the fear of persecution, and the nature of the defence against such fears. This last is the "schizoid", or split functioning, in which both people and events are experienced in very extreme terms, either as unrealistically wonderful (good) or as unrealistically terrible (bad). This state of mind tends to be characterized by an exclusive concern with one's own interests, by a sense of persecution in the face of pain and emotional distress, and by a focus on self-preservation at all costs. It is a natural and necessary state at this very early stage. For the infant is having to manage emotional experiences which he does not yet have the capacity psychically to digest by himself.

In the subsequent position, the "depressive", a more considerate attitude prevails, with a somewhat balanced, though ambivalent, relationship to the other. Feelings of concern arise, and the beginnings of a capacity to experience remorse for the harm which is felt to have been done to the loved one, or loved ones, by the frustrated and angry self. Such a recognition stirs feelings of guilt and the desire to make things better, to make reparation. These responses are organized around an experience of the other as separate from the self, as being a whole person, possessing his, or her, own independent life, outside the narrow concerns of immediate personal needs. Such an experience, in turn, arouses anxiety lest the fragility of the other may also endanger the self. At the centre of this anxiety is the perennially complex problem of the relationship between egoism and altruism. Such a problem becomes focused in the deeply mixed and ambivalent feelings which Klein describes as characteristic of the depressive position.

The shift in states of mind from what psychoanalytic theory describes in terms of paranoid–schizoid to depressive—or of primarily narcissistic to object-related[3]—is marvellously evoked in George Eliot's novel *Middlemarch*. The description is of a young bride's disillusionment both with herself and with her husband:

> We are all of us born in moral stupidity, taking the world as an udder to feed our supreme selves: Dorothea had early begun to emerge from that stupidity, but yet it had been easier for her to imagine how she would devote herself to Mr Casaubon, and become wise and strong in his strength and wisdom, than to conceive with that distinctness which is no longer reflection but feeling—an idea wrought back to the directness of sense, like the solidity of objects—that he had an equivalent centre of self whence the lights and shadows must always fall with a certain difference.
> [*Middlemarch*, p. 243]

This shift from one state of mind to the other is one which, though first possible in early infancy, is by no means fully achieved at that time. Rather it is a challenge to which there must be repeated response throughout life.

In Klein's work there is a sense of life-long fluctuations between a predominantly selfish and self-serving attitude to the world and an attitude of generosity and concern, albeit one which is always inflected by a concern for the self. Even after a more depressive stance has been achieved, it may be that under the sway of intensified anxiety, of the fear of separation for example, a person may lose his ability to see things from another's point of view and become obstinately convinced of his own. He may slip, in Klein's terms, from a capacity for depressive concern to a more selfish set of worries about himself. Likewise he may recover his previous empathic self when the testing time is passed.

Bion (1963) tended to see the relationship between the two attitudes as a matter of a more immediate kind of to-and-fro. He schematically represented this as a continuous movement between the two poles Ps↔D (p. 102). The Ps↔D formulation further suggests a notion specific to Bion: namely, that every move forward in development entails a degree of internal disruption and anxiety which temporarily throws the personality into disarray, that is, back into a more chaotic state of mind.[4] The turbulence stirred up by internal change is intrinsic to emotional growth, hence the two-directional emphasis in the diagram. Such a diagram also suggests a constant oscillation, moment by moment, between different temporary states of mind as well as between ones which, in a more extended way, belong to the broad developmental phases being described.

This idea of ever-shifting mental states, considered both by Klein and by Bion, offers an account of growth and development in which a number of different kinds of oscillation are always present. There is a constant interplay, for example, between the states of mind which generally characterize each developmental phase. But within each phase there is also an interplay between the paranoid–schizoid and depressive positions. Mental attitudes which appropriately belong to different stages of development, infancy, latency, adolescence, adulthood, will each, at any one moment, come under the sway of emotional forces which are characteristic of one position or the other, irrespective of the subject's actual years. An adult's state of mind may be found in the baby; an infant's in the adolescent; a young child's in the old man; a middle-aged man's in the latency boy. These various mental states will take effect in relation to whichever emotional attitude to the self and to the self-in-the-world has precedence at the time. Present, past and future are contained in any one state of mind. Such states flicker and change with the nuances of internal and external forces and relationships, forever shifting between egoistic and altruistic tendencies.

Drawing on one of George Eliot's metaphors, one might describe the to-and-fro as an alternation between gazing at the self in a mirror, and looking out through a window at the lives of other people. Perhaps under the impact of renewed anxiety or loss, the gaze may return again to the mirror.[5] Trying to determine with any precision which state it is that holds sway is often hard, but necessary in order to identify those experiences which are meaningful to the growing self and how they may, as a consequence, promote development.

*   *   *

A couple of brief examples will help to clarify this complex relationship between states of mind and stages of development. They highlight the importance, both for the self and for the other, of registering which aspect of the personality is predominating at any one time. Only then is it possible to ascertain what might be an appropriate, or possible, response—one which may encourage understanding rather than obstruct it.

The first is a vignette. It describes how eighty-nine-year-old Mrs Brown suffered intense jealousy over her belief that her husband, Eric, ninety years old and faithful for nearly sixty years of marriage, had become attracted to their recently widowed eighty-year-old friend, Gladys. When asked, one Sunday lunch-time, why she was being uncharacteristically quiet, Mrs Brown described the "miserable time" she had had the previous evening at a dinner. Mrs Brown had set forth with her husband to try to cheer Gladys up. She said that the evening had been dreadful because it was clear that her hostess "was just waiting for me to die so that she could move in with Eric". As Mrs Brown reported her suspicions, she looked anxiously at her husband who seemed puzzled, apparently not understanding what she was suggesting. He simply commented that he would not want to put up with "all her awful relatives". Mrs Brown was not reassured. Only on close and explicit questioning did her husband add that the widow, too, was awful and absolutely out of the question as a potential partner. His wife relaxed and began to talk animatedly and coherently about the current political situation.

Despite her mature years and her husband's constancy, Mrs Brown became temporarily overwhelmed by a type of anxiety which is first experienced very early in life, and which is characteristic of the Oedipal feelings of infancy, that is the longing on the part of the baby, or child, for sole possession of one parent to the exclusion of the other.[6] She was unable to think or to function properly until her mind was put at rest. She found herself in the thrall of early insecurities which had never been completely dispelled. What looked to others like the wisdom of years concealed a storm-tossed self, one that was vulnerable, fragile and prone to anguish and irrational fears whenever she was faced with loss, whether imagined or real.

Mrs Brown was beset by a persecuted certainty of betrayal and abandonment. This certainty bore all the hall-marks of an infant or young child's jealous belief of having been supplanted in the affections of the person who matters most. The child is forced to realize that that most beloved person also has important relationships with others, be they a partner or children. Mrs Brown was unable to hold in mind the kind of person she knew her husband to be. She ignored the real Eric and saw only a polarized and persecuting version of what she feared. It was as if she had lost her capacity for depressive concern and had become caught up in a paranoid–schizoid state, one more characteristic, in developmental terms, of a three-month-old baby than of an eighty-nine-year-old adult. In this state of mind, Mrs Brown could turn even the most loyal and caring figure into a fickle tormentor.

One witnesses, in an exchange such as this, the way in which, at any one moment, a person may be in a state of mind which is felt to be unmanageable and impossibly persecuting. These states have to battle with other forces in the personality which belong to a more stable, calm and hopeful self. An internal battle of this kind seemed to be going on in the course of a therapy session of twelve-year-old Leroy. Leroy was on the threshold of puberty and beginning to struggle with worries about his changing body and unfamiliar sexual feelings. He was also becoming increasingly preoccupied with a mixture of emotions about his absent and unreliable father, who had left home when he was a baby. Since then his father had been constantly on the move, having children by several different partners and keeping body and soul together as a jobbing musician. On one occasion, when Leroy had just been told that his father was unexpectedly coming home for a visit, he became especially confused about his feelings, both in relation to his father and more generally:

> He walked around and made odd noises with snatches of melody and "rapp" music. His air was arrogant and at the same time uneasy. He looked at me [his male therapist] in a way which felt intrusive and he then threw himself into a chair. Lying back, with his feet up on the table, he said, "I need some puuusssyyy!...". When I asked more about what he was thinking, he replied roughly: "Oh, I'll tell you. My mum beat me on the weekend and I've got seventeen slaps on my back. You can't see them now because they've got better". He spoke indistinctly but there seemed to be a link between the "slapping" and a garbled reference to drug-taking. I listened quietly. Leroy's rather excitable state began to subside. He suddenly announced that none of what he'd just said was true. His mum had not beaten him, but he *had* had a fight with his friend Ziggy. "He said that he doesn't want me to come to his birthday party. I said I didn't care and pushed him. Then he punched me and I fell over, and I got up and gave him an upper-cut and knocked him out and then I kicked him up." Leroy paused and said, in a subdued voice, that he now felt quite guilty. He didn't think that Ziggy was badly hurt. He [Leroy] didn't want to hurt anyone. "I'm a good person really."

In this short extract we can see how different states of mind and views of the world dominated Leroy's thoughts and behaviour almost from moment to moment. His therapist knew that he was worried about his father's visit. He was afraid that his father would be cross with him for getting into trouble and not doing well enough at school. Leroy's sexually-charged swaggering indicated not only a denial of how little and inadequate he really felt, but also, perhaps, a partial identification with an internal picture of his father as a person whom he boasted about but also feared. At times he saw him as good, and at times as just "a punishing, sexy, drug-taking musician".

Leroy wanted to be big, to be part of the older adolescent, macho world of drugs and raves. His tendency to dramatize and exaggerate things ("My mum beat me ... seventeen slaps") was an attempt to mask the vulnerable, frightened and guilty feelings underneath. Suddenly, from behind the swagger, his left-out-baby-self emerged ("He doesn't want me to come to his birthday party"). Behind the strapping twelve-year-old fighter was a hurt little boy, trying to inflict pain on the other, first verbally and then physically. It was as if, in classic bully-style, these two boys sought to relieve themselves of their own hurt feelings by getting others to feel just as hurt. By his actions Leroy was communicating to Ziggy how upset he felt to have been left out of the "party". But the timing and ferocity of the attack suggests that it bore the weight of hitherto unexpressed violent and distressed feelings about being left out of his father's life. At this particular time, he could well have been especially aware of, and upset about, the fact that he was not part of the lives of his younger siblings (he lived alone with his mother). Figuratively, he was not invited to their birthdays either. In the company of his therapist Leroy could begin to think about his deep grievances, and about how his difficulties with feelings of guilt and loss constantly propelled him into an extremely polarized picture of the way things were. In this picture, the good side of himself was always in danger of being set aside or forgotten.

In these examples we gain some sense of how shifts may occur between states of mind in which "thinking" is taking place of a realistic kind, one which is linked to the known-self, and those in which, under the sway of anxiety, thinking becomes separated from its emotional base and irrational or rigid ideas and attitudes begin to supervene. The examples convey how complex an impact different states of mind and views of the self-in-the-world can have on personality and on behaviour. An aspect of their complexity is that they are not naturally linked to the chronology of developmental stages. And yet they have to be taken into account in order to understand the subtleties of personality development. This is of the essence of ordinary mental functioning. Difficulties arise, however, if any one mental state predominates, excessively or too rigidly, at any one age: that is, if there is a lack of the normal fluidity of movement from one state to another of a kind which may become age "inappropriate". It is appropriate, for example, for an infant to be infantile, less so a civil servant; appropriate for a seven-year-old to be very ordered, methodical, perhaps even a bit withdrawn and self-controlled, less so for an adolescent; appropriate for a sixteen-year-old to be preoccupied with sexual identity and with challenging authority, less so for a latency child, and so on.

If someone has had the experience of an external observing and containing mind, available to discriminate between which part of the self may be "in charge" at any one time, that person will derive from the experience a measure of some similar "holding" function, one that can then enable the different parts of the self to be in touch with one another. For if the various mental states are felt to be received, held and somewhat understood, the intense feelings, whether of rage, fear, anxiety, jealousy or passion, can increasingly be recognized for what they are. They can be known about and assimilated into the personality (see Chapter 3). This is especially so in a group setting where individual feelings may be unmodified by recognition and understanding.

It is not difficult, for example, to see how Leroy, living as he did in a stressed and economically deprived community, could become drawn further into the kind of reactive, tough and sexually provocative behaviour just described. There was clearly a survival component in this role. It was adaptive socially and not without personal satisfactions. And yet it was in many ways profoundly at odds with the more tender and troubled side of Leroy's personality.

The examples described in this introductory chapter show that there is always the possibility that a particular state of mind may, at any one time, take over, inappropriately and worryingly. Disturbances can be spontaneously overcome, as with Mrs Brown; or a child may simply grow out of them. But the disturbances may be long-term, yet latent, only becoming manifest in some later life crisis. They can also, distressingly, lose their fluidity and harden into aspects of character which undermine, rather than encourage and support, the growing personality.

Notes

1. For the purposes of clarity, I am reluctantly using the masculine pronoun "he" throughout. Since so many of the early processes under

discussion describe interactions with the mother, the build-up of feminine pronouns simply became too confusing and the he/she formulation too clumsy. However, as Judy Shuttleworth (1989) points out, the functions being ascribed to mothers can be, and are, performed by fathers and by other caretakers who are in a close, sustained relationship to the infant (p. 203).

2. For the paranoid–schizoid position see Klein (1946); for the depressive position see Klein (1935, 1940, 1945). For an extremely clear and concise overview of Kleinian theory see Elizabeth Bott Spillius (1994) "Developments in Kleinian thought: overview and personal view", *Psychoanalytic Inquiry*, 14(3): 324–364. For definitions of Kleinian concepts and terminology, see Hinshelwood, R. D. (1989) *A Dictionary of Kleinian Thought*, London: Free Association Books.

3. At its simplest, the "object" and "object-relationships" can be described as the internal representation of figures and relationships which are emotionally significant, whether positively or negatively. For example, the baby has an internal experience of goodness and well-being as a consequence of being fed, not only physically but with love and attention. As such experiences are repeated, the baby will feel that he has a source of goodness within, which he feels to be some kind of concrete presence, one which is part of him and not only something which is offered to him from without. He has a good relationship to a good "object".

4. The term Bion uses for this kind of turbulence, which is the prelude to emotional growth, is "catastrophic change", see Chapter 7.

5. See, for example, *Adam Bede*, Chapter 15.

6. Freud describes a wish-fulfilling dream, or myth, of taking the place of one parent and marrying the other. The most basic version of this longing is expressed in the child's wish to keep the parent of the opposite sex for himself and to banish the parent of the same sex. Freud was struck by the way in which these, usually unconscious, wishes and desires were described in the Myth of Oedipus, as retold by Sophocles in the drama of *Oedipus Rex*. Here the hero unwittingly kills his father and marries his mother. Reflecting on the impact of the play on the audience, Freud wrote: "Each member was once, in germ and in phantasy, just such an Oedipus". The audience would see "the dream fulfilment here transplanted into reality" (1897b, p. 265). See Britton, R. "The Oedipus Situation and the Depressive Position", in Anderson, R. (ed.), *Clinical Lectures on Klein and Bion*, London: Routledge. See also Chapter 5 and Appendix.

CHAPTER TWO

Beginnings

> "'Begin at the beginning', the King said gravely 'and go on
> till you come to the end: then stop'"
>
> Lewis Carroll

K nowledge of the internal world of the baby may be gained, or inferred, from a number of sources and in a number of ways: from the behaviour and thought-processes both of those in relatively undisturbed and of those in recognizably disturbed states of mind; from the nature of the clinical relationship experienced in the consulting room; from psychoanalytic attention to the play and dreams of older children, adolescents and adults; from observational studies of babies and young children;[1] and, more recently, from studies of ultra-sound pictures of intra-uterine life.[2] When the internal world could be said to begin is a difficult question.

This chapter addresses the circumstances of the baby's psychological birth. The relationship between the fact of the physical birth and the timing of the psychological birth has been a much debated matter. Some locate the birth of the personality several months after the actual birth; others think of it as occurring *at* birth; the psychoanalytically minded tend to establish it as taking place some time during gestation in the womb. Freud (1925) was clear that the "impressive caesura of the act of birth" should not be over-emphasized (p. 138). A range of subsequent investigations, linking intra-uterine studies with psychoanalytically informed observations during infancy and early childhood have confirmed that "nature and nurture have been interacting for so long in the womb that it is impossible to disentangle them; even the idea of nature and nurture as separate entities comes to seem much too crude to be useful".[3]

Alessandra Piontelli (1992) has done extensive research on foetal and infant behaviour based on ultrasound monitoring which she has followed up with regular observations. This work, and that of others in the field, documents a striking continuity between life in the womb and life in the outside world. It confirms the long-held intuitions of those working without the benefit of modern technology. Piontelli convincingly describes how her interest in this work was stimulated during a brief psychotherapeutic consultation (a few sessions over a span of three weeks):

> A very young (eighteen months) and very intelligent child was brought to me by his sensitive parents whom he seemed to be driving mad with his incessant restlessness and lack of sleep. When I first saw Jacob, while his parents were explaining all his troubles to me, I noted that he seemed to move about restlessly, almost as if obsessed by a search for something in every possible corner of the limited space of my consulting room, looking for something which he never seemed able to find. His parents commented on this, saying that he acted like that all the time, night and day. Occasionally, Jacob also tried to shake several of the objects inside my room, as if trying to bring them back to life. His parents then told me that any milestone in his development (such as sitting up, crawling, walking, or uttering his first word) all seemed to be accompanied by intense anxiety and pain as if he were afraid, as they put it, "to leave something behind him". When I said very simply to him that he seemed to be looking for something that he had lost and could not find anywhere, Jacob stopped and looked at me very intently. Then I commented on his trying to shake all the objects to life, as if he were afraid that their stillness meant death. His parents almost burst into tears and told me that Jacob was, in fact, a twin, but that his co-twin, Tino, as they had already decided

to call him, had died two weeks before birth. Jacob, therefore, had spent almost two weeks *in utero* with his dead and consequently unresponsive co-twin. The simple realization of this, as well as the verbalization of his fears that each step forward in development, starting from the first warning signs of his imminent birth, might have been accompanied by the death of a loved one for whom he felt himself to be responsible, brought about an almost incredible change in his behaviour. [pp. 17–18]

With proper disclaimers to any certainties or definites, Piontelli does, very plausibly, demonstrate the post-natal import of pre-natal experience. As she points out, within the more general psycho-analytic literature too, not everyone regards the event of birth as the "turning point that sets mental functioning in motion" (p. 18). Rather, some believe that it marks a point on a continuum of an extraordinarily complex tangle of the physiological and psychological threads which interact, then and thereafter, to make up a person's "self". To the crude facts of genetic endowment are to be added those of the natural environment (degrees of freedom of movement in the womb; quality of the placenta; amniotic fluid, etc.). Yet the so-called "facts" of the natural environment are themselves already significantly affected by the mother's conscious and unconscious states of mind, in close relation to her body, and to her own environment and the quality of care available to her there. There are known links, for example, between the baby's physiological development and the mother's hormonal state, diet and mental and physical activity. Physical and emotional factors in the mother's life also affect the nature of the intra-uterine world more generally. That interior world is acutely sensitive to mental states, whether calm or anxious, and also responsive to the impact of physical stimuli, of sound, light and vibration, for example, whether soothing or disruptive in quality. As we shall see in detail, at this earliest stage there can be no easy distinction between physical and emotional, internal and external factors. Each pregnancy is unique, and in each case an enormous range of possibilities will have to be taken into account.

What does the pregnancy mean to the mother? To the couple? The family? Where does the question of gender, or place in the family, come into things? Is the baby wanted? Longed for? Feared? Is the pregnancy felt to be the mistake of a casual encounter, or the consummation of a loving union? A joyful addition or a painful intrusion? Is the foetus experienced as a disturbing, alien and foreign presence, or as a welcome and secure one? The pregnancy will never, in any simple way, be felt to be precisely any one of these. It will more likely be subject to a number of conscious and unconscious shifts, back and forth, of feeling and phantasy of a kind which will continue to be expressed as the relationship with this particular child unfolds.[4]

Depending on the underlying unconscious phantasy and the predominant conscious fantasies, birth itself will be experienced as a joy, as a wonder, a relief, a loss, a trauma, a discovery; probably a mixture of all these. The actual events of the birth also make a significant contribution, in terms of the quality of experience for parent or parents and, inextricably, for the baby: the degree of anxiety, of comfort or discomfort, of technological intervention; the nature of the birth environment; the amount of stress, of danger, or of confidence. The external reality of such events may be beautiful or harsh, but the meaning of those events, and the extent to which they are felt to be pleasurable, distressing, manageable or unbearable, will be intimately related to the internal, psychological disposition of all concerned.

The attitudes and responses of the parent, or parents, in the present, will be closely related to their own past experience, whether in reality or in phantasy. Pregnancy so swiftly, and understandably, mobilizes the infantile parts of the prospective mother and/or father, each of whom may, at times, feel a neediness as imperative and overwhelming as that of a new-born baby. Irrational anxieties may suddenly erupt or bouts of unfamiliar insecurity, fear or dependency. Whether or not parents' feelings can be kept within realistic limits depends on the quality of emotional care on which they can draw, both from the parental figures which they carry in their own hearts and minds (hereafter referred to as "internal parents"), and from their relationship to each other and to their families.

Piontelli's descriptions of obstetricians and parents as they watched the ultra-sound pictures of their babies, offer clear evidence of the specificity of personality so early attributed to these foetuses: "he is a nervous type"; "he is very calm"; "she is a sort of reflective type"; "she has a good character"; "look how badly he treats the cord". These apparent value judgements of actual behaviour and physical characteristics are based on observation, but they are also subject to the predispositions of the observers. They are, at least in part, correlatives of those conscious and unconscious ascriptions of character made by all parents to their unborn children (often so graphically expressed in pregnancy dreams), and are inseparable from the parents' own needs, hopes, past experiences, self-conceptions, social circumstances, ambitions and varying states of mind.

In the face of an undertaking as awesome as the life-long responsibility for the well-being of another, a responsibility which begins with an exceptionally long period of total dependency, the most confident of parents will feel some measure of timidity and anxiety. Day-time optimism may give way to night-time terrors in which dreams are filled with fear-ridden situations. Such dreams often express unconscious concerns about the enormity of the task of keeping alive this new and yet-to-be-known little being. One pregnant mother, Mrs Price, described such an experience: "I think I first took in that this was actually happening, that I really was going to have a baby, the week I started having terrible dreams about her. I would dream that she had been born and that I was forgetting her, leaving her behind somewhere, or neglecting to feed her." Mrs Price then recounted two such dreams, ones which expressed characteristic anxieties about the strength of her maternal capacities, anxieties which turned out to be closely linked to her own early experiences. In one dream,

> I put the baby to bed in a drawer. I shut the drawer and, to my absolute horror, only remembered two days later that she was in there. I rushed to the drawer and found that she had shrunk to the size of a doll. She was all shrivelled up but still had a beautiful, smooth face.

As she thought about her dream, this mother-to-be remembered that her "starving baby" looked exactly like a china-faced doll which had belonged to her own mother and which she had been given as a child. Her mother, she recalled, had on one particular occasion, told her not to play with the doll, in case she broke the face. She had disobeyed. The doll did, indeed, get broken and was put away in a drawer with the injunction that it should never be played with again.

In Mrs Price's dream the apparently lasting guilt and distress about this unhappy episode was linked to an ongoing unconscious fear about the danger of inflicting damage as a result of disobeying the voice of an internal mother; a voice which forever threatened disapproval and punishment. With pregnancy she had become especially sensitive to early fears and anxieties. Would she again, as her dream suggested, metaphorically disobey that voice and, as a consequence, hurt her baby, just as she had hurt her doll? Was she a bad person who had no right to think that she could be a real mother if she had failed to be a pretend-mother? It was significant that she seemed so clear that her baby would be a girl. It was as if, unconsciously, she had already linked this real child to the doll of the past, and to all the complex and lasting worry and guilt connected to that terrible day.[5]

It seems very likely that the doll also represented her little sister, about whom as a child, Mrs Price had had deeply ambivalent feelings, as the next dream makes clear. She reported that on the following night she dreamt that,

> I went to a swimming pool and put my new-born little girl in a locker while I was in the water. Then I dressed and went home. Only much later did I remember the baby still in the locker. I dashed back and discovered her, hungry but still alive.

Mrs Price immediately described a second occasion on which her parents had been very angry with her. As a teenager, she had taken her little sister to the local swimming baths. Her sister had been playing happily in the baby-pool when she herself had encountered some of her own friends. Forgetting her charge, she went off with her friends, later to face the unforgettable music of "dereliction of duty", of "self-centredness", of "not-to-be-trusted". In the light of her dream, Mrs Price realized that the abandoning of her sister was probably linked to her thinly-veiled murderous aggression towards her. As an adult, she was now unconsciously terrified lest some element of this destructive part of herself might find its way into her relationship with her baby. That is, she feared that she would somehow inflict on her own baby the same kind of harmful negligence which belonged to unresolved aspects of her past relationships, both to her parents and to her younger sister.

This example invites many thoughts and possible interpretations. In the simplest terms, it becomes clear that, from the very
first, the baby's task of establishing a sense of who he, or she, is, in
this extraordinarily complex picture of inter-relating facts and
fantasies, is bound to be a very difficult one—a life-long endeavour.
Developmental potential is bound up in these earliest interweaving
skeins of physical and psychic life, in the connections and
disconnections between mother and baby, already so deep and so
subtle. No conclusions can be drawn about the precise impact of
any of these factors. But their presence is powerfully felt among the
myriad forces which subsequently bear on the distinctiveness of
temperament and disposition, aspects of which are so apparent
from the moment of birth, and in the first few hours and days of life.
The baby arrives with his *own* complex emotional life. He is also
already invested with an extensive range of others' feelings, hopes
and fears, with anticipated or imputed similarities and dissimila-
rities, for example, to parents or siblings, and with expectations of
what he will do for the parent, or couple, of what place he will have
in the family. The most powerful and incontestable of these
influences and determinants are those of his most immediate
environment, his world, the world of his mother's body and mind.

As Piontelli suggests, much thought has already been given to
the way in which physical factors and experiences affect the unborn
child (pp. 18–19). Less is known about the impact on her baby of the
mother's state of mind and of the relationship between that state of
mind and the disposition of the baby, both before and after birth.
Clinical research with children is constantly providing evidence of
amazing, and still far from understood, links between the mother's
unique experience of each pregnancy on the one hand, and the
baby's physical and psychological experience on the other. In the
following example we can understand something of the impact
upon one little boy, Tommy, of the intricate correspondences
between the circumstances of his conception, gestation and birth,
his mother's pre-natal fantasies and post-natal attitudes, and his
own early emotions and behaviour.

Tommy was referred for therapy when he was three. He had
many worrying problems. Of particular concern, were the states of
extreme terror and desperation which he would fall into when in
enclosed places. When "released" he would remain limp and

regressed for several hours. He found separation of any kind extremely difficult, especially from his mother to whom, when absence threatened, he would cling as if his life depended on remaining in physical contact. Tommy's mother was very candid about her feelings of deep ambivalence towards this, her only baby. Believing herself to be an "immature and bad" person, she had long set her face against the idea of having children of her own. Indeed, she seemed to have dreaded the idea of any kind of intimate relationship. The conception was the result of a brief encounter with a stranger with whom she had totally lost touch. She discovered that she was pregnant too late to have the wished-for abortion and became convinced that the baby she was carrying would either be deformed or some kind of monster. She suffered an intensely traumatic delivery. The pregnancy ran overterm and her eleven pound baby became stuck in the birth canal. An emergency Caesarean was performed during which the anaesthetic failed. The horrors of the "blood and gore" were compounded by the mother's agony. In the aftermath she was unable to breastfeed this monster/baby who was felt to have caused her so much torment. She lapsed into a profound and protracted depression.

Tommy was described as being acutely anxious from the first, especially over physical closeness which he seemed desperately to seek and equally desperately to reject, almost at the same time. His distressed mother described him as being simultaneously claustro-phobic and agoraphobic. His anxieties were particularly evident in his behaviour over feeding. He would characteristically hold on to the teat with all his might and then suddenly spit it out, as if it disgusted him.

Not surprisingly, Tommy found the therapy-room to be, by turn, a dangerous, persecuting, imprisoning place, and a comforting and desirable one. A particularly disturbing and poignant aspect of his behaviour from early on was, what can only be described as an apparent repeated re-enactment of the appalling experience of his own birth. Time and again Tommy would seem to re-live the terror of being totally stuck and suffocated and then of being suddenly precipitated into the chaos of dazzling light, of screaming and general mayhem. One can imagine that his mother, herself so traumatized, was scarcely able to relieve her son's terror or to render it in any sense bearable for him. At this point she had little to offer of the kind of peacefulness which might have gathered up Tommy's trembling psyche in the warmth of a mother's thoughtful, if troubled, devotion. For the experience of her pregnancy with Tommy, culminating in so painful a birth, had not felt bearable to his mother. The size of her baby, and her difficulty in helping him out into the world seemed to confirm an extreme reluctance on her part to let him be born at all. She actually said that she was afraid of setting eyes on him. It was a long time before, despite (and to her surprise) loving him, she could modify her hatred for this child who had "inflicted such agony" and who, she believed, had nearly killed her.

Tommy seemed constantly to go through sequences of terrified entrapment, followed by what looked like an experience of disintegration, ending with a weak and dazed exploration of his surroundings. He would, at times, recoil from his therapist, or from the therapy-room, as if in horror, apparently fearful of being shut up within an utterly dreadful and persecuting place. It was often the corridor (birth-canal?) that lay between waiting-room and therapy-room which seemed to engulf him with particularly overwhelming feelings. Over the weeks and months, the ferocity of his terror slowly diminished. It was as if it could be brought to more manageable proportions as a result of being re-played in a setting where, as well as re-experiencing it, Tommy could also talk about it and think about what it might mean.

The following session took place when Tommy was just four. On this occasion his therapist had felt that his initial fear of her, and particularly of the corridor, was so intense that even words might be experienced by him as too hard and intrusive. As he lay crumpled in a chair, screaming and sobbing and trying to cover his eyes and ears at the same time, she had quietly begun to hum to him, in a calming and responsive way.

> As his crying subsided, he started to uncurl from his enraged, desolate and petrified foetal position, and, tentatively, not unlike a frightened little animal, to look around the room. He began to touch different surfaces, as if to discover their texture anew. First those of his body and then of the chair on which he was huddled, and later, of the objects nearest to him. All the time he was clutching his "ba-ba-di" [his special blanket]. He glanced out of the window, gazed at his therapist and solemnly spread his "ba-ba-di" on the floor. To the

suggestion that this blanket might remind him of his Mummy and that this was a comfort to him, Tommy nodded and replied, "It's got a hole in it". He immediately began to tell his therapist the story of Peter and the Wolf, describing the dangers of the scary wolf "getting out" into the garden, frightening the other animals and eating them up. He quickly added, "It's not real, it's only acting, because it goes into the tape-machine and it plays again and again."

This short exchange seemed packed with possible meaning. Tommy appeared to be experiencing some kind of emergence from a terrified state of mind which felt to his therapist to be like a replication of the experience of an eleven pound, full-term baby first confined within the womb, and then clamped by the muscles of the birth canal, as he and his mother strained, physically (and psychologically) in different directions. We see how this emergence was closely linked in his mind to a source of comfort which was associated with his mother—the blanket. But he immediately pointed out the "hole". It is certainly possible that Tommy was indicating that he felt there to be something missing in his mother. He was, perhaps, representing his sense of her depression, of her absence of mind, or even some intuition that she wished *him* not to be in her mind, that is, that there be a hole where he actually was. On another level, however, he may have been describing an internal pre-birth experience, one in which there had literally been a hole in his Mummy, whether a birth canal or a Caesarean cut, through which he had either escaped, or been expelled, or been released, or even fallen—perhaps a mixture of all of these.

The "hole" seemed to put Tommy in mind of the story of Peter and Wolf, the account of which was immediately followed by his remark about the tape-recorder. It was as if he was impressing on his therapist that the dangerous events described in the story were not to be experienced as really going on, but were simply being "played" again and again. This sounded almost like a commentary on the events that had just occurred in the session. Tommy seemed to be stating that this "scary wolf" story was not *so* frightening because it was not actually happening. It was a "re-play" of the actual event, rather than the event itself. Perhaps he was reminding *himself* that, scary though the re-telling and re-enacting of his own birth story might be, it was, nonetheless, something which, at that moment, unlike a few minutes ago, he was able to re-play rather than actually having to go through it. He was now able to think about it, to find a symbolically effective way of expressing it, rather than having concretely to experience it. There may have been an accompanying sense, more in phantasy than in fact, that the playing and re-playing could be under his control, that it was *he* who could put the tape in, or choose not to. Nonetheless, some anxiety did seem to have remained, for he hurriedly told his therapist that although there are still real wolves, they are in zoos. "They are behind bars and cannot get out."

Tommy then said something, which, bearing in mind his initial being-in-the-world, was quite stunning in the immediacy of its unconscious insight: "How do you know if you are a scary thing?" He elaborated, "What if you are born a scary baby-thing?" In an exchange later in the same session, Tommy became preoccupied with a hole in the skirting-board. He thought it might be a mouse-hole. His therapist linked this notion to what Tommy had been puzzling over, suggesting that mice too were very little, and people were often scared of them, but that the mice themselves might be more scared than scary. Still later in this session, Tommy pulled up his sleeve to show his therapist a patch of what he called "scary skin", where his elbow had been grazed. The damage to his bodily skin seemed to be associated with the fear of there being a frightening hole in himself, as in his mother. Was there anything which could reliably hold him together? (See Chapter 4).

From these few details we can gather quite a rich sense of Tommy's urge to make his bad experiences more bearable by thinking about them, and of some of the measures which he adopted to help himself psychically to survive. The example offers a very immediate sense of how extraordinarily complex is the pattern of influences and determinants at this beginning stage. By the age of three, Tommy seemed to have a very distinctive picture of himself, based both on his actual experience and on what his mother conveyed to him. He carried a conviction that he was a scary baby-thing, a frightening baby/monster who could distress and repel the one whom he most needed, his beloved mother. His question to his therapist was how he was to know (that is understand and internally make sense of) how it was that he was a scary baby-thing. He feared himself to be, and felt himself experienced as, a scary wolf-figure who devoured the lives of others (the life-threatening baby which his mother so vividly described). And where was he better off? Was it outside, where he seemed to arouse particular horror (the wolf "getting out" and into the garden); or inside (behind bars)? Was he more scared and scary as a born-child, or as an unborn child? Both places were intensely alarming, as he so dramatically displayed; hence, perhaps, the agoraphobia and claustrophobia which so concerned his mother. Both places were extremely unsafe, impelling him to cling on, at all costs, lest he fall through some terrifying "hole".

This example describes, writ-large, experiences which resonate with the kinds of internal turmoil and ambivalence that the pregnancy and birth of a first child so often bring about. There are profound anxieties in many mothers about loss, and fears about change, which often cause anguish and uncertainty, though they may be concealed beneath the more available emotions of joy and anticipation. There is always a degree of the kind of inner disturbance which Tommy and his mother suffered particularly acutely. In their case, they each had a capacity to communicate that suffering, and, as a consequence, they found some measure of relief from its unbearable impact. The account of their difficulties may convey some sense of the intense reality of the psychological, as well as of the physical world into which babies are born. Beneath the observable "facts" of the beginnings, lies the most intricate conscious and unconscious interweaving of longing and loving, of hope, of fear, and of hate; threads which, tenuous and minute though they may be, each make their particular contribution to the tapestry of a baby's life to come.

Notes

1. Regular weekly observations of babies and young children in their home environment, introduced as part of training at the Tavistock by Esther Bick in 1948, have contributed to the understanding of their inner worlds and of their family relationships.

2. It is beyond the scope of this book to draw on the extensive range of ideas and important research into these areas from the perspective of the developmental psychologist, particularly on the subject of early infancy. Those whose research bears most directly and illuminatingly

on my present concerns include, for example, T. G. R. Bower, T. B. Brazelton, A. W. Liley, L. Murray, D. Stern, C. Trevarthan. But discussion of their work does not appear in a text which is primarily focused on the difficulty of determining the meaning to that particular person of that particular aspect of observable "development", or on the difficulty of knowing how such an aspect may be registered internally as well as externally. The two approaches are by no means antithetical, as Anne Alvarez (1992) makes very clear in *Live Company: Psychoanalytic psychotherapy with autistic, borderline and deprived and abused children*, London: Routledge.

3. Elizabeth Bott-Spillius, in Alessandra Piontelli (1992) *From Foetus to Child: an observational and psychoanalytic study*, London: Routledge, p. ix.

4. Phantasy, with a "ph", is a term used in psychoanalytic writing to describe the content of the continuous inner, unconscious mental life of a person. Fantasy, with an "f", denotes the term for everyday, conscious imaginative life.

5. There is an important ongoing debate about the construction of gender difference and the ways in which development is inflected by expectations according to gender. A clear outline of the main issues and arguments is to be found in Parker, R. (1995) "Does Gender Make a Difference?", in *Torn in Two: The experience of maternal ambivalence*, London: Virago.

CHAPTER THREE

Infancy: containment and reverie

"... a Babe, by intercourse of touch
I held mute dialogues with my mother's heart ..."

Wordsworth

Melanie Klein understood the utterly dependent baby to inhabit a world of deep gratification and extreme discomfort, even terror; in the grip of passionate feelings of love and hate, and constantly oscillating between experiences of integration and disintegration, fearing at times for his very survival. Very simply, with the nipple in the mouth, surrounded by loving arms, lulled by the sound of the mother's voice and by the gentle attention of her eyes and mind, the baby will have an experience of being loved.[1] He will have a sense of coherence, of having a centre, one which may hold even in temporary absence. Deprived of sufficiently good experiences of this kind, by too prolonged an absence, for example, or too insistent an impingement of pain and frustration, the baby's experience of the lack of good things becomes an intensified feeling of the active persecutory presence of bad things inside him. He inhabits a polarized world and inevitably the

29

ordinary turbulence of infantile life causes him anxiety, the intensity of which we can only surmise.

Bion (1962b) conjectured that what enabled a baby to bear these pains and frustrations was a rudimentary form of thought, one that became possible if the impulse to evade painful experience was not too strong, nor the experience itself too overwhelming (pp. 83–87). Whereas Freud highlighted the baby's primary conflict as centring on the life versus the death instincts, and Klein emphasized the conflict between states of love and hate, Bion added to these a radically new conceptualization. He saw the conflict as the predicament of having the desire to know and understand the truth about one's own experience on the one hand, and the aversion to that knowing and understanding on the other. The authenticity of the quest for the truth of one's experience is lodged, he maintained, in the capacity actually to *have* the experience, in the sense of staying with it, of really undergoing and suffering it, rather than seeking to dismiss, or to find some way of bypassing it.

In Bion's thinking, the model of the growth of the mind becomes an alimentary one, in which the mind is nourished by true experiences and poisoned by false ones. This kind of food for thought is less a cognitive matter than an emotional and imaginative one. Bion's notion of the process by which this very particular kind of "thinking" comes into being locates it in the quality of the original communication between mother and baby, in the availability of what amounted to a "thinking" breast. He suggested that an aspect of the primary maternal capacity to feed was, metaphorically, to offer some kind of shape to the infant's rudimentary "thoughts", initially a confusion of impulses and sensations. At the same time, that capacity to feed provided the beginnings of an apparatus whereby these rudimentary thoughts could be organized, and thus become available *properly* to be thought, and to be rendered meaningful. The "thinking" breast referred to a particular maternal function, one which would seem to follow from Freud and Klein, but, in fact, suggested a rather different model of mind, one which offered a new perspective on the nature of development. Whereas in Klein's thinking the breast had stood as a metaphor for primary maternal functions—those of feeding, gratifying, satisfying, with Bion, it stood as a metaphor for the mind. The mother brings not only her straightforwardly nurturing and loving qualities to the baby, but also her thinking self, the mental and emotional states which, in encompassing the chaos of her infant's psychic life, establish a precondition for more integrated capacities, for a more integrated self.

A helpful analogy for these rather elusive ideas is that of a child trying to do a jigsaw puzzle. We might imagine a situation in which a child is unable to see where a jigsaw piece fits into the puzzle as a whole and is becoming increasingly anxious and upset. There may be a variety of responses on the part of different mothers (or even, at different times, of the same mother), each affected by any number of complex causes. Her child's inability to complete what she thinks is a quite simple puzzle may engender in one mother feelings of anxiety (about the child's incompetence), and therefore irritability. The child, sensing this, becomes more anxious and thus less able to manage to do it, finally bursting into tears. He not only learns nothing from the experience but, having had the fun of completion drained out of the puzzle-making, he becomes inhibited about trying again—"puzzles are boring". Or else he may enter into rivalry with his "no-good" self. He may attempt to master anxiety and, in the process, to win back his mother's esteem, by intensively renewed efforts.

Another mother, sibling-like, might take the piece and simply put it in, thinking that thereby the problem will be solved, or, more likely, not thinking much at all, simply wanting to clear things away for tea. From a child who has not yet given up the fight for a measure of autonomy and a desire to come to his own conclusions, or from one who has given up and passively accommodates to whatever is meted out, tears of rage or glum acceptance are likely to follow.

A third response the mother might make is to begin by observing attentively and suggesting that the child takes a bit longer to try. A little time may be needed to gauge the degree of the child's difficulty. The problem might, to some extent, be relieved simply by the mother's being emotionally available and receptive to the source and the intensity of the distress. As a consequence the child may now be able to put the piece in himself. But no, the stress continues. Realizing that her child is still unable to think for himself, the mother turns the jigsaw piece around so that its shape more readily corresponds to the hole it is to fill. With an exclamation of delight, the child puts the piece in. By thus holding the emotional state and neither acting prematurely nor excessively prolonging the frustration, this mother enables her child to "see" what had been impossible only a few moments earlier.

In this third response one witnesses the mother's unconscious capacity to gather in the bits and pieces of the child's upset and scattered self and to offer him a sense of an emotional fit, a coherence between his mind and hers, which was then expressed in the recognition of the external shape which was now also seen to fit. Something happened between mother and child which enabled the child to feel understood. From that experience the child was able to derive a sense of achievement and self-esteem. Inseparable from this, no doubt, is an experience of being loved and of loving, and the deepening expectation of similar feelings to, and from, others.

This situation concerned an older child where matters are more certain, but a much earlier version of the process in which Bion was so interested is visible in the following sequence from an infant observation recorded when the baby was three months old:

> Mother put her baby to the breast. He sucked steadily making snuffly noises. He seemed quite relaxed, but then suddenly coughed, continued to suck for a moment and then began to cry. Mother sat him up on her lap to wind him. He was giving thin, high cries followed by a few sobs. He moved his head from side to side. His face was pink and puckered. This behaviour would stop and he would relax for a time and then repeat it. He didn't bring up any wind. He didn't ever cry wholeheartedly, just in this spasmodic way. Mother lifted him to her shoulder and his shrieks increased. She put him on his tummy on her knee and he still shrieked, throwing his head back. She sat him up for a while saying that this is how he felt most comfortable. All the while she was talking to him soothingly. She told the observer that one could feel how stiff his legs and tummy were. She decided to put him back to the breast "to see if that would help". The baby sucked quite eagerly and seemed to relax. He dozed off. She held him in this position for a little while and then, as she moved him, he woke up. She sat him up to wind him. He brought up some wind. He sat in his mother's lap looking sleepy, his head nodding forward. But when she offered him the breast again to see if he was still hungry, he sucked noisily, his cheeks going in and out at a furious rate. The rest of him was quite

still. He gradually slowed down and stopped feeding. Then he lay back in his mother's arms and gazed at her face. She smiled and talked to him. He cooed in reply and waved his hands.[2]

This mother's capacity to hold her baby's anxiety and her own, to go on thinking in the face of puzzling and increasingly intense protest and distress, drawing on and offering her inner resources, beautifully exemplifies what Bion (1962b) called "reverie" (p. 36). The mother gradually dispels the baby's distress, seeking to engage with it rather than to explain it. She is able to tolerate not knowing its source. She restrains herself from diverting the true meaning of the experience by prematurely imposing a solution of the "he must have a dirty nappy" variety. She gently talks, rocks, strokes, feeds, reflects, until her baby, basking in the calm of trustful intimacy, begins to recover. The baby is experiencing some kind of internal pain and anxiety. Physical pain and psychic pain are indistinguishable. As the pain intensifies, he becomes unable to understand or to manage it himself. With all the resources that his little frame can muster, he seeks to expel the pain. Through his mouth, his lungs, his musculature, his eyes, he tries to project (get rid of) the terrible sensations in an effort to relieve himself of them. Fortunately for him, there is a "thinking" breast/mother available who is able to take in the projections, to resist being overwhelmed by them, to render them manageable and, in a sense, to hand back to him a quality of experience which makes him feel divested of terror and capable of reintegration.

Crucial to this experience of integration was the fact that the mother had, on this occasion, understood and contained her baby's distress. The baby had been offered, and had been able to receive, a true version of himself, not one that was distorted by anxious preconceptions on the mother's part, or by imputations of something that she took to be his experience but that really stemmed from her own impatience, or her anxiety. She was not taken over by second-hand views about what was likely to be the problem rather than what she *felt* to be the problem. A baby who has this experience often enough will be able to take in these same mental functions. He will be able psychically to absorb them, that is to introject them. Slowly, as he learns these functions, they become built into the structure of his personality. In the end he will acquire the sense that he possesses an inner strength of his own and is not wholly and anxiously dependent on external help to hold him together. (For an exposition of the processes of projection and introjection, see the Appendix.)

In the *Prelude* Wordsworth describes the beauty of the mother and baby relationship, the complexity of their pre-verbal "heart to heart", the inchoate origins of the infant's first perceptions and yearnings; his reaching towards a feeling of reciprocity which might help him to make conscious and unconscious sense of his world.

> Blessed the infant Babe,
> (For with my best conjectures I would trace
> The progress of our being) blest the Babe,
> Nursed in his Mother's arms, the Babe who sleeps
> Upon his mother's breast, who, when his soul
> Claims manifest kindred with an earthly soul,
> Doth gather passion from his Mother's eye! [ll. 236–240]

A few lines later Wordsworth describes how since as

> a Babe, by intercourse of touch
> I held mute dialogues with my Mother's heart,
> I have endeavoured to display the means
> Whereby the infant sensibility,
> Great birthright of our Being, was in me
> Augmented and sustained. [ll. 283–288]

Here Wordsworth captures something of the impact and the beauty of a mother's capacity for the kind of "reverie" just described. It is Bion's term for the state of mind in which it is possible for the mother unconsciously to be in touch with the baby's evacuations or communications of pain, and of his expressions of pleasure, to receive them, to be able to engage with and savour them if calm and loving, or to modulate them if distressed and hating, and to hand them back to him in recognizable and now tolerable form. Bion thought of this capacity as being essential to the baby's ability to get to know, to centre and to understand the different parts of himself and his relationships with others.[3]

According to this way of seeing things, the mother becomes the "container", and the baby's fragmentary impulses and emotions, the "contained" (1962b, p. 90). The container/contained relationship constitutes Bion's model for the thinking of thoughts, a model for processing emotional experience which, in-so-far as it is repeatedly reproduced in the infinite flux of life thereafter, makes a fundamental contribution to the structuring of the personality. Impulse life may thus become bound by thought rather than merely enacted and re-enacted. Initially the mother thinks *for* the infant. Slowly the infant learns to perform that function for himself, so that later the mother, or parent, may think *with* him.

The process is captured in J. M. Barrie's description in *Peter Pan* (1911) of the child's sense of his thoughts being "sorted" by a mind capable of understanding and holding his mental states.

> Mrs Darling first heard of Peter when she was tidying up her children's minds. It is the nightly custom of every good mother after her children are asleep to rummage in their minds and put things straight for the next morning, repacking into their proper places the many articles that have wandered during the day. If you could keep awake (but of course you can't) you would see your mother doing this, and you would find it very interesting to watch her. It is quite like tidying up drawers. You would see her on her knees, I expect, lingering humorously over some of your contents, wondering where on earth you had picked this thing up, making discoveries sweet and not so sweet, pressing this to her cheek as if it were as nice as a kitten, and hurriedly stowing that out of sight. When you wake in the morning, the naughtiness and evil passions with which you went to bed have been folded up small and placed at the bottom of your mind; and on the top, beautifully aired, are spread out your prettier thoughts, ready for you to put on. [p. 12]

Inner states of disparate and confused sensation can only be understood and thought about (in the sense of emotionally engaged with) if they correspond, in some ordinary and basic way, to external experience. What is felt can then become imbued with meaning in that it accords, often enough, with the response to it from the outside world. Initially this response is on the part of the mother or mother figure. Such a congruence was evident in the infant observation described above and in the jigsaw puzzle example. The issue is that of being able to make sense of one's own feelings as a consequence of having had sense made of them by a thinking other (1962a, p. 119).

A distressed baby who is "hungry", be it for food, for attention, or for company, will do his utmost to communicate that distress. He is unable to locate it in any way other than the undifferentiated expression of pain. He cries. Disregarding the fact that he has recently been fed, his intuitive and discerning mother may think to offer him the breast before he becomes too upset to take it. Thus not only does she meet his physical need, but also, psychically she gives him the experience of being understood. If this happens consistently enough, gratification may come to answer need in acts of intimacy that the baby can begin to count on. In this reciprocity of feeling there is a sense both of beauty and of truthfulness (1962a, p. 119). The baby experiences an integration of the different parts of himself which originates in his immediate environment, in his mother's heart and mind, but which may slowly be felt to become part of his own internal self, of his very backbone, the centre of his being. It is an experience of being held in a primary emotional "psychic skin", equivalent to the physical skin which holds the parts of the body together. In good circumstances, that is if sufficiently held—psychically and emotionally—by a containing presence, the baby slowly derives a sense of having an internal holding capacity of his own, an experience of integration which is a necessary prerequisite to continued development.

Implicit in Bion's idea of the maternal capacity for reverie is the presence of an unconscious process of a particular kind, one which forms a basis for the sort of reflective self-consciousness which defines the difference between theories of mental development (cognition) and of personality development (character). The essential elements of this unconscious process are caught in a thought of Yeats's: "It must go further still: that soul must become its own betrayer, its own deliverer, the one activity, the mirror turn lamp" (1933).

The reflective and transformative qualities evoked by the metaphor of "the mirror turn lamp" are inherent in Bion's model of the mind. The metaphor defines the divide between a notion of mind as a mere reflector of external objects, or, by contrast, as "a radiant projector that makes a contribution to the object it perceives".[4] It is this latter conception which, as we have seen, is conveyed in the idea of the "thinking" breast. Bion deepened and extended existing theory of early infantile development into a sense of a very particular relationship in which the mother proffered not only loving, nurturing, nourishing qualities to the baby, but also formative mental ones, of the sort that could be drawn on to *make sense* of experience; that could make meaning available and thus could *actively* contribute to the growth of the mind.

The mother's relationship to her infant is not one simply of reflecting moods and impulses, and thereby enabling the baby to get to know himself by a process of mirroring, of recognition of self-in-other, but rather one of having an actively participatory role in *doing* something with the projected emotions. What is being described as taking place is an unconscious processing of the baby's instinctive communications and evacuations, which can be depicted as a sort of chaos of impulse, pain and desire, in which mental and physical, self and other, are hardly distinguishable. These, as yet meaningless, fragments of disconnected sensation are what Bion (1962b) referred to as sense data or sense impressions (pp. 6, 26). For the baby to turn the sense data of experience into his own reflexive mind, he needs a primary experience of *active* holding by his mother's mind.

To this process of actively holding the baby's mental state, Bion (1962b) ascribed the term "alpha-function", his way of designating the very earliest unconscious means whereby the mother may mentally "serve" her baby, by contrast with merely meeting his creature needs (pp. 25–27). It constituted a containment of fragmented aspects of psychic experience of a kind that lent shape and form to the baby's *own* emotions: neither imposing feeling from without nor merely reflecting it back. Another term for the process, synonymous with alpha-function, is "symbol-formation". These notions will need some clarification. The example of the jigsaw puzzle described the difference between a response which fosters a child's capacity to find shape and form, and one which impedes it. A degree of receptivity to the distinctive nature of the child's anxiety and frustration is necessary in order to transform that troubled state of mind into something that is reasonably manage-able, that is, manageable enough for him to be able to understand the nature of his experience. Once the experience has been understood, it becomes possible to express it symbolically, to learn from it, and to develop beyond it. In other words, a prerequisite for the finding of shape and form in recognizable symbolic terms (be those of word, or of play, or of song) is the unconscious process of the gathering up of disparate emotion and sensation—the process of unconscious symbol-formation, or of alpha-function. This is a capacity which, in good circumstances, is slowly acquired by the baby from the mother. It is an unconscious process which is continuously worked on in the course of a life-time and may, therefore, be described in the sixty-year-old (see Chapter 13) quite as much as in the six-month-old.[5]

*   *   *

That such a process was in train could be inferred from the way in which Anne, an eleven-year-old, began to emerge from her habitual frozen and uncommunicative state and to risk entrusting some of her thoughts and feelings to her therapist. Details from her first session of psychotherapy may give further insight into the difficult area of what is meant by "symbol-formation", as opposed to the more familiar process of forming symbols. Anne had been a victim of severe child sexual abuse and, as a consequence, had been fostered into a supportive, though busy, family. She was deeply unhappy and very disturbed. Her foster parents' main concerns were that she compulsively masturbated, pulled out her hair and resisted any form of intimacy. She was suspicious, provocative, reticent and apparently unable to learn. In desperation they referred her to the local Child and Family Consultation Service. Her three assessment sessions had taken place just before the long summer-holiday break, after which she was due to begin regular therapy. The assessment had been characterized by extreme resistance on Anne's part: darkly untrusting, she had met her therapist's comments with silent dismissal or contemptuous rebuff. Her therapist had felt inadequate and disliked. She had struggled hard with her own feelings of guilt about her distaste for such an icy, quietly sadistic and unsympathetic child. In the last meeting, however, there had been a slight thaw. Anne had made a couple of "play-doh" figures with some care. Her therapist had preserved them over the holiday in a plastic container which she had placed in Anne's box of therapy toys.

Anne returned to therapy in September to discover, to her astonishment and pleasure, that her figures had been carefully kept intact. She smiled fleetingly at the recognition that she herself had been kept in mind. Unusually, she began painting, and as she did so her therapist reflected that she was herself experiencing an unwonted feeling of warmth towards Anne—a change of mood from the assessment sessions which had been so cold and agonizing. She asked Anne about the painted figures. Anne shrugged and, for the first time, smiled properly. With some reticence she ventured that she wasn't very good at painting, and that she had made something better at school. With her hands, Anne made a shape that looked like a vase. Again in gesture, she added what seemed to be a lip and a handle. "Oh, you made a *jug*", said her therapist. "Yes", Anne replied, "but I didn't do it on one of those things (again she gestured), I made it myself". "So you didn't use a *wheel*?" "No, but it broke in the thing" (another gesture). "You mean it blew up in the *kiln*?" She nodded and turned back to her figures, which she now began executing with extreme accuracy and precision.

Anne had had very little experience of being kept in anyone's mind in a genuinely consistent or thoughtful, as opposed to sporadic or abusive way. The impact of the discovery that her therapist had preserved (remembered and thought about) something which she had made and which mattered to her, was immense. It could be suggested that such a realization (in this, her first proper session of therapy) enabled her to take further tentative communicative steps. In the context of what was beginning to be felt to be a safe place/mind. It emerged that the object which she had tried, and failed, to make was, indeed, a jug—a container, one might say—which had exploded in the kiln. Anne had not been able to find a specific word for "handle" or "lip". She had merely gestured and hoped to be understood. Her therapist *had* understood. She articulated the gestures, giving them a voice (lip) and therefore offering Anne a "handle" on the matter. She did, indeed, provide "symbols", of a kind, for Anne's efforts to communicate the jug/handle/lip/wheel/kiln aspects of her achievement.

Despite Anne's unhappy and fractured life she was able to draw on her therapist's capacity to bear her pain and to keep her in mind. As a consequence, she herself became able to begin to engage with the meaning of her experience. In technical language, we could say that, by way of symbol-formation, Anne's therapist was able to gather up the as-yet-unthinkable aspects of her experience, the senseless bits and pieces (what Bion, 1962b, called "beta-elements"), into more meaningful bits and pieces (alpha-elements) (p. 6) which could then become the basis for further, and more recognizably symbolic forms of expression, of the kind found in dreaming, playing or naming—the jug, the wheel, the kiln, for example. The containing structure of the therapy and of the therapist's mental and emotional capacities provided "a local habitation and a name" (*A Midsummer Night's Dream*, V, i, l.7) for Anne's fragmentary thoughts and impulses. She could experience the cohering power of the process whereby words were given to feelings. She could feel something of the creative, indeed transformative, effect of that process.

Writing of the inexhaustible nature of the unconscious and of the creative processes, Hanna Segal (1994) offers what is, in effect, a description of what happened between Anne and her therapist. Segal quotes:

> To give a thing a name, a label, a handle; to rescue it from anonymity, to pluck it out of the Place of Namelessness, in short to identify it—well, that's a way of bringing the said thing into being.[6] [p. 63]

The individual details of Anne's early life would echo innumerable stories of children fostered, or in care, whose experiences of being dropped or passed on are etched deeply in their frantic searching for sources of comfort. Yet, despite her difficulties, Anne seemed to have the capacity to sustain hope. In her therapist she found someone who had not only undertaken to be available to her for the foreseeable future, but who was, indeed, still there after the summer holiday, unlike so many of her care-workers in the past. The therapist was physically there, but she was also mentally and emotionally there. She had valued, remembered and preserved the first creative attempts which, at the time, Anne had fiercely disparaged ("They are nothing really, just rubbish"). The therapist had thereby established the beginnings of a securely dependent relationship. The meaning that emerged from Anne's scarcely articulated "story" of the jug and the kiln, indicated that behind her defensive retreats into sensual and self-mutilating behaviour, there remained a capacity, in the receptive environment of another's mind, to "think" about her experience, however catastrophic, and therefore potentially to learn from it. That experience had hitherto been so painful that it had been impossible for Anne to make any sense of it.

The state of mind in which symbol-formation, or alpha-function, can occur, the unconsciously receptive capacity which initiates in the baby, the child or adult, the potential for making sense of himself-in-the-world, is one which is bound to be variable. The opportunity to know oneself, and hence to develop *as* oneself, requires the availability of a presence which has qualities of receptiveness and responsiveness, based in self-knowledge and in a sense of inner worlds which are honest, not counterfeit. As a consequence, a view of the world may develop which is based in the desire to understand, rather than in the need to "know". (Bion differentiates between "becoming a walker" and "learning about walking", a distinction between an extension of the capacities of the self, by contrast with an addition to the stock of knowledge; see Chapter 7.) Experience is transformed into growth when it is possible to learn from that experience. This process is dependent on the quality of interaction between container and contained, on the integrity and reciprocity of that interaction, by contrast with the "subtle proliferation of mythology and lies which in differing degrees obstruct the search for truth" (Harris, 1981, p. 322).

A figurative way of expressing the significance to the infant's psychic well-being of this mutually concordant relationship is that he needs to have access to a breast which is perceptive and transformative. By no means does such a relationship have to be available all the time but it should be available enough of the time for the child to be able to "grow through" the absences, whether of body or of mind. Harris writes of "a mind that grows through [the child's] introjecting experiences of himself in the world, impelled to think in order to retain internally relationships with needed and valued objects in their absence" (p. 322).

If the mother rightly interprets the source of distress and the communicated need sufficiently often, the baby will have the experience not just of having his physical discomfort relieved but also of being understood. Most mothers have an ordinary unconscious amount of attunement to their baby's needs and communications, simply by virtue of the love they feel for their child. Winnicott's notion of the "good enough mother" conveys precisely this sense. Moreover the good mother is not the one who denies her hatred and aggressive feelings but the one who knows about them and is able to tolerate them in herself.[7]

By contrast, a baby whose mother defensively "knows" what is wrong and answers a cry of hunger with "he's got a dirty nappy", or a cry of fear with "he's tired", will have an experience, if this happens too much of the time, of being actively *mis*understood, such that a mother hostile to understanding will be experienced and taken in—a frightened self perhaps, divested of meaning, because there is no "common sense", no experience of correspondence between the need felt and the response given.[8] Such a baby will have more difficulty in getting to know and to accept himself, as distinct from trying to accommodate to what appears to be required, or attempting to reject the projected picture of, for example, "he's a difficult baby, he'll be the death of me" (see Chapter 4).

Those experiences that make sense do so because they are underpinned by emotional authenticity. They are therefore the ones that can be learnt from. Those experiences which do not make sense have to be either artificially accommodated in the personality (the roots of Winnicott's "false-self") or extruded elsewhere, coming to hinder rather than to foster growth. The question of whether or not an experience is one which promotes development depends on the quality of interaction which occurs in the complex communications between child and mother from the earliest stage—the mother's own idiosyncratic capacities being matched with those of her baby.

The main purpose of this chapter has been to convey something of the subtlety and complexity of the earliest communications between mother and infant, in particular those which promote individual thinking capacities and further the child's confidence, spontaneity and interest. If the quality of these early infantile relationships is sufficiently good and true, not only will a prototype for subsequent relationships and modes of learning from experience become established, but a capacity will be engendered for sincerity and trust between self and other as the basis for further development.

Notes

1. It should be emphasized here that Klein referred to the "breast" as an emblem for intimacy. She always stressed that what was important was the quality of intimacy and not the issue of whether the feeding relationship was literally one of breast or bottle. In Klein's thinking the

breast represented the feeding relationship, both literally and metaphorically.

2. Judy Shuttleworth (1984) "On containment". Unpublished manuscript.
3. See also, Britton, R. (1998) "Wordsworth: The Loss of Presence and the Presence of Loss", in *Belief and Imagination*, London: Routledge. For a brief account of the processes of projection and introjection; of projective identification and introjective identification, see the Appendix.
4. Abrams, M. H. (1953) "Changing Metaphors of Mind", in *The Mirror and the Lamp: Romantic Theory and the Critical Tradition*, Oxford: OUP. Abrams uses the lines just quoted from Yeats as the epigraph to this book.
5. It is the process on which Theseus reflects towards the end of Shakespeare's *A Midsummer Night's Dream*:

    And as imagination bodies forth
    The forms of things unknown, the poet's pen
    Turns them to shapes, and gives to airy nothing
    A local habitation and a name. [V, i, 14–17]

6. Segal, H. (1994) "Salman Rushdie and the sea of stories: A not-so-simple fable about creativity", *International Journal of Psychoanalysis*, 75: 611–618; repr. Steiner, J. (ed.) (1997) *Psychoanalysis, Literature and War*, London: Routledge.
7. Parker, R. (1995) *op. cit.*
8. Bion (1962a) used the notion of "common-sense" in a very specific way. It described an integrated view of the world which was based on a corresponding integration of the self, a balance between those different aspects of the self which were founded in, or relied upon, data derived from the different senses, such as sight, hearing, touch etc. He regarded the sense of truth as being based on the combining of different emotional views of a person, or a relationship (p. 119).

CHAPTER FOUR

Infancy: defences against pain

"That element of tragedy which lies in the fact of frequency, has not yet wrought itself into the coarse emotion of mankind; and perhaps our frames could hardly bear much of it. If we had a keen vision and feeling of all ordinary human life, it would be like hearing the grass grow and the squirrel's heart beat, and we should die of that roar which lies on the other side of silence"

George Eliot

I n the previous chapter we saw how, if sufficiently held psychically and emotionally by a containing presence, the baby develops a sense of his own internal holding capacity, an experience of integration, of having a centre. But many babies do not have the opportunity to discover themselves in a mind that is able to register their gusts and storms, passions and pleasures and to respond accordingly. For in many mothers birth arouses joy, but also unforeseen difficulties. Their own emotional life becomes shadowed by depression, by unfamiliar feelings of loss, ambivalence or confusion. Responsibility for the very survival of a new life may weigh heavily and the physical and psychological disturbance be felt as a burden rather than as a discovery. The infant may only occasionally find the resonance and reciprocity he seeks and may, from very early on, have to struggle with the impact of emotional absence, despite physical presence.

Adverse experiences of any kind will be marked in the personality, rather as shakes in timber give evidence of periods of drought (to use Meltzer's metaphor, 1988, pp. 25–26). The tree continues to grow and perhaps to flourish but the core has been affected. So too the inner life of the growing child is marked by periods of emotional drought. Defensive measures against the experience of pain may have to be adopted from the earliest age, ones that are drawn on to protect the vulnerable self from experiencing the fear of disintegration which is felt to be potentially overwhelming.

Distracted, depressed or puzzled by, for example, the restlessness and distress of her baby, despite having been recently fed, a mother may decide that his nappy needs to be changed, or that he wants to be put to bed. This mother may have difficulty in being in touch with the quality of her baby's communications and may also, perhaps, prefer "doing" to "being". This baby will have the experience of *not* being understood which, if too frequent, will be confusing to his ability to investigate, and therefore to organize, an integrated sense of the relationship between the experience of hunger which he has inside himself, and what seems to be happening outside. A persecutory feeling is aroused in relation to something which is felt to be hostile to understanding. In such circumstances the baby not only has no sense of coherence between internal and external experiences, but he is also subjected to a malign mismatch, in the face of which he has to find alternative sources of strength to bolster his fragile efforts at psychic survival.

This experience of an absence of primary containment on the part of a mother who, for whatever reason, cannot be available and responsive to her baby's communications, is part of normal development. Any number of factors will bear on whether or not a mother is able to make sense of her baby's tentative, or tyrannical emotional cues. Externally, she may herself be ill-supported, depressed, pressurized by circumstantial worries, traumatized by a difficult birth. Or, internally, she may be especially affected by her private hopes and fears about the baby's role in her life and his relationship to past and future figures. She may manage emotionally to be present some of the time, but with an inconsistency which will puzzle and confuse her baby.[1] Too much emotional absence is felt as an insecure or "leaky" form of containment. It may be inferred from later accounts of very fragmented states of mind, that the baby feels that he is literally falling apart. In the face of an experience of not having his feelings taken in and understood, or of having nowhere to put them, that is, lacking a "psychic" skin to hold his emotional self together, the baby can draw on a range of tactics to help him to tolerate temporary absence or adversity.

The infant's immediate impulse, as we have seen, is to get rid of the painful experience by pushing it elsewhere, by projecting it. Crying, farting, defecating, urinating, vomiting may be impulsive attempts, emotionally as well as physically, to expel the discomforting feeling. In good circumstances this will occur in the context of a breast, or "thinking breast", which has the capacity emotionally to digest the pain and thus to render the experience meaningful, in the sense that its source and the nature of its impact have been understood. Inherent in this experience is a feeling that it has been possible to push, or put, emotions elsewhere, that is, *into* something (the other), and also to take them back inside, likewise *into* something (the self). In other words, this is a three-dimensional experience of the existence of an interior, or inside space.

In the absence of a containing presence, the individual, at whatever point in life, will resort to an array of defensive mechanisms to help him retain as great a sense of integration as he can muster. These mechanisms are detectable in infancy and thread themselves through the different phases of the life cycle. They will necessarily be drawn on, in the short-term, as immediately available measures to alleviate anxiety and to retain, or retrieve, some kind of equilibrium. But if they have to be resorted to too often, or for too extensive a period of time, they may become "built-in" as aspects of character, rather than functioning as temporary respites.

The central question is whether powerful emotions are felt to be bearable; whether there is a sense that mental states of intense love or hatred, of gratification or abandonment, can be engaged with, borne, processed and digested; whether a genuine link can be established between a mother and child which is felt to be a thoroughfare for feelings.

If the emotions are not felt to be bearable the consequences are stark:

> Normal development follows if the relationship between infant and breast permits the infant to project a feeling, say, that it is dying into the mother and to reintroject it after its sojourn in the breast has made it tolerable to the infant psyche. If the projection is not accepted by the mother the infant feels that its feeling that it is dying is stripped of such meaning as it has. It therefore reintrojects, not a fear of dying made tolerable, but a nameless dread ...

> The rudimentary consciousness cannot carry the burden placed on it. The establishment internally of a projective-identification-rejecting object means that instead of an understanding object the infant has a wilfully misunderstanding object—with which it is identified. Further its psychic qualities are perceived by a precocious and fragile consciousness. [Bion, 1962a, 1967, pp. 116–117]

The epithet "nameless dread" (1962b, p. 96) describes the experience of a baby who not only does not have available to him a mind into which he can project his distress, but whose distress becomes terrifyingly augmented both by the discovery that this is so and by the fact that the weight of his own feelings is thereby being added to. For the primary presence which should be relieving him of his distress is now actively increasing it. The term "nameless dread" catches the essence of such an experience: the experience has no nameable shape or form of a kind which could render it meaningful, even negatively. The epithet describes a losing of any vestige of meaning because the incipient capacity to establish possible meaning has been reversed (Bion, 1962b, calls this process the "reversal of alpha-function", p. 25). No correspondence of thought or feeling can be found. Even a terrible one, for example that the fear of dying has been understood, is stripped of the sort of resonance which might make it more bearable. Ronald Britton describes such a state of mind as one of "psychic atopia".[2]

When psychic pain is felt to be unheld and therefore unbearable, there may be a withdrawal into a closed-off state of petrified emotional isolation. The baby, or child, may retreat to a deeply withdrawn, or borderline state, unable to allow anything in, so traumatic to the self's emotional survival has the "loss" of the needed presence (physically or psychically) been felt to be. In some cases there may be a literal refusal to take things in, whether partial or regulated, as manifest, for example, in eating disorders—even in infancy. Such a refusal is not an uncommon response to what Gianna Williams (1997) describes as a "convex container", one that pours projections into the baby rather than receiving them from him.[3] Alternatively, a child may attempt to project all the more forcefully, mentally, and later perhaps physically, battering away at the resistant surface of the mother's mind—sometimes with the tragic result of being physically battered in return, as the mother, unable to bear the anger, tries to "push it back" into the baby.

Unless he is to give up, or to give in, the deprived or frantic child has to make desperate attempts to deal with his unbearable emotional experiences. These constitute primitive and extreme psychic defences against overwhelming pain and anxiety. As long as the ordinary pain and anxiety of everyday life is not felt to be unmanageable, defensive measures may be observed which offer necessary and appropriate balm. It is only if resorted to too much of the time, that these defences result in a lasting impact on the personality.

Esther Bick posited a stage prior to the three-dimensional world of projection and introjection, a more primitive two, or even one-dimensional mode of functioning. This is a defensive system which may be drawn on when an experience of psychic containment has been lacking from so early on that scarcely any external or internal holding capacity is felt to exist. The baby will seek some psychic equivalent to the physical skin which enfolds his body, in an effort to create for himself a sense that the rudimentary parts of his personality can somehow be made to cohere. Attempts can be observed to create a kind of continuous, containing, skin-equivalent —what Bick calls a "second-skin". There are many ways in which the infant tries to bring such a defensive structure about, each with a distinctive "sticky" or adhesive quality: for instance, by fixing attention onto a sensory object, whether visual (for example, a light bulb); auditory (possibly a repetitive sound); tactile (the experience of being clothed, or of surface contact); muscular (the tensing, or clenching and unclenching, of bodily parts); or by repetitive movement (stroking, tonguing, fiddling). These babies seem to be attempting to hold themselves together as if threatened by a sense that they may at any moment fall to pieces. In later life, the tendency literally to be "buttoned up", or to stride up and down, never to stop talking (to have the "gift of the gab"), may serve a similar function. The "second-skin" phenomenon constitutes a form of primitive omnipotence and is felt to serve a primary survival function.

The following example illustrates the survival mechanism provided by holding on to a visual sensory stimulus:

> On arrival the observer noticed that the mother looked tired and depressed. The mother had commented on the dark winter afternoon, and on her feeling of isolation with her baby. Later in the observation, after the baby had been bathed and fed, the mother brought her into the kitchen and sat her in her baby seat on the table. At this point, the husband returned home from work and, having greeted the observer, immediately began telling his wife of some incident at work. The baby began to make demanding noises, getting louder and louder as she was ignored. The mother noticed this and went to the baby, lifting her up briefly and then putting her back in her chair. She turned back to her husband who was also wanting her attention. The baby squirmed and wriggled in apparent distress, looked upwards, saw the light and stared at it. Her face and body relaxed and she smiled at the light, making a brief cooing noise. On turning back to the baby to see what had quietened her, the mother's face registered distress, even hurt. She asked why the baby was staring at the light, as though she feared that something was wrong, and that she may have driven the baby into this sort of behaviour by her intolerance. [Symington, J., 1985, p. 482]

One can observe the ordinary ways in which the infant resiliently and appropriately seeks a temporary source of solace and coherence in the absence of a focus for the needed sense of integration. Yet if babies have to draw on their own devices for too much of the time, living within a second-skin can be felt to be a necessity and become a habit. This kind of shell can protect the baby from feelings of psychic disintegration and panic, but it also cuts him off from the external world. Bion invoked the term "exo-skeleton" for this form of psychic defence, one which forms in the absence of an endo-skeletal structure of the kind which develops out of confident dependency on internalized containing functions. The "second-skin" can constitute a pseudo-independence; *as if* the individual were autonomous, while really psychically, if not actually, he is always seeking to stick himself to a surface in a way which is felt to be essential to ongoing existence. George Eliot has an image for such a personality: she describes Hetty in *Adam Bede* as being like one of those climbing plants which, when torn from their native nook of rock or wall to which they cling, have such shallow roots that they will, if simply laid over an ornamental flowerpot, immediately attach themselves and "blossom none the worse".[4]

In her therapy sessions, an adult patient, Miss Pearce, would often describe her emotional states in "Bick-like" language. With great articulacy she would talk about feeling that she was "falling apart", "disintegrating", "liquefying", "falling through holes", "spilling out". Around the time of weekend or holiday breaks in particular, she would speak about her sense that she could not hold anything in. On one occasion she said that the best she could do was to try to exercise her "psychic muscle". This turned out to mean her mind.

This young woman had suffered terribly as a child. She was brought up in a violent and loveless household and her troubles had begun early. When she was four months old, her mother had suddenly stopped breastfeeding her on discovering that she was again pregnant. The mother had apparently said that there was "no room for two"—a striking statement of her sense of the absence of mental or emotional space for herself or for her baby. The story went that Miss Pearce had been inconsolable. She had screamed for a week and refused any other form of food. She became seriously ill and finally had to be fed by tube.

Versions of the trauma of this separation were constantly relived thereafter. Miss Pearce had, nonetheless, become professionally successful, having developed a particular kind of very marketable cleverness. In the early stages of her therapy, her inexhaustible stream of words and ideas did not seem to be *about* anything, in the sense of being connected to genuine thought or feeling. Rather, they seemed to function as a constant flexing of her "psychic muscle" (a description which she associated with her fear of being identified with her father whom she regarded as "pseudo-potent"). This "flexing" functioned as a defensive manoeuvre against the pain of being in touch with her intolerable feelings of loss and fragmentation. Her extraordinary verbal fluency, especially about emotional states, served the purpose less of communicating, than of ensuring that there could be no experience of her therapist as someone with her own mind and therefore as someone who was different and separable from herself. It was a long time before Miss Pearce was able to trust her therapist's constancy and in so doing to begin to give up her tendency to keep herself insulated from any form of intimacy, from "the dread of allowing another to become precious".

Her mode of using her mind and speech was equivalent to a continuous wall of sound and muscle. It seemed to function as a "second-skin" to hold her fragile self together. Very little emotional development could go on within this wall. She was aware of this and would often refer to the extreme agility with which she had adapted to environmental requirements. But there was a brittleness to her smooth and well-ordered exterior and she constantly felt the threat of disintegration. At times of stress the shell would crack and, like Humpty Dumpty, she felt that all the best interpretative thoughts could not put her back together again.

Miss Pearce's defensive system was not unlike that of a much younger patient, a little four-year-old, Peter, who had also already undergone many traumatic experiences by the time he began therapy. His parents had separated amidst his mother's increasingly severe psychotic episodes and frequent hospitalizations. Despite her deteriorating mental state, Peter had stayed with her. He too was extraordinarily articulate for his age and had developed an encyclopaedic knowledge of monsters, dinosaurs and reptiles which passed for intelligence. This "knowledge" felt to his therapist to be an acquisition of facts and information in the attempt to master his anxieties rather than to engage with them. When he was not talking, Peter was moving around at great speed in the therapy room. He would leap from surface to surface with terrifying agility. Rather surprisingly, despite this activity he was considerably overweight. Apparently he would eat the food off his emaciated mother's plate, as if trying to glean physical resources from her in the absence of meaningful emotional ones. He was terrified of her disappearing or dying and had enormous difficulty detaching himself from her in order to go to his sessions. His cleverness was matched by his jokiness. A rather manic stream of witticisms often accompanied the flow of information which he would impart to his therapist. To the therapist it felt like a desperate attempt to keep himself going and certainly to be an effort to "revive" his mother's spirits. He was utterly delighted when he managed to make his mother laugh or when she told him how brilliant he was.

In one particular session his therapist commented upon how anxious Peter seemed to feel about his taking up too much space.

> Peter became increasingly excitable, countering that it was true that people did get pushed out and animals got pushed out when there wasn't enough room for them, and then they started killing and eating each other. "That's to make more room", he said. He then recounted having seen a film of Popeye who was floating over the ocean with a cut in his leg, "which is the worst place to be if you happen to have a cut in your leg". When asked why this was so, Peter replied "Because of the sharks". His therapist suggested that Peter felt that he could not afford to let himself be weak and little, for then he would be destroyed and eaten up himself. Not surprisingly, Peter's reply was a clever intellectual comment to the effect that sharks could detect one millilitre of blood in a hundred thousand litres of water. "If they were hungry", he said, "they would eat anything, even their own children". With an anxious look, he modified his last statement, "Well, perhaps not their own children, maybe they wouldn't be able to find them". He then stated that not all sharks were man-eaters, although people thought they were. There were some, like the Woebegone and the Thrasher sharks, which didn't eat people. The Thrasher shark rounded up little fish into smaller and smaller circles and then lunged at them.

The session continued in this vein, with his therapist listening to, and briefly commenting on what he said. Peter began to calm down and asked if it was known whether sharks could survive in fresh water. He thought there was a place, perhaps called Nicaragua, in which sharks had swum through a tunnel and attacked people anyway, even though they were not by the sea. Underlying this statement was the sense that one could not feel safe anywhere. In this session Peter's vulnerability and anxiety come through very clearly, despite his constant mental, physical and verbal activity. That is, the so-called "facts" were no protection from his more infantile fears. His last comment suggested that, on some level, he feared that sharks might even swim up the water pipes and attack him while he was in his bath.

This example is introduced both as further illustration of "second-skin" functioning as a mode of defence, and also as a way of conveying, whether in a therapeutic or in a family setting, the difficulty of being on the "right wavelength" with so anxious and insecure a child. What needed to be thought about was not so much what Peter was saying as how he was behaving, that is the excessive speed and energy in everything that he said and did, in addition to the way he was using his mind. Of note was the fragility of the "performances" which were being elaborately mobilized in an attempt to fend off his more persecutory feelings.

Because Peter was so anxious and behaviourally so disturbed, his difficulties came to light when he was quite young. But for many, the modes of defence which may, to an acute observer, already be detectable in infancy, can take years to become evident, whether to the self or to others. The brittle, protective façade may suddenly crack, exposing an absence of inner resources and a panic about being torn away from the supportive structures which had been felt to hold the personality together, albeit only externally.

The experience of eighteen-year-old Sophie, urgently referred to an adolescent unit, would seem to bear out some such situation. Sophie had become panic stricken. She was unable to go out, scarcely even to get up. She could neither stop crying nor allow her mother out of her sight. An arrangement was made that she should be assessed for psychotherapy. During the first meeting she simply sat and sobbed. The therapist spoke to her very simply about the degree of her distress, about her need for somebody to understand the pain of it, and also about her hope that it *could* be understood and made sense of. Sophie was unable to articulate anything beyond a request for permission to go to the lavatory and, when it was time to conclude the session, a statement that it felt impossible to leave.

The three meetings which followed were more coherent. With a flicker of a smile, Sophie said how relieved she had felt that her therapist, unlike her family, had seemed able to bear her "wailing and snivelling". It was true that at the time her therapist's thoughts had focused on the importance of just trying to "hold" Sophie's infantile state, in the sense of wrapping her up with words, less for their interpretative content than to provide some kind of seamless web of continuous and containing sound—a sort of descriptive lullaby.

Slowly a picture began to emerge. Sophie lived with her mother and twin brother. Her father and an older sister had been killed in a car-crash when the twins were six months old. Haltingly Sophie described how she felt that she had got through life from an early age "by subterfuge". Unlike her twin brother, who had gone out and excelled at everything, she had kept close to home, modelling herself on her beautiful and steadfast mother, identified with her mother's pain and stoicism, fitting in with the family culture, as if she understood it and supported it. In fact, Sophie felt that she had nothing of any value inside herself at all, certainly not what was routinely attributed to her—"how lovely she is"; "what an angel" etc. Sophie felt that she simply stuck to a surface accommodation to the exigencies of her complex circumstances without "a thought of my own in my head". The current crisis coincided with major separations: her boyfriend was going abroad; her mother was beginning full-time work. To her amazement Sophie herself had been accepted at drama school. "Of course I can't really act—it's all imitation, perfect for me since I haven't the faintest idea who I am. It's just like my drawing—brilliant still-lives!—a con." A few minutes later she started crying again: "There really is *nothing* inside me, or only rubbish".

Sophie's predicament is not unfamiliar. Her response to the difficulties of her early infancy and childhood seemed to have been to make an attempt at emotional survival by way of conforming as much as possible, to the point of experiencing herself as "stuck" to the surface of those she loved in what is being described as an "adhesive" way. This sticking was indeed felt to hold her together but in a manner which, in fact, offered her little lasting strength and no sense of having a centre of her own. "I'm just a fraud", she said, "people think I'm so intelligent and deep. I try to provide what I think is wanted without really understanding anything." Now that her boyfriend and mother were both working away from home, and her twin was off "getting on with his life", Sophie was having to confront her sense of inner emptiness. No longer in a position to cling to external figures, she had to find the courage to be herself.

In the early days, it seemed that mother and daughter had each found their own rather fragile and two-dimensional defences against the pain of their lives by clinging to one another. When she was twelve Sophie had been very shaken by her mother unexpectedly marrying again, finding in her new husband the emotional support which she had previously sought from Sophie.

Sophie herself had remained as "stuck" to her mother as ever but now, threatened with physical separation, her survival mechanisms were felt no longer to hold. The fragile, externally erected structures broke, leaving Sophie unsustained by any capacity internally to limit her distress. It simply, and literally, spilled out of her. It would seem that her mother, burdened by grief and by the sole care of the twins, had had minimal emotional resources to cope. The boy twin had become precociously independent early on, removing himself from the family and pursuing an intensive interest in sport, latterly becoming a passionate body-builder. One might speculate that his preoccupations were also evidence of a need to be held together, in this case by a muscular carapace which might protect him from having to engage with his own particular pain of loss and the sense of deprivation within.

Each child had, in different ways, conformed, adjusted and appeared to be capable and talented. Sophie was more vulnerable at this point, partly because of the closeness of her attachment to her mother, but perhaps also because of a willingness to address her sense of internal emptiness, an alarming task which her highly performing twin was not yet ready to undertake. Sophie's good-girl-self could not sustain the impact of separation, of being torn away from her supportive structures. She "fell apart", as she put it.

To return again to early infancy, a final, brief example will indicate how thoughtful intervention can rescue a situation which might otherwise have led to the development of the kinds of defensive structure just described. We have seen how the hapless, helpless baby is born into a maelstrom of new and startling sensations over which he has no control. Bombarded with sensory experiences which both relate to, and yet feel wholly distinct from, anything known hitherto, he struggles to maintain a sense of coherence. There will be moment by moment shifts from the panic of feeling wholly uncontained, under the pressure of unsustainable emotions whether of isolation, over-impingement, physical pain, confusion, to the bliss of being securely and lovingly held by nipple and gaze. Terror then gives way to satisfaction, overwhelming disintegration to the beauty of integration, fragments become a whole.

Much depends, as we have seen, on how the primitive anxieties, issuing from this kind of psychic pain are managed in early infancy.

And yet as the child grows up, different qualities of experience may variously affect the early patterning. Indeed, that patterning may itself change and modify, enabling a floor to be put into what, for some, may have felt like a bottomless and terrifying abyss. An example of the impact of a sensitive approach, offered by a young health visitor to a troubled family, illustrates the hopeful effect of well-timed understanding. In the grip of post-natal depression, Mrs Thomas seemed to have been drained of any shred of positive feeling towards her baby, Jane. The health visitor found her to be feeding her baby listlessly, silently, heavily, scarcely even holding her. And yet Jane, whose disposition appeared to be that of a fighter rather than a giver-up, was observed rooting for the breast, reaching for it, and holding on to it, in an effort, it seemed, not just to survive, but to instil in her mother some confidence in the capacity to feed her.

However, the health visitor described how, as the weeks went by, Jane found it increasingly hard to sustain her endeavour. Her faltering spirits set in train a descending spiral of depression, frustration and rage. There was a sense of desperation in both baby and mother. It was as if Jane's capacity to remain on the side of life in the face of her mother's depression had dwindled and, unable to engage with any loving light in her mother's eye, and having access only to a lifeless rather than a lively breast, she seemed to feel herself on the edge of despair. Jane became withdrawn and lifeless herself. The health visitor became extremely anxious about this struggling pair and was at a loss as to how she might help them. During one of her visits she picked up on some asides of Mrs Thomas's about her own mother's difficulties in feeding her and about how she traced her later eating problems to what she had been told about the distress of this early relationship. The health visitor tentatively wondered whether perhaps what had been described as the "moral imperative" to breastfeed was not one that, in practice, Mrs Thomas found manageable. She suggested that she might try the bottle instead.

After a few days a much more happy feeding situation became established between Jane and her mother and, to her astonishment and delight, the health visitor witnessed the baby being changed by a now smiling and engaged parent. Each was able to greet the other with transports of giggles and delight. To suggest the bottle rather than the breast was an apparently simple idea. But the result was transformative. The consequence of the health visitor's understanding, her capacity to take in and process the nature of Mrs Thomas's anxiety, was that she was able to respond in precisely the way that was needed.

Feeling uncontained in the mother's mind, the baby anxiously seeks some means of holding himself together. A range of defences against the fear of disintegration can be observed from earliest days. In terms of their impact on a person's character, it is those defences which affect the relative shallowness or depth of the personality which are of particular interest. Early on psychoanalytic work with very disturbed children and adults revealed states of mind which seemed to have a paper-thin, adhesive quality. As time went on, such states began to be detected in younger and younger children and even in descriptions of infantile behaviour. It was as if there was little or no sense of an inner world in such children, a world where experiences of the self and of the other might be engaged with and found meaningful. Instead, there was a fragile quality of superficial attachment, initially to sensory objects and experiences and later to certain kinds of relationship, whether to people or to things. With the two-dimensional view of the world go particular kinds of learning (see Chapter 7) which may bring social rewards, as with Miss Pearce, but which offer little opportunity for emotional growth and change.

In exploring the beginnings of these patterns in infancy and in describing some of the internal and external relationships which underlie them, we can begin to see how deeply the baby's experience affects the potential growth of his personality. Subsequent events may modify, or even alter, these early patterns of relating but, broadly, infancy constitutes the foundation for the way in which the developmental process unfolds, functioning as a model for the child's later relationships with family, school and the wider world.

Notes

1.   This was an aspect of mothering which particularly concerned Winnicott, for example (1965) *The Maturational Processes and the Facilitating Environment*, London: Hogarth (1972), p. 183.

2. In "Subjectivity, Objectivity and Triangular Space", Ch. 4 of Britton, R. *Belief and Imagination*, London: Routledge (1998).

3. *International Journal of Psycho-Analysis*, 78(5): 927–941. In *Internal Landscapes and Foreign Bodies* Williams (1997) explores the way in which early experiences of absence and loss can stir up a defensive "dread of allowing another to become precious". Winnicott (1948) discusses the impingement of the mother's state of mind on the baby, in particular in "Reparation in respect of mother's organized defence against depression", in *Collected Papers: through paediatrics to psychoanalysis*, London: Tavistock, (1958).

4. *Adam Bede*, Ch. 15, p. 199. This aspect of Esther Bick's thinking is very similar to the "as if" personality described by Hélène Deutsch (1934), and to the concept of the "false self", extensively discussed by Winnicott (1958).

CHAPTER FIVE

Early childhood:
weaning and separation

"A pity beyond all telling
Is hid in the heart of love"

W. B. Yeats

With integration and self-knowledge as common goals, psychoanalytic practice and the process of growing up share a number of congruences. The aim of psychoanalysis could be described as seeking to make available to the patient more aspects of the self. In this sense helping someone to grow up has similarities to what one tries to do in an analysis. Parents' aspirations towards being able to help the developing child are affected by their own capacities to reflect on how insight is impeded or facilitated, on how understanding and thinking can be encouraged. This issue of how insight may be "impeded" or "facilitated" in the ordinary, challenging process of a person's development assumes particular importance when it comes to leaving infancy and embarking on the early childhood years. The central emotional tasks are those of weaning and separation, ones which will be forever internally worked and re-worked, whether in life generally or, for some, in the particular setting of the consulting room.

Weaning usually occurs during a limited period of time and probably at some point during the baby's first year. Yet the feelings and responses aroused by weaning reach furthest back in life and farthest forward. They belong to the fact of birth and to the fact of death. In that weaning can be thought of as the prototype for all separations and losses, the way in which it comes about cannot but have a profound impact. The first, and primary, separation it evokes is probably that of birth itself. It stirs anew every early experience of being cut off from what is felt to be the primary source of love and sustenance; of being left alone when company was needed; of being starved when food was required; of being deprived of a cohering presence when holding was wanted. A baby lacks all capacity for individual survival. When left alone, his fear of dying is never far away. Subsequently, at whatever age, terror may threaten and panic pervade when he feels back in a situation, or in a relationship, which is evocative of these early fears.

These overwhelming states in an otherwise emotionally secure adult might be short-lived versions of an experience which is wholly familiar and ordinary in the infant. In these early days they can usually be relieved by the sound of a voice, by loving arms or proffered breast. At any one moment in a baby's experience, night will threaten, and at any other day will break. The experience, in the earliest weeks, of terror being relieved and hope fulfilled is affected by the baby's own internal capacities and go on to influence how he responds to sorrow and to joy for the rest of his life. At its simplest, there is, for the baby, one life-saving presence. The lack of that presence is experienced as a pain and possibly a trauma, arousing feelings which he will not willingly suffer. If these feelings are inflicted on him, he may respond with a degree of rage and destructiveness which is felt to be equivalent in magnitude to that infliction.

From very early on babies and small children adopt an extensive and diverse armoury of defensive measures in order to protect themselves from the pain of loss. These measures are most easily detectable in their primitive forms: denial, belief in the self's omnipotence, projection and splitting (i.e. the splitting of experiences and perceptions of the self and the world into extremes of good and bad; see Chapter 1 and the Appendix). But self-defensive measures also take much less dramatic forms and filter subtly into the fine grain of the personality. Here they may provide a "sense" of integration, but, as we saw in the last chapter, this is not the experience of genuinely having a centre of self, of really being oneself.

Much depends on how desperate or extreme these self-defensive measures are, on how deeply they become entrenched in the personality, and on how easily they can be relinquished. A simple example of one eighteen-month-old's negotiation of his feelings about his mother's absence is given by Freud in the famous cotton-reel game (1920). Freud's grandson was observed throwing away, with some considerable force, a cotton-reel which was tied to his cot. The repeated flingings-away alternated with a satisfying pulling-back again. Each throw was accompanied by a clearly articulated *"fort"* (away), and each return by *"da"* (here). Freud suggested that his grandson was dealing with separation anxiety by means of the illusion that he could, in his symbolic play, omnipotently control the comings and goings of his mother. It has since been observed that the child may also have been giving vent to some quite hostile and sadistic feelings towards his absent mother, ones which alternated with calmer and more reparative impulses.

Freud's grandson was thought also to be demonstrating the satisfaction of feeling in possession of his mother. Maybe such a child does, for a time, actually become controlling. Bossiness, or being-the-one-in-charge, may be part of his personality, at least for a while. Other experiences will later modify or alter such character-istics, and new anxieties will, in turn, bring about new ways of behaving. As soon as the baby has this idea that his mother is a separate person, that she is not, in fact, his own possession, that she is someone who can independently come and go, there is the inevitable awareness that she may be with another, some hated third being. Thus, the powerful realities of love and hate are, from the start, built into the human experience. The mother, so loved, becomes also hated for having betrayed a primary trust. Envy of her has already arisen, for being the one who has the needed resources and is in control of them. Then the conviction that precious things are being offered to somebody else adds jealousy to envy; jealousy of him to whom those loved, and loving, resources are now being given. The struggle with the vicissitudes of triangulation begins.

That the capacity for such perception sets in around the time of physical weaning, whether from breast to bottle, or to cup, or to solids, gives a special centrality and poignancy to the relationship to feeding. At the same time as gratifying, interesting, sensuous and emotional experiences are becoming available, arousing joyful exploration and exciting new urges, so too are experiences of deprivation, of loss and sadness, of nostalgia for a state of being which can never be "home" in quite the same way again. The self-defensive measures with which, hitherto, the baby/child has sought to protect himself from the painfulness of these experiences, may not any longer be adequate to the task. Or the experiences themselves may be felt to be too overwhelming. The pain will then induce anxiety, rage, resistance and, even at the infantile stage, murderous, biting, destructive feelings which forever flood unbidden into subsequent struggles against jealousy and the anguish of separation.

One of the reasons for the centrality of weaning in Kleinian thought is that it is so closely associated with the beginning of the Oedipal constellation, which is experienced primarily in oral terms at this point, by contrast with the later genitally-centred "Oedipus complex" described by Freud. Weaning often takes place at the time when the infant is beginning to experience his mother as a whole person, a coming-and-going person, sometimes there and sometimes not there. There is, at this stage, a dawning awareness of an integration between various of her functions which had hitherto been experienced in discrete and "partial" terms: the feeding, the looking, the sounding, the holding. New defences will now need to be drawn on, defences which will protect the infant against the anxiety stirred by powerful feelings of loss, and by experiencing such rage towards the mother whom he also loves. The baby begins to move away from the paranoid–schizoid position which has hitherto provided him with the necessary defensive structure, one so organized as not to allow him to experience his mother as a whole person.

Once the mother is felt to be a whole person, the world begins to be experienced from a different point of view—from the depressive position. This involves having in mind the terrible damage that has, in phantasy, been done, or is being done, by the enraged or terrified baby to the one whom he so loves. This new kind of experience, in turn, brings into being new kinds of anxieties and necessitates new kinds of defences.

In this state of mind the well-being of the self is felt to be intimately bound-up with the well-being of the mother, and of the infant's internal version of her. The belief in the sole possession of her has to be given up, and the pain of loss and sorrow sometimes turns to rage, sometimes to excitement, sometimes to despair. What has to be given up is a belief in there being access to a unique, uncomplicated and blissful experience. What is mourned is the time when that experience was felt genuinely to be available.

The depressive position and early Oedipal anxieties are closely entangled. Early on the difficulties of relating to "threeness" rather than "twoness" are focused on oral issues of feeding and starvation, as enshrined in so much myth and fairy-tale (in the story of "Hansel and Gretel", for example, or "Snow White"). Later, the pleasure and pain, the excitement and the frustration tend to become focused in the genitals, arousing powerful sexual feelings of passion and aggression. At whatever stage, the anxieties aroused and the defences against them can become sticking points in development, affecting later relationships and capacities to grow emotionally. The locus of this struggle, whether in the four-year-old, the fourteen-year-old, the forty or the eighty-year-old, characteristically becomes the triangular relationship in which, over and over again, these matters of love, hate, possession and separation have to be negotiated.

As we have seen, the myth of Oedipus describes what Freud came to believe were the universal phantasies and desires in the young child to possess the parent of the opposite sex and to get rid of the parent of the same sex (see Chapter 1). He found these longings to be epitomized in the bare facts of the story as already noted. Klein saw this pattern of relationships as beginning much earlier, in the infant's first awareness of not being the only one, of his mother's attention being directed elsewhere, and in his belief that when the milk is not being given to him it is being given to this now hated rival. The phantasy of having the beloved parent all to himself thus originates in very early need. Initially that need is felt to be for the mother, to the exclusion or detriment of the father: "When I grow up I'm going to marry Mummy" is uttered by two-year-old girls quite as often as by boys. It is a wish for sole possession which takes on the much more recognizable sexual connotations, associated with Freud's picture of things, only later, at around the age of four or five.

The part that Oedipus's parents, Laius and Jocasta, play in the myth is also of interest. Fearing the pronouncement of the Delphic oracle that their son would commit murder and incest, they had exposed him to die on the mountain where, unbeknownst to them, he was rescued by a shepherd and later adopted by the king and queen of Corinth (see the Appendix). Unable to contain their anxieties, Laius and Jocasta had sought to kill their own son. The father feared being surpassed and eventually superseded (represented by the idea of being murdered), and the mother feared loving her child more than she loved her husband (represented by the idea of being married). These fears would seem to stem from the "Oedipus" whom they felt to be somewhere in themselves and in every child. Likewise, every parent knows that, in the natural course of events, they will watch their children outlive them. This knowledge brings hope and optimism for the future, but also some sense of anguish, and even dread, about being displaced and left behind. It is a joy, but also a struggle, to allow children to grow up and to move on, figuratively expressed in the events in the myth. In this, and in many other ways, parents' anxieties interact with those of their children, inevitably affecting the course of development.

The parental capacity to know about, and to contain, these anxieties is fundamental to the outcome of their children's lives, forever interacting with the children's own dispositions. The Oedipal story which had so arrested Freud in the very earliest days of his psychoanalytic thinking was thus not only one of incest and murder, but also one which draws attention to the necessity of understanding oneself, including those murderous impulses and incestuous desires which one would rather disown. Moreover, the story establishes links between the parents' lack of understanding of these aspects of themselves, and the implications of that "not-knowing" for the child. The interplay between the parents' internal world and the child's is powerfully enacted.

* * *

This interplay of relationships will be explored in later examples, but more immediately a sequence from the observation of an eleven-month-old boy, Billy, may clarify some of these issues. For Billy's behaviour vividly conveys a sense of the intensity, and complexity, of the intrapsychic, triangular relationship in which he is clearly passionately engaging, even at so young an age. Billy is being observed waking up:

> He looks dazed. Sitting up with his back against the wall-side of his cot, he seems to be about to cry. Inside the cot there are three objects: a large teddy bear, a Fisher Price activity centre and a small teddy. Billy notices the yellow and pink cylinder of the activity centre and tentatively spins it. This completely changes his whole mood. He smiles. Each time he manages to spin the cylinder, he turns to face the observer and makes a little laugh. He looks delighted with himself and his whole face lights up. He concentrates on two parts of the toy, the cylinder and a small plastic dome which, if pressed hard, causes a bell to ring (this is much more difficult for Billy to do, yet he persists). Billy is obviously very happy to repeat the sequence: playing with the toy, turning to the observer and laughing. But out of the corner of his eye he suddenly notices the large teddy at the end of the cot. He looks at the teddy and scowls. Teddy's presence seems to pose a difficulty as far as continuing to play with the activity centre is concerned. Billy can't seem to get back to the toy. He makes one or two attempts to recapture his pleasure of a moment ago, but the presence of the teddy appears to have become somehow too threatening. Billy glares at the teddy with a look of baleful malevolence, as if the threat is passing both ways. Billy's gloomy look fast becomes one of distress.

At this point in Billy's play one can observe the persecutory impact of the sudden awareness of the competing presence of a third factor (the big teddy). The happily confident possession and control of the "two-person" game of self and cylinder/breast is shattered, and hostile attempts at vanquishment ensue.

> Quite suddenly Billy makes a lunge for the teddy. Grasping it tightly in one hand, he brings it close to his nose and starts shouting at it: "Di-di-der-der!". He pokes his fingers into the teddy's face. Then he pushes it through the bars of the cot and onto the floor. He is overjoyed. Laughing and making urgent sounds at the same time, he returns to the cylinder and then to the dome. Everything about his behaviour has now become insistent. He is almost hitting the toy in his excitement. Indeed, he finally makes the bell ring and his pleasure seems complete.

Yet somehow, in the midst of all this agitation he hesitates. He comes to the side of the cot, looks down onto the floor for the teddy, and when he sees it, starts pointing at it and "calling" for it. The observer restores the teddy to Billy and he brings it close to his face again and repeats, now almost shouting, "Der-di-di ... der!". Then he pushes the teddy back out through the bars. All the previous excitement and energy come back into his play as he again turns his attention to the activity centre. This sequence is repeated, almost exactly, three or four times, with Billy's attention shifting back and forth between one object and the other. Suddenly he stumbles across the small teddy, which, in all the excitement, has become wrapped up in the blanket. He immediately pounces on it, shouting: "Der-der". He is even more violent with the second teddy. He pushes at its face in the same way as he had pushed the button on the activity centre. He squeezes and pulls at the little teddy's head and then takes great delight in squashing it out through the bars. With both teddies out of his cot, Billy makes a perfunctory effort to go back to his toys, but his mood now seems rather flat and he is unable to regain his former enthusiasm.

Billy's experience poignantly describes the eleven-month-old's version of depressive anxieties. He repeatedly, but only momentarily, recaptures the blissful situation in which the object of his passion completely responds to him. It does exactly what he wants. But then he becomes aware of the presence of something else, something which he can't control, something which he wishes to get rid of but then experiences as something lost, and lost by his own hand. With that awareness comes the anguish that he cannot get back what he has thrown away.

It seemed that Billy's relationship to the teddies was as if to hostile intruders who were going to spoil, or break up the exclusive relationship he was conducting, whether that was felt primarily to be with the activity centre or with the observer, in whose presence he felt secure and able to play with his toys. He ferociously attacked and did away with the opposition, but his manic triumph left him rather defeated, and the joy of the original encounter could no longer be maintained. In seeking sole possession he had lost what he also realized he needed.

Central to any possibility of successfully negotiating the complex triangularity with which Billy is struggling, is the capacity to mourn what is felt to be lost or is having to be relinquished, and to take responsibility for whatever part the self is felt to have played. For those few moments at least, Billy was unable to let go of his exclusive two-some relationship and to share with a third. Nor was he able to continue playing now that a rival had so disturbed him. As a result, the teddies posed a threat rather than a comfort. They had to carry Billy's projected feelings and to suffer torture, even "murder", simply because they were "there".

The process of mourning is one which, at whatever age or stage it occurs, is to do with managing to experience oneself as separate from the loved and, even if only temporarily, lost other. Only then is a discrimination possible between what really belongs to the other and what belongs to the self, and a sense of self-sufficiency, albeit initially quite brief, may obtain. The process involves the undoing of all those complex bonds and ties by which the self had sought to feel not only attached to, but even the same as, the other. To evade the experience of being separate and different, the baby will draw on whatever means he has at his disposal.

Weaning epitomizes a central aspect of growing up. In its explicit and concrete way, it can come to represent any number of later struggles to give up an attachment to childish things and to be an older self. It becomes possible to be dependent less on the physical presence of the external person than on having been able to take in, and to hold internally, in short to introject, a version of their functions and capacities. Negotiating this situation involves being able to bear relinquishment, to encounter new experience, hitherto untried; indeed, to change. For change to be possible in a relationship each party has to be able genuinely to let go of the fantasies and projections of what is, by turn, longed for, or feared, in the other person, and to appreciate whatever he or she actually is, as distinct from what they may have been needed to be. This may painfully involve giving up quite complex idealizations or narcissistic aspirations (see Chapter 11). The baby is greatly helped by the mother to give up the intensity of the early experience, though also greatly troubled by the loss. Mothers also find this process difficult. They lose their relationship to a baby who completely adores them. Different ways of assuaging the pain will be sought, most characteristically perhaps, by going back to work. A mother's sense that she is indispensable to her baby is narcissistically pleasing but also burdensome. The recognition that the baby can, at whatever age, be kept alive by sources of care and nurture other than herself is a complex mixture of loss and of gain.

A myriad of responses in the baby will be found to the very idea of weaning, even when that idea is still only in the mother's mind. Sensing a change in his mother's attitude, one baby stopped feeding from the breast overnight, as if in a kind of omnipotent protest: "If you don't want me, I don't need you". Another avidly clung on, rooting for the breast with far greater insistence than ever before. A third seemed to want to hang on to the experience of an available and gratifying breast and to reject the breast which was sensed to be part of a denying and depriving mother. The psychic split was accompanied by a physical right/left split, one which enabled this baby not to have to recognize that she who gave and she who withheld were one and the same person. He sucked blissfully from the right breast and rejected the left breast as if in terror. He turned, seemingly in fear and loathing, from the left breast, as if it were genuinely "sinister", filled with devouring and persecuting demons, but he remained sensually entranced with the "right" one.

All babies have to suffer a degree of discomfort, fear and anxiety. Each one will develop his own particular strategies to help him to manage. If he has too little opportunity to take in good experiences, or indeed too little capacity to make use of them, or if his early experiences are especially painful, these strategies will, as we have already seen, have to be all the more extreme. In the most general terms, they could be thought of as representing the difficulty of being able to mourn. For they represent a range of overt or covert ways of holding onto, or remaining entangled with, the primary loved one, often making it difficult to sort out to whom feelings, emotions and impulses really belong. One of the most subtle, and in some ways insidious, of all these strategies is that of projective identification (see the Appendix).

We have seen how the baby may project in different ways, with different intensities and for different reasons. If moderate, the projection may be about being understood, the basis for empathy, and for communication generally ("I can feel that my feelings are being understood if I feel that you have those feelings too"). But when anxiety runs high, the baby may be impelled to project much more forcefully in order to get rid of feelings which stir in him intolerable anxiety and disturbance. The baby/person seeks to protect himself from the unbearable experience of, for example, pangs of envy, or the terror of separation, by feeling that it is possible to identify with mental or emotional characteristics in the other, characteristics which are really a projection of those very parts of the self. In the case of envy, the unconscious motive might be something like, "If she is merely an extension of me I don't have to worry lest she have something which I don't have"; and, in the case of fear of separateness, "If she and I are really the same, I do not have to experience myself as apart from her". The capacity to confront the reality of loss and to go through the mourning process seems to be essential, at whatever age, to the possibility of projections being retrieved from the other and returned to the self, that is to the possibility of actually becoming oneself.[1]

*   *   *

The close links between the capacity for mourning and the capacity for emotional development will be explored in many different ways in subsequent chapters, as the balance is traced between projective and introjective processes. The two examples that follow here may convey some aspects of these links in the complexity of two little boys" negotiations with love and loss, in relation to their Oedipal anxiety in particular. Nick was twenty-two months old when his mother became pregnant with her second child. In a sense, Nick was having to be weaned, or to wean himself, not in literal "feeding" terms, from breast or bottle, but from his experience of being the only child. His parents may also have been having complex feelings, involving loss and perhaps guilt, about the forthcoming changes for Nick, his pain at being forced to give up his exclusive rights as well as his pleasure about being the new baby's big brother.

Since he became aware of the pregnancy, Nick's behaviour had changed in quite striking ways. Even before he was officially "told" about the new baby, his play had suggested that he had a sense of what was going on. He had become passionately interested in railways generally and in Thomas the Tank Engine in particular. These interests were closely associated with his father who went to work every day by train. (Nick's mum thought that his idea of what his dad did when he went to "work" was to stay on the train all day; that is, that his "work" meant the ideal state of being-on-the-train.) Much of Nick's play had begun to focus on excitedly pushing his train into a tunnel and pulling it out again. Meanwhile his relationship with his mother had been altering. He began to call her by the same name as his father used, and suddenly to acquire both words and skills precociously fast, much to his mother's delight. He tended to be given disproportionate rewards for being "grown-up". It was as if his mother needed him to be a big boy in order to leave room for another baby. This led to Nick's more infantile needs at times being ignored.

Seemingly in response to his anxiety over the new baby, Nick's charm and precocity rapidly increased. He became very adept at winning over his mum by ever new feats of competence and verbal agility. There were many delightful exchanges between them. For example, Nick would recite the days of the week to the accompaniment of claps and smiles. His more mixed, even angry feelings, were confined to his play, and to some extent to his increasing sleep difficulties.

> On one occasion, soon after the observer arrived, Nick's mum went to the kitchen to make some tea. Nick began brandishing his model of Thomas the Tank Engine in the air, saying "Train". He then climbed up on his father's armchair and threw the train over the back. "Gone", he shouted in glee. Excitedly he began to clamber off the chair via the arm, on which he was standing, precariously balanced, as his mother came back into the room. She told him to get down and not to be naughty. Nick leapt quickly onto the seat with a slightly guilty, yet seductive, grin and jumped up and down joyously exclaiming, "Babs, Babs" (his father's pet name for his wife). She firmly told him to get off the chair. Grudgingly he did so. But as soon as her back was turned he climbed onto an upright chair (again the one his father usually sat on) and, holding the back, began violently to rock to-and-fro. His mother said, "No, naughty" several times, but Nick took no notice and continued to rock and to grin. His mother said "No" more urgently. She lifted him down and tipped over the chair to show what could happen, telling him how cross and upset daddy would be. Nick glanced anxiously in the direction of the thrown-away train and said "Up", clearly wanting the chair swiftly to be righted again.

As time went on Nick seemed unable to concentrate in his usual way on the book about having-a-new-baby-in-the-house which his mother was trying to show him. Suddenly he said "Thomas". His mum asked where Thomas was. Nick pointed first to the chair and then out of the window. He went to the piano and said "Thomas" again. His mother said, "Oh, you want me to play Thomas's tune", and she did so. Nick looked happier and asked for some different tunes, Postman Pat and so on. Some moments later, he again seemed restless and started muttering "Thomas". He picked up a Thomas the Tank Engine comic and began studying it intently, pointing out and naming different parts of the various trains. His mother seemed pleased about the breadth of his vocabulary and then asked him to tell the observer what had happened that morning. Nick looked very glum. He said, "Cried", but would not elaborate. He suddenly left his comic and, now more anxiously, repeated "Thomas" several times. His mother again asked him where Thomas was and this time Nick ran to the chair and tried, rather desperately, to squeeze behind it to retrieve his engine, unsuccessfully. He looked at his mother entreatingly. She reached round the chair and restored the engine to him. He danced around with excitement, took his engine to the track and began pushing it back and forth and through the tunnel. He then carefully attached a carriage to the engine and later, quietly and as if as an afterthought, also attached a small truck to the carriage. He was chatting to himself meanwhile: "tunnel": "laddy, ladding". Understanding the gist of what he may have meant, his mother asked him where his daddy was. "Train", said Nick delightedly.

This brief extract suggests several possibilities, centring on Nick's anxieties about the new baby and the complex feelings stirring in him in relation to his parents. One way of dealing with the difficult situation was to get rid of daddy (the thrown-away engine) and to be triumphantly King of the Castle/mummy in his stead (the jumping and rocking on the chairs). But it is interesting to note how he tries to deal with what appears to be his mounting anxiety about what he is feeling. Perhaps he is beginning to experience a sense of loss and guilt over the banished engine. He attempts to find symbolic substitutes for it (the Thomas tune and the comic) but these have only limited effect and he increasingly needs the reassurance of the engine itself. A solution is to allow mummy and daddy to be together as the train and tunnel (with the reassuring phantasy, perhaps, that they can thus be kept under his control). In order not to feel excluded or left behind, he attaches his own "carriage" to the daddy/engine and then, rather touchingly, manages to add on the baby/truck behind. What he may have meant by "laddy, ladding" is intriguing. His mother's response suggests that he is describing what he thinks it is that daddies do with mummies.

The sequence describes Nick struggling, quite successfully, with the Oedipal feelings of wanting to banish daddy and have mummy all to himself. He is also struggling with his fears of being displaced by the new baby. In his play he is trying to master his anxiety about exclusion by doing the excluding himself. He draws on symbolic representation (engine, tunnel, carriage, truck) in order to sort out these worrying phantasies and identifications. It turns out that he cannot long sustain the experience of having vanquished his father, nor the heady excitement of having taken his father's place with his mother. As the absent "father" turns present persecutor, Nick attempts to stave off anxiety by further symbolic play. His omnipotent sense of control, and his fear that it is failing, is only reduced when, unable to retrieve the engine himself, he has to ask for his mother's help. At this point Nick has to undergo painful depressive feelings of guilty recognition, as well as of relief, that his mummy has daddy in her mind and can bring him back, at the moment when his own fear is that, in wanting to get rid of daddy, he has actually done so. When the engine has been safely restored to him it becomes possible again to contemplate the triangular relationship, to busy himself in symbolically conducting it, and, finally, to allow the new "baby" a place as well.

In this everyday little episode we can see very clearly the relationship between anxieties about separation and loss and the capacity to form symbols. It is Nick's concern, both about being left out of the parental couple, and about forcing his way into it, which spurs his ability symbolically to represent his worries through his play and his words. It is clear that he has already developed a self which is separate enough from his parents to be able to represent both them and himself in the way that he does.

His use of symbols is a way of not having to have his actual parents available to him every moment. Nick can draw on words and toys to represent relationships between himself and others. When, however, he is under the sway of intensified anxiety, his guilt and fear of loss become too acute, and the toys are then felt actually to be the people whom they once represented. Toys and people become equated, and Nick is unable to continue playing until his mother comes to the rescue.[2]

By contrast, a sequence from a therapy session of a three-year-old twin, Sammy, offers a rather more troubled picture of early anxieties, one in which, under increased pressures, the symbolic mode for expressing these difficult feelings frequently broke down. The phantasy would all too readily be felt to be reality. Often little distinction between "pretend" and "real" could be made, not only briefly, as we have just seen with Nick, but in more extended and alarming ways.

Sammy had had a very difficult beginning. He had been born prematurely and with several quite serious physical problems which had resulted in his being kept in hospital for two months after his mother and twin sister had gone home. His mother had been very depressed following the birth and had been convinced for a long time that Sammy would die. Sammy spent his first three weeks in an incubator and suffered many brief stays in hospital thereafter. He was referred for treatment because of his parents' distress over his nightmares which had begun around the time when his mother had started to wean him from bottle to cup. Scarcely a night passed without his mother having to spend long periods attempting to calm him down and to try to render more manageable the persecuting world in which he would find himself. She described how, when he awoke, he would often seem to experience her as a frightening, rather than as a comforting figure. This increased her own distress. There seemed to be a complete split between the happy, chatty, day-time Sammy and the terrified and tyrannical night-time Sammy. He could now demand his mother's reassuring presence, unlike before when, as a tiny infant, he was not only helpless but frequently physically separated from her as well. He may also have sensed in her the lack of an emotional capacity to contain his own fear of dying since she was so frightened of death herself.

As time went on and he began to experience his therapist as someone who could bear the naughty, messy and destructive "boy" as well as the charming and chatty "Sammy", the terrifying nature of his inner world, hitherto confined to his nightmare life, started to appear in the sessions. Violent fantasies began to be played out, usually attributed to the "nasty, biting crocodile", or to "Jenny", his twin, or to "Spencer", one of his soft toys. The play was only very occasionally preceded by the pronoun "I", for Sammy, at this stage, found it almost impossible to take any responsibility for his rage and aggression. Primitive, persecutory fears were expressed which were clearly linked to Oedipal anxieties concerning the seduction of the good, maternal figure, who might, at any moment, turn into something bad and witchy ("There are lots and lots of witches and they"ll put the boy into a cauldron and make him into frog-soup and eat him all up"). There were also fears of punishment by other frightening figures who were increasingly represented as one huge, ever-watchful and punitive "God".

The role and function of Sammy's "God", and of his devouring witch figures, would seem to have much in common with the psychoanalytic concept of the primitive superego. In the light of such material, it is not difficult to understand that the monstrous, terrifying figures which Klein discovered in the inner worlds of the young children whom she treated, figures which she regarded as making up the early superego, were not so much the *outcome* of the classical Oedipus complex of Freudian theory, but actually ushered it in. In simple terms, Freud's view was that as the child became too anxious to sustain his passionate and murderous feelings towards his actual external parents, he relinquished them in the external world. But in order to retain his relationship to them he internalized versions of them in the form of censorious or encouraging internal presences, roughly corresponding to what became known as the superego and the ego ideal. Klein, on the other hand, felt that, however passionate or murderous a child's relationship with his actual parents might be, such a relationship would be preferable to trying to cope with the sorts of archaic and terrifying figures with which Sammy was having to contend. Thus the child would begin to intensify his loving and hating feelings towards his parents externally, in order to escape such persecutory internal parental figures, or "imagos", as she called them.

Although in many ways extreme, Sammy's difficult experiences and the nature of his attempts to deal with them, are on a continuum with the ordinary, internal processes of young children. Being able to bear the loss of what is felt to be the needed person derives from the "knowledge" that, for example, although the mother may not be physically present, she has not died nor disappeared forever. If she is with the father, whether actually or in phantasy, that does not mean that the little one is totally excluded. He can be out of sight without having to be out of mind. Bearing separation and loss will be helped, as we have already seen, by having mentally and emotionally available, enough of the time, a "thinking breast", a mother who, in that she is herself able to bear loss and, ultimately, the fear of dying, can understand those same fears in her child, and can discriminate need from greed in his desire for her presence. Not only was Sammy deprived of this initially, but later too, his mother found herself scarcely able to bear her own anxieties let alone his.

Not surprisingly, Sammy's fears and desires greatly intensified whenever there was a holiday break and his therapist was not available to see him. At these times his jealous and murderous feelings became quite overwhelming. The following extract from the first session after a two-week holiday clearly shows how the absence plays into his Oedipal anxieties and fears of abandonment. These are anxieties common to all children although they may not be as starkly felt, or clearly expressed, as by this disarming and disturbed little boy.

Sammy brought Spencer, to the session. Anxiously he asked his therapist if she liked Spencer, commenting that he was a bit fat and glancing at his own tummy. Then he started cutting and re-joining strips of sellotape, in the course of which he announced that he was going to wash the window, "It's got horrid bits on it". When asked what he thought had made the window dirty, Sammy replied, with a crescendo of anxiety, "I think it was the hammer, no, the ladder . . . no, the man . . . no, . . . your husband". He began trying to rub the dirt off, but when he realized that it was on the outside of the window, he became frantic and started throwing all his toys around, kicking his therapist and her chair, stamping and shouting, "bombs", "bombs", and, as he spun the bin across the room, "I"d like to *kill* everyone".

His therapist was mindful of how worried Sammy was about her feelings for him during the break ("Do you like Spencer?"), and of how he had then re-enacted the experience of being cut off and reunited (the cutting and joining of the sellotape). She also realized that the intensity of his distress must stem from his mentally linking the unexpected presence, a few weeks previously, of a window cleaner at the window, with his phantasies about whom she had been with over the two weeks when she was not with him. The spots on the window which Sammy could not remove seemed to have made him desperate about not being able to control his therapist's life or relationships, and about feeling so left out himself. She had betrayed him with this "husband" person, and it made him feel that he wanted to kill her, as well as everyone else, so that he wouldn't have to have these awful feelings anymore.

As she spoke to him in these terms, Sammy began to calm down. He stopped kicking and shouting and eventually even started to clear up the mess. He decided to throw away the "bits" of sellotape which he had not managed to rejoin, and also to keep the remains of a torn crayon packet: "This is a magazine", he said importantly, "It's for my work". [In the past Sammy had explained how his father takes a magazine to work every day.] He ended by an unprecedentedly coherent rehearsal of the days and times of his next sessions.

As a consequence of experiencing his therapist as able to tolerate his unbearable feelings of anger, jealousy and distress, and realizing that she could take in and hold these feelings without being dominated by them, or driven into action herself, Sammy was able to re-engage with his "thinking" self. With the reminder of his sense of exclusion during the break, he had become overwhelmed by an infantile state of terror of a paranoid–schizoid kind. He had attempted to externalize an internal situation by projecting the part of himself in distress into his therapist, who would then, it was unconsciously hoped, identify with that baby-Sam self. The therapy session provided a safe place and time for thinking about the meaning of Sammy's feelings and actions. In being so receptive and understanding (Bion's "reverie"), his therapist was eventually able to divest Sammy's feelings of the excessive anxiety and to return to him a "thought-about", and therefore meaningful, version of his pain. At first he had had furiously to reject the sense of being broken (the "bits" of sellotape) and excluded (thoughts of the man on the ladder), but he was now able to take them back in more manageable form and to re-establish his friendly, accommodating self. He was helped in this endeavour by a temporary identification with his father-in-his-work-world. Perhaps as a consequence, he was able to take a small step forward, represented by his new-found ability to sort out the times and days of his sessions. Whether Sammy's temporary identification with an adult, together with his impressive mental agility, are evidence of developmental steps genuinely being taken (because he was able to digest his anxiety), or whether they represent a glimpse of pseudo-maturity, in the service of mastering anxiety, cannot be inferred from these brief details. Much depends on the feeling and tone in the room at the time, and on the nature and negotiation of subsequent experiences of separation and loss.

In the event, it was only a short time later that, under the impact of his father's prolonged absence on a business trip, Sammy's anxieties about what again became a very horrible and persecuting man/husband/person, exploded into behaviour that was both increasingly violent and overtly sexual. He renewed his threat to kill his therapist: "Because of your husband, your man and your bloody old self." Sammy was having a much harder time than most boys in managing his feelings of jealousy and possessiveness. Never having had a sufficiently secure relationship with his mother, at times he found it unbearable to share her. It seemed that sharing with his twin was something that he had grudgingly had to put up with, but the awareness of any further claims on his mother's affection felt unbearable, arousing the kind of anguished hostility which we see enacted in his relationship with his therapist.

Development involves some kind of process of mourning at every stage and, in this sense, it cannot be said that the weaning process, or the Oedipus complex, are strictly ever "resolved". They are simply re-worked, over and over again, at different times and on different planes. Fortunately for Sammy, he had the opportunity at a very young age to learn about his impulses and fears and to begin to understand them.

As the child approaches five the early Oedipal anxieties described here will be yielding to the more recognizable triangular struggles between child and parent, and the excessively harsh and cruel characteristics of those early internal figures will begin to lessen. Some children will have more difficulty than others in negotiating these difficult times, depending on the complex interplay of disposition and experience.

The degree to which it has been possible, in these early years, to process the internal tumults and attachments will have a very important bearing on the major external step which now has to be taken: going to school. Some children will already have had experiences of small play-group settings in which, to some extent, they will have been able to test out, for example, their willingness to separate, to share, to make friends, to trust other adults, to join in. But it is the beginning of "proper" school which significantly tries the robustness of the internal gains so far. Each child's readiness to embark on, and to manage, this next phase of his life will very much depend on the nature and outcome of the developmental processes discussed in this chapter.

The capacity to bear loss, to risk change, to widen experience, to extend relationships, is based in the degree of containment and security which a baby and young child has initially experienced in the primary relationship, and which later function as resources to support and sustain the still fragile ego through new and challenging endeavours. That security stems from the availability of a containing presence which is itself able to bear and to learn from both good and bad experience and, as a consequence, to develop and grow in relation to the child's changing sense of himself-in-the-world. The internal experience of such a presence can then become the core of the developing self.

Notes

1.   These issues are explored in detail by John Steiner (1996).
2.   This distinction between symbolic representation and symbolic equation was first made by Segal, H. (1957), "Notes on Symbol Formation".

CHAPTER SIX

Latency

"The air was thick with a bass chorus
Right down the dam, gross-bellied frogs were cocked
On sods; their loose necks pulsed like sails. Some hopped:
The slap and plop were obscene threats. Some sat
Poised like mud grenades, their blunt heads farting.
I sickened, turned, and ran. The great slime kings
Were gathered there for vengeance, and I knew
That if I dipped my hand the spawn would clutch it"

Seamus Heaney

The purpose of the present chapter is to explore the nature of the state of mind known as "latency" and its function in the developing personality of the child. Chronologically the period characterized by "latency" roughly corresponds to the primary school years of five to eleven. But the "latency mentality" may be present at any age thereafter if, for particular reasons, the personality needs to continue with a mode of functioning which developmentally belongs to these early years, or needs to revert to it. Whereas each child will have his own unique experience of this stage in life, certain broadly identifiable modes of learning and behaving tend to prevail, modes which are closely related to the underlying tasks of the child's age. Initially I shall be drawing on clinical examples to illustrate both theoretical notions about latency and some of the characteristic anxieties and problems of the age. The latter part of the chapter explores some aspects of children's literature, especially those which lend further life and clarity to the complexities of latency states of mind. These aspects also stress the creative and imaginative ways in which stories and make-believe can enrich the child's capacity to negotiate some of the developmental hurdles which are particular to this age group.

In the most general sense, latency falls between the time when the turbulent passions of the Oedipus complex are beginning to subside, at around five, and the time when those passions are stirred again, with the onset of puberty at eleven or twelve. Latency, as the word suggests, is a period when these passions need to lie dormant for a time, while the child gathers resources in preparation for the major psycho–sexual changes to come. The laying down of this emotional provision is the central undertaking of these years. At the same time it furnishes the individual child with a sufficiently strong sense of inner identity to enable him to undertake the psycho–social tasks of, for example, going to school in the first place, at five, and contemplating "big school", at eleven.

Although many children will already have spent time at nursery school or in various day-care settings, a different kind of separation now impends, one that is both more extensive and more formal. The family relationships, even though they are still central to the child's world, nonetheless begin to loosen slightly to include, for example, wider friendships, the school day, perhaps also brief stays elsewhere. The success or otherwise with which these social tasks may be accomplished depends to some extent on the degree to which the emotional ferment which has preceded them is felt to have been, and to be, under control. If it is so, the child may be free imaginatively to explore the social world which is beginning to open out to him and to engage with it in a way at once playful and diligent. The exciting experience of multiplying skills and of amassing information is a new kind of flourishing. But underlying anxieties expressed through, for example, somatic complaints, sudden phobias, eating fads etc. are by no means uncommon. These may result in characteristically rigid patterns of defence against fears which originate both internally and externally. For the child usually finds the challenges of the outside world worrying as well as stimulating. And he may also become unconsciously troubled by what are felt to be dangerous internal situations, terrors of something unmanageable or uncontrollable, anxieties which need to be kept at bay if at all possible. These threats are felt, to some extent, by most children of this age. Sometimes they make for a tendency to timidity or obsessionality. They may inhibit the child from exploring and taking initiatives and limit the more imaginative side of the self, resulting in the repetitive and monotonous activities so characteristic of these years. Such activities, if exaggerated and extreme, may lack any great fervour or creative interest and instil boredom, even indifference, in those exposed to them. But in the more moderate expressions of ordering, of learning "about" and learning "how", a very distinctive sense of pleasure and achievement may be discernible in the child who relishes the increasing ability to manage his world and whose activities arouse interest and encouragement from the adults involved.

For some whose latency years have not provided them with the inner strength necessary to embark on the explosive sexual conflicts of adolescence, the restricted mentality can extend well into adulthood. In such cases attention to procedure and method may continue to be depended upon to protect the self from disturbing emotions. One particular patient, Mrs Adams, demonstrated precisely this history. It seemed that an excessively rigid latency period had extended far into her adulthood, draining her life of joy and vitality, indeed of any genuine interest in anything beyond the narrow concerns of her work-world. Mrs Adams was always meticulously dressed and had spent thirty years as a successful business woman. She came into treatment during her sixties because she had begun to experience panic attacks. She linked these states of acute anxiety to the time when, as a little girl of seven, she had been evacuated during the war to stay with a hitherto unknown family.[1] The states of panic coincided with her thirtieth wedding anniversary when she first acknowledged to herself that she had never really loved her husband and had never been sexually satisfied by him.

Although she could describe the difficulties, and sometimes her awareness of her own role in them, Mrs Adams was unable to attach any feeling to her exhaustive narrative of grievance and complaint. She could recognize that she might have a part in her husband's unhappiness. She could also recognize that she had only a distant relationship with her children (about whom nothing was known to her therapist except their ages and the ages of the grandchildren). She could register scarcely any emotion towards them. Little was known of her own childhood because little was remembered, beyond the horrors of the wartime evacuation. She had a practical, common-sensical and rather contemptuous response to everything her therapist suggested and seemed to think that to engage with feelings in the sessions would be an interference rather than an asset.

On the whole she dreamt very little, but a year or so into treatment she did report a dream which seemed to reveal something of her predicament.

> There was a fire outside the kitchen window of her house and she felt anxious.

This was all there was to the dream and there were no thoughts or associations. It was only much later in the session that Mrs Adams recalled that there had been two actual fires during the last few years which she had watched from that same kitchen window: one fire was some way away and the other much nearer. In the light of this information it seemed that the dream might suggest an anxiety lest a fiery part of her personality (possibility with sexual connotations) would get too close to her house/mind (or marriage?) and that the conflagration would destroy everything. Perhaps the therapy was beginning to bring up dangerous, angry, sexual feelings of an adolescent or infantile kind, against which she had spent so much of her life protecting herself. These feelings threatened the armour of conformity, respectability and efficiency in which emotions were kept separate, distanced and "organized", lest they trouble her more fragile and undeveloped self.

Mrs Adams treated her therapist's suggestions as if they were bits of scientific data which she could bring to bear on the subject of investigation, namely herself. One might surmise that the traumatic disruption of Mrs Adams's life when she was evacuated and separated from her parents for several years, was an experience from which she had not been able to recover. She had, as a consequence, developed her own impenetrable defensive structures which had served her external self reasonably well, but at enormous cost to her personality.[2]

This account of a latency state of mind in a middle-aged body is reminiscent of a therapist's description of her first session with an actual latency child, ten-year-old Vicky.

> Vicky sat expectantly on the couch opposite me, her short, straight hair neatly parted and pinned back in Kirby grips. She was dressed carefully with white, knee-length socks, which she frequently adjusted. She had a little purse on a string tied across her shoulder. She spoke politely and rather softly but looked at me with friendly eyes and an eagerness to please. Vicky paralleled this physical appearance and demeanour with an account of herself in terms of dates and places of residence, the external appearance of members of her family, and the physical location of the rooms in her house. She engaged in some doll-play in which the dolls were arranged into a neat and static line. However, she hurriedly told me at the end of the session about two disaster stories which emerged as associations to her mother's recent marriage. The first was that her father had also remarried but his new wife's mother had suffered an accident and required looking after, "the hospital had tried but could do nothing for her". The second was that a friend who had attended her mother's wedding had had a minor car crash when she was on her way to visit her baby who was ill in hospital. Vicky left our first meeting with the remark "it has taken a long time to get here and on the way I heard a noise and caught a glimpse of the underground". Perhaps Vicky was unconsciously expressing her relief that at last she had found a place to which she could bring her disasters and was also showing me a glimpse of the area in which her difficulties lay—a glimpse of "the underground".[3]

This "glimpse" of things sensed but not known, frightening things, which seemed to involve destructive impulses, guilty fears, disasters, was like the dream "glimpse" of the conflagration. Yet though clearly anxious, Vicky was far readier to engage with her problems than was Mrs Adams, and Vicky had an opportunity to explore them before they became rigidified in her personality. By contrast with Mrs Adams's, Vicky's response to a series of disruptions and separations in her early years had been to fail: she was referred for help with learning difficulties and temper tantrums. Her parents had separated early on and both had recently found new partners. Vicky had just discovered that her mother was soon to have another baby. Her anxiety about being displaced by this baby was evident. From the start of therapy she conveyed a desire that her therapist see only her and no other children. "I thought it would not be just me", she said, sadly, during her first session, when she registered the other children's lockers in the therapy room, and realized that between her 4 p.m. session one afternoon and her 8 a.m. one the next day, her therapist would be going to her own home.

During this first session Vicky absorbed herself in drawing, "in great detail and with careful precision", the inside of the local community centre, the main feature of which was a stall filled with rows and rows of neatly potted plants and vases of flowers. As she drew she commented on a new shop that had just arrived, having moved into a space vacated by another shop. The material seemed to highlight Vicky's notion that there could only be room for herself if others were moved out, or only room for another if *she* were moved out. Her drawings suggested a wish to keep everything static and under control, to hold at bay her anxieties about babies who might come alive and push her away.

It seemed likely that Vicky's early difficulties and her parents' separation had meant that she had lacked a sufficiently present and constant container of a kind which could help to mitigate her ferociously jealous and envious attacks on her image of her parents and, later, on their respective partners and on any new baby, fantasized or real. She seemed to have responded to her early anxieties by redoubling her angry attempts to get her mother's attention: screaming and throwing tantrums. As a result she had brought about what she most feared, that is, anger and withdrawal on her mother's part and detachment on her father's. Without a mother who could take in her distress, at least some of the time, Vicky seemed to lack the capacity to take in or to make use of any potentially helpful experience. It appeared that her learning and imaginative abilities had become reduced to a minimum. They began to emerge only slowly, with the increasing evidence that this sexually desirous and murderous little Vicky could also be tolerable, acceptable and even understandable to her therapist and, in the course of treatment, also to herself.

Vicky's particularly rigid ordering and controlling of external reality was a means of keeping at a distance the dangerous impulses which so insistently assailed her. But her behaviour did not serve her well in any genuinely developmental way. By contrast, with a child who has had a less disrupted early experience than Vicky's, these kinds of ordering, arranging, sorting, quantifying activities can also include a considerable degree of learning, of acquiring skills, of expanding knowledge both in range and in interest. These new accomplishments may, in part, be in the service of keeping unmanageable aspects of the self outside the sphere of conscious knowledge, but they may, nonetheless, also allow for more flexibility and for more sense of achievement and integration than was possible for Vicky.

* * *

Latency constitutes one of the three periods of human sexual development, according to Freud's original theory. It is described as beginning as the Oedipus complex ends, and was regarded as a biologically determined stage, during which sexual impulses were not so much absent, as less evident, and less actively engaged with. Freud (1905) suggested that energy was diverted from sexual aims to other ends:

> It is during this period of total or only partial latency that are built up the mental forces which are later to impede the course of the sexual instinct and, like dams, restrict its flow—disgust, feelings of shame and the claims of aesthetic and moral ideals. [p. 177]

To this diversion of interest, which he considered extremely important in terms of cultural achievement, Freud gave the name "sublimation", placing its beginning in the period of sexual latency in childhood (p. 178). The dams, or restrictive forces, were not felt to be the product of education. Rather it was thought that the more appropriate role of education was to follow the psychological lines already laid down and to impress them somewhat more clearly and deeply (p. 178).

The link with the dissolution of the Oedipus complex lies in the notion that if parents have to be relinquished as external figures, because the libidinal and aggressive attachments are felt to be too disturbing (and to threaten punishment), then one way of not losing the parents altogether is to install them internally, by way of introjective processes (see Chapter 5, p. 68). There they become part of the child's internal world, as a mixture of loving and encouraging presences on the one hand (the "ego-ideal" aspects), and of punitive and frightening ones on the other (the more classically castrating or conscience-ridden "super-ego"). As Freud, and later Klein in particular pointed out, these internal figures do not correspond exactly to the actual parents and their views and attitudes in real life. For the internal figures also carry the weight of the child's earliest projections onto the parents, whether in love or in hate. Thus, for example, the father who was hated for coming between the child and the longed-for sole possession, the mother, might be experienced internally as a much more hating and punitive figure than he ever actually was or wished to be. Fears of censoriousness and criticism related to these unconscious anxieties are particularly common features in this age group, often linked with an intense struggle against masturbation. For the general picture seems to be that in the child's mind this internalized parent objects to the child's sexuality. The introjective emphasis is very important, for it represents in particularly clear terms at this point, the way in which the development of the adult part of the personality is dependent on the child's beginning to let go of external Oedipal ties, in favour of a much more internally-orientated mode of relating.

After the passions and storms of the first five years of life, which are mostly dominated by infantile states of mind, there is a need for relative stability in order to manage the new demands of the external situation, full of untried experiences and anxieties, epitomized, perhaps, by going to school. A child, at this time, may be having to deal with a whole new range of sources of psychic stress. The more he becomes aware of himself in relation to the family and the outside world, the more aware he also becomes of what he does not have, and cannot do. He may have less parental attention than he thinks he needs; he may feel he has had to yield prematurely to younger siblings; he may fear that he is being excluded, aware now of the wider aspects of his parent'(s)" world. He has to recognize the limitation of his skills, in tying shoe laces, for example; or his difficulties in reading and writing, or in performing other tasks. Even as the world opens up in its richness and diversity, it becomes more tantalizing and more frustrating.

There is, then, a very particular combination of pressures on the latency-aged child, originating both internally and externally. Psychically he has the opportunity to shift to a situation in which he is less totally dependent on the external figure towards whom he has been directing such intense feelings, and more securely related to internal figures. How well this shift is managed depends on the capacity to internalize and identify with his parental figures. It also depends on whether these figures, in their turn, are predominantly benign or malign, and on how benign or malign they are felt to be. In this way, the child is starting to experience a sense of having an internal world of his own, a world in which the gusts and storms, pleasures and passions begin to be recognizable as belonging to an individual personality—to himself. The internalization of these figures is part of the struggle which is developmentally necessary to resist excessive sexual ferment and to provide the mental equipment which will then enable the child to deal with the current pressures and with those of puberty to come.

When these internal shifts and struggles are made harsher by the external social challenges—of having to co-operate, to share, to make friends, to separate—particular strategies tend to be adopted which between them contribute to the "latency" mentality being described. At this age these strategies may often divide the kind of learning which focuses on the acquisition of skills and knowledge from the learning which is to do with getting to know and understand the self (see Chapter 7). For reasons already suggested, the learning "about" mode now becomes more dominant and visible in order to support the new abilities necessary to engage with wider and more complex experiences.

The "establishing" of a secure latency period of the sort that can effectively prepare the individual for life to come depends, in part, on the strength of the instinctual energy (in terms of unconscious anxieties and impulses) which has to be diverted. Thus it depends on how rigidly this energy has to be kept apart from the rest of the personality, or to be repressed. If, on the one hand, the internal forces of the "underground" and the threat of "conflagration", and, on the other, the external stresses of school and family, are not felt to be too alarming, that energy may be used to foster learning and development of an expanding and helpful kind. But if, as in Vicky's case, these areas of the self are potentially too over-whelming, then an excessively closed off and emotionally blocked state of mind may prevail. There may be a tendency towards obsessionality and bursts of anxiety or temper if the measures taken to defend against psychic pain are felt to be inadequate to the task.

*   *   *

Nine-year-old Joe was a child who seemed to have changed from his bright, ebullient, articulate little self, precociously able to read and do puzzles, to a rather bigger boy who was uninterested either in his school work or in the world more generally. He had become quiet, nervous, withdrawn and uncommunicative; stiff in posture and sad in expression. By turn thoughtful and exasperated, his worried parents brought him to therapy, where, before long, not only did the nature of his anxieties begin to become apparent, but the method whereby he was trying, and failing, to keep them in check also started to be enacted.

It emerged that during the early years of his life Joe had suffered many changes of primary care and enforced separations from his parents because of their work. It may be that his intellectual and verbal precocity at this stage had a defensive side to it. Perhaps it constituted an attempt to hold himself together and to bind his parents to him by impressing them, rather than anything more genuine and serviceable to his personality. A change of school when he was eight seemed to have stirred in him something which he found quite unmanageable. A deep anxiety about anything new and unfamiliar, and about loss and separation generally, began to express itself, together with an over-close enmeshment with his family and an incapacity to move away and to make friends. He began to show a measure of guilt about all the early changes and absences, as if he felt personally responsible for them. Beneath this lay an intense fear of death which began to appear first in dreams and then in more conscious anxieties.

By the time the following exchange took place Joe had instituted a system within his sessions which he would often write out on the chalk board. His therapy time was divided into neat categories:

4.00 p.m. to 4.05, talking about my problems;
4.05 p.m. to 4.35, talking about what I have been doing;
4.35 p.m. to 4.50, playing.

The timetable was headed "What I do, a schedule."

This structure, though extremely mechanistic in form, none-theless seemed to provide Joe with a boundary within which he was able to risk further exploration. At times he would add "talking about my dreams" to "playing", and occasionally he would allot five minutes to "my feelings". At 4.35 p.m. on this occasion Joe said,

"I have been having some dreams about dying. Last night I dreamt about being dead and not really being dead but being buried in a coffin. I woke up in the dream and I heard this knocking and realized that I was in a coffin."

When asked about the "knocking" he said that it was "like someone trying to get through," but had no other thoughts about the dream. His therapist suggested that his dream might be about feeling that he was not as alive as he wished to be, that he felt trapped inside some quite deadly state of mind, as if something had got killed off while he was living. Maybe the knocking person was someone like his therapist whom he hoped might yet get through to him, to reach him and help him to come alive.

Joe looked at her intently and said "yeah, and the other night I just could not sleep. I went to bed at 10 o'clock but was still awake at 3 o'clock in the morning. I was so scared I would die. I was thinking that my pulse would stop and people would think I was dead and I would be buried." His therapist agreed that these were indeed frightening worries, both that he might actually die and that people might give him up for dead. At this point Joe was becoming increasingly agitated and asked if he might play "Hangman". [This is a game in which one person has to guess the word or phrase which another person has in mind, by suggesting different letters of the alphabet which might contribute to the spelling of the word or phrase. Each wrong guess becomes an additional part of a gallows structure on which the figure/"guesser" is hanged, unless the correct answer is arrived at before the drawing is complete.] Joe said that it was "too worrying" to talk about his feelings. His "Hang-man" phrase turned out to be, "worried about being dead and not waking up". It seemed that in the course of literally "replaying" his worries, they did become somewhat diffused. Five minutes before the end of the session, Joe sat down saying, "now for the last bit, talking about my feelings". He appeared pleased to be keeping to schedule and to be on the home strait, but suddenly again expressed doubt. He briefly commented that he felt proud because his dad had just got a new and better job. When his therapist suggested that he might also feel worried that he wouldn't succeed like his dad, so that his parents would be proud of him, he nodded and then went blank and said, "I do not have any other feelings." He seemed to look inside for evidence of this and then said, "No, I have no other feelings", and asked to play a last game of "Hangman".

Joe clearly demonstrated his own persecutory fears of being locked up within a dead state of mind and of not being able to come alive again, or of being thought to be dead without the trapped-little-boy being known about. He also revealed how these fears may have been closely associated with more aggressive impulses about which he knew very little, impulses stemming from infantile rage and fear about being left or abandoned. The unconscious, punitive and murderous feelings (the Hangman-Joe) which had not been registered or understood when he was younger, were now making their appearance and requiring a range of rigid and obsessional mechanisms to keep them in check, at great cost to his developing personality.

In contrast ten-year-old Annie seemed to be a much less troubled little girl. She performed outstandingly at school and seemed content, though a little isolated at home. None of her worries were known about until she came home after a holiday with her cousins.

She said to a sympathetic teacher that she had been worried about not making friends at school and about being bullied, but most especially about her parents separating while she was away. The only way she felt she could control her fear about this was to kill herself. With unusual articulacy she said that this fear was mainly about losing her mother. She described it as feeling like "a strong current under water which pulls at me and I can't escape from it, however hard I try". Her teacher agreed that that sounded very alarming and that he had a strong sense that Annie was terribly worried about dying. She replied that it was funny that he should say that because no-one in her family seemed to be worried about dying except her. "I'm just so scared. It's like not existing any more and then, well, something like milk in the morning—just something like that. You just wouldn't have it and also you don't know when. I mean, I might live till eighty years old or I might go out into the car-park now and be killed by a car. I can't know when it might happen."

Later in the conversation her murderous impulses became quite apparent, although she was herself wholly unaware of the implications of what she was saying.

She described how she had begun to carry a knife to deal with the bullies until another teacher discovered it and took it from her. This led into a description of how furious she often felt and how she managed to hide it, hoping it would just go away. It tended to happen when she felt excluded from something because that seemed as if no-one wanted her. "I feel as if I've been left, put down." As she spoke Annie had, with extreme precision, been drawing a map of the area in which she lived, with distances between home and school and her parents' work-place measured and marked with careful accuracy.

As with Joe, Annie seemed to be expressing anxieties which were very immediate but which also reached back to early years. Each child revealed areas of passionate attachment, fear of being left, and repressed fury which belied the more seemingly detached exterior.

*   *   *

Both these children became explicitly troubled, but the kinds of anxieties which they were trying to manage are typically those of any latency child, though usually to a lesser degree. Likewise the methods of control are recognizable, though not in so extreme a form. Socially acceptable channels for infantile urges will be found during these years. For example, destructiveness may be "contained" in an apparent delight in structured games and rules. A craving for order and discipline often develops as a way of supporting the fragile boundary between disruptive impulses and acceptable social behaviour. The acquisition of knowledge and skills allows for unconscious, feared internal "badness" to be repaired in the external world by a growing sense of effectiveness and control. The boy's propensity to enjoy "fixing things" with dad, or the girl's desire to cook and clean up with mum, or indeed vice-versa, will represent the ways in which each may be experimenting with different identifications, but these activities may also represent an important psychic need to restore and repair. The mechanism of "reaction formation" sets in, in which, as Freud and Klein describe it, the wish to wet and soil becomes the desire to wash, clean and order; the impulse to bite and spit becomes an interest in food and cooking, etc.

*   *   *

In general terms the latency struggle concerns the deflection of sexual and aggressive energy and its investment in the enlargement of other types of activity. Klein tended to place less emphasis upon the creative benefits of "sublimation" than upon the drain and strain of those processes on the young ego. She described the attitude of reserve and distrust which sometimes sets in, and the cost to the imagination of the repression of curiosity. While a child may still be happy to take an interest in, for example, poos, pees and farts, more serious sexual enquiry will often arouse acute anxiety. Such anxiety is vividly expressed by Seamus Heaney in his poem "Death of a Naturalist". Heaney recounts the intense pleasure of the young naturalist as he gathers frog-spawn into jam pots and watches them hatch into little swimming tadpoles. He describes the information given to the class by their teacher, Miss Wall, without the boys ever putting together the fact that the frog-spawn was the product of a sexual encounter between the "daddy" frog and the "mammy" frog. Once he put two and two together the whole process became horrifying to young Heaney and his days as a naturalist were suddenly over. He powerfully evokes the disgust and terror which this first-hand evidence of sexuality arouses in the small boy whose interest in natural things has not, until this moment, encompassed the reality of the processes:

> Then one hot day when fields were rank
> With cowdung in the grass, the angry frogs
> Invaded the flax-dam; I ducked through hedges
> To a coarse croaking that I had not heard
> Before. The air was thick with a bass chorus
> Right down the dam, gross-bellied frogs were cocked
> On sods; their loose necks pulsed like sails. Some hopped:

The slap and plop were obscene threats. Some sat
Poised like mud grenades, their blunt heads farting.
I sickened, turned, and ran. The great slime kings
Were gathered there for vengeance, and I knew
That if I dipped my hand the spawn would clutch it.

The Oedipal threat implicit in the last lines is a marvellous evocation of the unconscious sexual terrors of a boy of this age.

An aspect of the resistance to knowing the meaning of things is often reflected in the preferred modes of learning and the distinction between a hunger for information and a thirst for knowledge becomes especially clear (see Chapter 7). Meltzer (1973) describes the characteristic learning mode as follows:

> This drive of the latency child to amass information is very social in its nature and lends itself to competition, display, secrecy, commerce. But also, of course, delinquent forms of acquisition arise: theft, scavenging, fraud. Discrimination as regards value tends to be poor, just as the insight is shallow. Thus a child may eagerly memorize the names of football players or flowers without concern to recognize the objects visually. He may memorize a poem without concern for its meaning; dates of battles without any idea of human slaughter; names of capitals without any certain realization that it is cities and not the spelling in capital letters which is involved. [p. 159]

The toy market and the media generally have been swift to "cash in" on the latency tendency to collect, to barter, to buy and sell. The tendency is based in part on the anxious greed for acquisition, and in part on the desire to enter into the world they find themselves in, and to feel that they can have some impact on it. In bringing about their own versions of that world, ones which are based on their unconscious sense of internal relationships, the children also meet their need not to stand out as individuals, but rather to be "part of" something. It is this desire to be doing the same as the others, the necessity of sorting out the internal relationships between siblings and parents which, as Meltzer (1967) points out, leads to the external formation of groups in which

> the pattern of family life and of adult social and political structure are mirrored. His clubs, secret societies and teams tend to be stable

as regards roles, with more aggressive and imaginative children as leaders (parental functions) while weaker, more passive, younger or less intelligent children are dragooned into submission to the rules and procedures laid down (children functions). The obsessional tendency of this age group with its desexualisation of object relations through omnipotent control thus finds expression. [pp. 96–97]

*   *   *

Social hierarchy tends to be reproduced in a caricature of classification and categorization, the big 'uns and the little 'uns, the strong and the weak, the clever and the stupid. The crudeness of the categories is mirrored in the simplicity of the morality: goodies and baddies; Cowboys and Indians; "them" and "us". More creative children's literature tends to challenge these polarized versions of things by speaking to the more complex and thoughtful parts of the child.[4] These are the kinds of story which, as Margaret and Michael Rustin (1987) describe, make possible an identification with the practice of reflection on emotional experience which is especially valuable to personal development.

By contrast, the literature of comics and magazines and the contemporary programmes on television to which this age group tend particularly to be exposed (especially after the mental and emotional exhaustion of the school-day) merely reproduce the crudest versions of these already limited ways of thinking. Their popularity lies in the fact that they reduce to a minimum the unwelcome confusion and anxiety which lie so close beneath the surface for this age group. The tendency is to confirm the rigidity of the mindless categories rather than to diffuse them and to encourage instead a less limited and more imaginative alternative. And yet this latency world of acquisitiveness and commerce, of competitiveness and hierarchy, of collecting for the sake of it (football stickers, match boxes, rubbers, beads) is by no means merely a kind of caricature of the adult world. It may, especially for the more secure and enquiring child, involve a way of beginning to discover the meaning of his own world, one which may strongly resemble, and yet be importantly different from, that of his parents and family. There is an increasing need to develop a world apart, a world of one's own, separate and yet not cut-off from that of the adults. Time for engaging with one's own experience is needed, for experimenting with it, and developing a stronger sense of self as a consequence. Paula Fox's story, *A Likely Place*, describes such a process in nine-year-old Lewis's struggle to find for himself a place in twentieth-century Brooklyn. This painfully disarming story offers, in the details of Lewis's thought processes, a fine counterpoint to the well-meaning, progressive, and ultimately intrusive and confusing intentions of his parents and teachers. Lewis has difficulties, "for the place he is looking for has no inner representation in his imagination as yet". One of his problems at school is of not being able to distinguish "there" and "their". When asked what is on his mind, he tends to think of the surface of his head. So worried is he about the permeability of the boundary between himself and others that he attempts to hold himself together more firmly by constantly wearing a woollen cap, even in bed.

What a relief for Lewis to find an alternative to his interested and ever constructive father ("Lewis do you have a plan for those batteries which you're soaking in your spare fish bowl?") in eccentric Miss Fitchlow, "Something on your mind?" she asks Lewis, "So have I". "If Lewis could have a wish, it would be to make people stop asking him how he felt or telling him how he felt", a wish in some sense realized through his relationships with Miss Fitchlow and with the equally eccentric Mr Madgruga. In depicting these two figures' capacity to allow a child space and time to think (the older child's equivalent to the baby's space and time to find his way to the breast), Paula Fox offers a beautiful rendering of how a good experience is internalized and becomes the source of creative development and of the sense of identity. Well-meaning as parents may be, as in Lewis's case, other figures can also perform important aspects of the parental function for children in this age group. Sometimes a slight emotional distance will allow a recognition of, and an engagement with, the child's preoccupations or mental pain of a kind which parental over-involvement may preclude, or at least limit (see Rustin and Rustin, 1987, pp. 215–224).

The fictional worlds of the best children's writers offer places that a child may go to in his own mind, where there is the opportunity, though perhaps not consciously recognized, to engage with the complexity of response to their internal as well as to their external tasks and experiences. The rather organized and formal mental and behavioural bent of children of this age offers little scope for the mysterious and contradictory impulses which break the surface of what may otherwise be a fairly ordered existence. At a time when, in many ways, creative capacities are at their lowest, there is, nonetheless, much evidence for imagination being "a foraging impulse: it will find food for thought in the desert" (Meltzer, 1988, p. 17). The enduring nature of some children's literature is testament to its ongoing emotional significance. Two of Frances Hodgson Burnett's stories express the keeping alive of internal hope and of a sense of self in the hearts of the children she describes. This can occur despite the difficulty of external circumstances and the harshness and lack of understanding which the adult world imposes on the children, with which they have necessarily to contend. The two stories offer accounts of how it may be that, in the face of adverse circumstances, children of this age may nonetheless psychically survive. It may be that the lasting quality of these stories, which certainly have their mawkish and sentimental side, arises from the emotional closeness to the author's own experience, to her own capacity to survive external hardship through internal creative capacities.

In *The Little Princess*, "princessly" attributes are those of the internal world: of trust in sources of goodness from which derive qualities of selflessness, restraint, emotional generosity; a capacity to retain a sense of dignity and self-worth in the teeth of degradation; to resist succumbing to, or being overwhelmed by, the traumatic experiences of the external world. The story describes the way in which eleven-year-old Sarah Crewe, already bereft at birth of her mother, emotionally survives the loss of her adored and adoring father, and with him all the extensive material resources she had hitherto enjoyed. Far from being comforted in her plight she is immediately deprived by the school authorities of all her previous luxuries. She is cruelly treated as a servant and a pauper. To the mystification of those around her, however, she not only preserves her own integrity but also engenders in others, especially in the most needy, the strength to bear the day-by-day humiliations and hardships of their shared institutional life.

Sarah's sustaining qualities lie rooted in the keeping alive of her private and idiosyncratic imaginative world; in her ability to imbue her surroundings, however meagre or persecuting, with meaning; to sustain a sense of life and purpose despite appalling mistreatment by the adult world. At the heart of her inner resilience is her capacity for make-believe. This functions less as a manic escape from hardship, or as a denial of it, than as a way of managing to undergo it; to suffer the pain of it. The metaphor of the princess does not relate to material resources. These are proved irrelevant to the strength which Sarah displays. Princessliness is about internal matters of value. It is about moral not material qualities.

In *The Little Princess*, as in the later book, *The Secret Garden*, it is established that the life of the mind, particularly if it is shared with another or with others, functions as an internal source of love and of life. The eventual resolution of Sarah's predicament, contrived though it may be, has to be seen in the tradition of the nineteenth-century novel—as abandoning verisimilitude for a more significant psychic truth. The truth is that the capacity to refresh the imaginative wellsprings offers resources of untold depth, available to enrich those who come in contact with them in-so-far as they are themselves open to the experience. Earlier on in the book, the repository of Sarah's hopes, fears and passionate feelings had been her doll, Ermintrude. Ermintrude was felt stoically to receive all Sarah's projected communications and to hold them for her, in the absence of a more effective container. Later on, younger, needier or more damaged children functioned for Sarah in a rather similar way—children who could temporarily be felt to represent her own damaged and needy parts, thus enabling the more coping, caring and resilient aspects of her personality to hold sway.

Sarah's eventual benefactor, "the Indian gentleman", turns out to have suffered years of remorse for his (unintentional) part in Mr Crewe's financial ruin and death. The emotional recovery of the Indian gentleman is related both to the degree of his suffering and to his desire to make reparation. By contrast, there are some characters, epitomized by the wicked, cynical and self-seeking Miss Mincham, who are depicted as being unavailable to any modifying influence. There is a suggestion that there are unregenerate, and therefore unshiftable, destructive forces lodged so deeply in the personality as effectively to exclude them from the life of the mind. Such ideas are, perhaps, akin to Klein's later, more pessimistic, notions about human nature (1958).

In real life, the question of whether the reparative or the destructive tendency will prevail is rooted in an extraordinarily complex interaction of internal and external forces. Initially the balance depends both on whether or not there is a sufficiently containing presence available to the infant, and on the infant's capacity to sustain a relationship with such a presence from the first. As we have seen (Chapter 4), an excessive degree of persecutory anxiety, whether originating internally or externally, interferes with the opportunity of engaging with or trusting anyone, be it an external or an internal figure. Or it may be that the experience of engagement is so shadowed by the fear of absence and loss that dependency and commitment are felt to be impossible. The needed person may then be successively tested, even tortured and rejected, as if being willed to be the one who lets down or who fails. Such a description could just as well apply to an infant's relationship to the breast, as to a five-year-old's relationship to his parents or to his tentative friendships, or, indeed, to a fourteen-year-old's early essays with boy or girlfriend, or to an "adult's" attempt to establish a lasting and loving partnership. The nature of these later experiences will be deeply affected, though not necessarily determined, by earlier ones. One person will have the capacity to be open to those experiences which are genuinely different from the past, another will be bound to the ceaseless repetition of previous events unable, perhaps, to understand, to regret, to mourn and to move on. Patterns may be repeated, but they can be broken too. It may be that the wider world that begins to open out for the latency child offers opportunities to establish relationships which can help to heal the wounds of earlier suffering and deprivation. As a consequence, the pain of insight and then of determination, imagination and courage, can support the struggling self towards greater integration and towards moral and emotional development. These stories of regeneration and reparation attest to such a possibility.

Like *The Little Princess*, *The Secret Garden* also centres on the restorative power of goodness and integrity. In this story, these qualities are represented by the physical bringing-back-to-life of an actual garden (locked up by Mr Craven under the impact of the unsustainable grief of his wife's death, as a result of an accident there). The implication is that the trauma of the loss and of the "craven" inability to bear it, have resulted in a kind of psychic death, an aversion to feelings, especially the painful ones entailed in the care of Mr Craven's sickly (because emotionally deprived) son, Colin.

The metaphor of the garden and of its reclamation, expresses the gradual coming-back-to-life, the mutually restorative effect of the two young cousins' relationship with one another and with the few others around them. Both children had been deeply traumatized by losing their mothers in sudden accidents. Mary has also lost her father, and her Ayah and the whole world of her Indian childhood home. Slowly each child develops. The joyous, hopeful, down-to-earth, generous, even homely, aspects of their respective natures had hitherto seemed quite foreign to them, indeed to have resided elsewhere (the warmth and common-sense of Dickon's family, for example, who "serviced" the Craven household). Gradually these sides of the children's personalities begin to awaken and to become more integrated as the physical/psychic task proceeds.

There is a distinctively allegorical quality in each of these stories. The experience of loss, specifically that of a parent or parents in early childhood, is intimately linked to a tale of emotional growth, drawing centrally on imaginative and creative capacities. The stories were written primarily for an age-group in which, as we have seen, moral values tend to be rather polarized and simple (the goodies and the baddies). In these narratives the adult world also tends to divide, at least in the children's minds, between those who are heartless, exploitative and self-seeking (*The Little Princess*), emotionally remote, cold and cut-off (*The Secret Garden*), and those who are, by contrast benign, generous and philanthropic (*The Little Princess*), or wise, kind and thoughtful (*The Secret Garden*). The actual restoration of the garden by Mary and Colin, and of the family fortune to Sarah Crewe, can be construed as the confirmation and restoration of inner resources, still possible despite the exigencies of the external world. The latency child can thus engage with the hope and possibility of finding his way to a life of good, even of splendour, in the face of what may hitherto have been quite painful, bleak, and negative experiences.

Significantly, the process of restoration begins to occur in secret places—respectively in the private "attic" of Sarah's mind (which begins mysteriously to be furnished by the unseen hand of the Indian gentleman's servant) and in Mary and Colin's locked, walled-garden, sequested from the adult world. These are the private places where, particularly at this age, important aspects of growing-up occur. Their very privacy and separateness provide a much-needed, if temporary, sense of independence, of control even, and mastery, while their actual location is usually intimately and necessarily linked to the world of the "grown-ups". Few children at this age have whole gardens to build in and to occupy as their private places, or as the external expression of their internal worlds. But many find, or create, some equivalent, whether in themselves, in response to fiction perhaps, or externally in the worlds of the den, the hide-out, or the camp. Such hide-aways may later be resurrected in the shed-culture of the garden retreat or, more intimately and intensely, in the makeshift allotment structures where rusty bolts, planks and corrugated iron provide islands of solace and nostalgic rumination, where pottering in "one's own little world" is quite as significant as any actual potting that goes on. These are all versions of a "room of one's own"—the personal place/space which Virginia Woolf regarded as a prerequisite for the expression of women's creative capacities. Such private places in the mind/world are different expressions of interiority, where the exigencies of external reality, like "tea-time!" for a child who is absorbed is something else, horribly intrude on the life of the mind and disrupt the imaginative endeavours which are being undertaken in the make-believe, "let's pretend" place.

For children, the building, arranging, weaving, propping up, organizing (a stick here, a broken cup there) of these places, the thrill of the odd bit of cardboard found, or the button chanced upon—the fruits of scavenging—link dependency on the adult world with the blissful illusion of separateness, heightened, perhaps, by the excitement of "theft". A pseudo-adult and yet passionate air of importance often obtains, a purposefulness, a busyness, a sense of hierarchy as well as co-operation, lending scope both to obsessional and to creative qualities. The tasks the boys and girls take on will often conform to a stereotype, perhaps those of "constructing" and of "furnishing". The vigour and enthusiasm with which boys build and girls service or supply may appear as spontaneous expressions of internal identifications and relation-ships, whatever the division of labour in the external households. And yet they may often also be precisely the opposite, expressions of a fluidity of gender-role and function, a delightful freedom from the clichéd modes of identification which characterize the more gender-conscious struggles to come when the children enter puberty. Memories of the period during which it was still permissible to be a "tom-boy" are much treasured by girls who, later on, may have had to relinquish this intoxicating licence. There is often a sense of certainty and reassurance about roles and prerogatives, of something being "played out", despite an underlying confusion, which has comforting links with the adult world, while yet being felt to be independent of it.

Preoccupied with the questionable benefits of growing up, for this culture, whatever its contemporary and more organized permutations, versions of the Wendy House, may long continue to offer charms. It is a world which has very clear affinities with that of *Peter Pan*. Peter was so daunted by the prospect of growing up that he mistook the "role" for reality and believed it to be life: "to him make-believe and true were exactly the same thing" (p. 91). The "let's pretend" food on the table for the "lost boys" could provide no actual thought. When asked to be the boys' mother Wendy replies "but you see I am only a little girl. I have no real experience" (p. 95). Wendy knew that you could only be a mother by becoming one. Peter, caught up in omnipotent projection, mistook role-playing for really "doing". He spoke for all those who find themselves trying to bypass the painful process of development— the challenge of learning from experience, the difficulty of acknowledging littleness and ignorance. A tempting alternative is to try to adopt a pseudo-adult state of mind—a Doll's House version of being "grown-up", in which external form is looked to in order to obscure lack of internal content (see Chapter 8). Mrs Adams's life, described earlier, could be seen in such terms. But for the panic attacks which belied the professional exterior, Mrs Adams might have continued her rather two-dimensional existence without ever engaging with the uncomfortable disparity between surface and substance.

Genuine growth and development during these latency years depends on a delicate balance between acquiring the necessary skills and knowledge to manage the fear of the "underground" and of the "conflagration", and doing so in such a way that order, quantity and concreteness do not crowd out the qualities of the more imaginative self. For this latter self will be struggling, with varying degrees of difficulty, to keep alive the process of self-discovery, often in the face of what feel like overwhelming internal and external demands. Unexpected fears and phobias may, at any time, burst through an apparently ordered exterior. Learning about things, as an intellectual mode, is both socially necessary and developmentally helpful. It is even exciting, and a way, in good circumstances, of building a framework which may contain the more turbulent impulses and anxieties. For the moment those impulses and anxieties must be kept relatively quiescent, while the personality gathers strength to meet them again later, in more frightening and unpredictable shape.

Notes

1. In 1939 John Bowlby, Eric Miller and Donald Winnicott wrote to the *British Medical Journal* to point out the psychological dangers for children of the kind of separation that was entailed in the policy of evacuation. They suggested that the risk of psychic damage from such separations surpassed even that of the physical dangers of remaining in the inner cities. See *British Medical Journal*, (1939), 16th of December, pp. 1202–1203. See also, Rustin and Rustin, M. & M. (1987) "Inner implications of extended traumas: *Carrie's War*", in *Narratives of Love and Loss: Studies in modern children's fiction*, London: Verso.

2. The degree to which Mrs Adams had had to wall herself up could even be described in terms of a second-skin or of a paranoid–schizoid defence system (see Chapter 4). Nevertheless, I describe her here because her mode of functioning had so much in common with that of a particularly rigid latency child.

3. I am grateful to Vicky's therapist for this example but have not been able to reach her personally to give formal acknowledgement. As with all other examples, the case itself is disguised in order to avoid any possibility of recognition.

4. For example, in Phillipa Pearce's *Tom's Midnight Garden*; E. B. White's *Charlotte's Webb*; Paula Fox's *A Likely Place*; Nina Bawden's *Carrie's War*, Lynne Reid Bank's *The Indian in the Cupboard*.

CHAPTER SEVEN

Models of learning

"God guard me from the thoughts
Men think in the mind alone
He who sings the lasting song
Thinks in a marrow bone"

W. B. Yeats

A child's capacity to develop and grow internally is closely related to the kind of learning that has been going on from the earliest phases of his life. Depending on the predominant task, or function, of the phase in question, different models of learning will come into play. During latency, for example, a child may both need and enjoy the sense of an extension of skills and an amassing of information. At another stage, perhaps adolescence, this kind of learning may seem to run counter to the more imaginative and creative capacity of beginning to think for oneself. But underlying such shifts of emphasis between one phase and another, there is a further fundamental distinction. It is the one which Yeats so impressively describes as being between the thinking which goes on "in the mind alone" and that which occurs "in the marrow bone". A similar distinction pervades Bion's work: he was interested in the contrast between learning "about" things, and being able to learn from the experience of the-self-in-the-world.

Thus a chapter on "Learning" belongs at the heart of a book which is focused on the ordinary ways in which a person may grow up—internally as well as externally. The aim is to differentiate between the sorts of thinking and knowing which contribute to character strength and the capacity to think for oneself, and those which encourage the mere proliferation of qualifications and expertise—the "learning" which may measure external success without increasing internal growth. What concerns us here are not matters of social values and priorities, but the most specific and personal of issues—the kinds of identification to which a child has been drawn from the very first.

In over-simple terms the question may be posed: do the child's primary identifications (with externally significant figures or their later internal representations) seem to be of an adhesive, of a projective or of an introjective kind? There will, of course, be constant movement between these. But in any one child it is usually possible to discern the underlying predominance of one mode over another, despite shifts and changes. It is the predominance of one of these modes over others that determines whether learning takes place by way of imitation, of a mimicking, parroting, adhesive kind; or by the child's anxiously seeking to be someone that he or she isn't, projectively acting in role or even experiencing the self as if it *is* the other; or by the child's resiliently seeking understanding by engaging with his or her own experience of a secure, inner sense of self, derived from a capacity for introjective identification with good and thoughtful qualities of mind.

The importance of the link between these broad types of identification and the different learning modes which are embedded in them is that it both characterizes and illuminates fundamental developmental processes. The present task is to try to explore the origin and nature of different kinds of learning and the possible consequences for the personality when one mode takes precedence over another.

The following dreams of three adolescents in treatment may lend definition to the different kinds of identification in question. In the first example, the adhesive mode seems to have predominated from early on and seriously to have inhibited development. In the second example an excessively projective mode had also significantly impeded emotional growth. The third example, however, offers some evidence of early adhesive and over-projective tendencies yielding to a more benign introjective capacity, with a consequent enrichment of the personality.

The first patient, John, was nineteen when he began therapy. He was the son of a successful writer. His dream will be seen to characterize the type of identification in which it may look as though development is occurring, but, in fact, that development is very superficial, offering little genuine internal support. John's primary identification was one of slavish observation, imitation and mimicry of the social behaviour and appearance of those to whom he was close, particularly his father. He described himself as dressing, speaking, gesturing and behaving exactly like his father. It was as if he needed to be stuck onto the older man's skin, surface-to-surface. He adopted his parents' taste, their way of life, their interests and goals. He was frequently overwhelmed with panic at the idea of having to make an independent choice. Not surprisingly, when he began therapy his personality seemed rather shallow, as if two-dimensional. At this point his state was one of total dependence upon the thoughts and views of those to whom he attached himself.

John had survived his mid-adolescent years by appearing to be mature, although perhaps excessively self-concerned and lacking much genuine feeling for others. His behaviour was socially adaptive at the expense of any internal development. He had had no meaningful sexual relationships or friendships and appeared to have only a meagre capacity to think for himself, getting through the educational system by rote-learning and a parroting technique of the "in one ear, out the other" variety. This method left him with little feeling of confidence in having any knowledge of his own, with the result that the knowledge that he did acquire made no lasting impact on his personality. He was a teenage isolate, presenting to the world a rather fraudulent appearance of stability which on the whole attracted little attention from the adults concerned. He only came to anyone's notice when he started becoming seriously depressed at the point at which his age meant that, educationally at least, he had to take steps to separate from his family. Separation was felt to be both traumatic and damaging, not only to himself but also (at least in his mind) to the individuals from whom he was having to tear himself free. (He became morbidly preoccupied at this time with the idea of his father's death.) The characteristic defence against this kind of primitive sense of being torn apart is familiar in Esther Bick's notion of "second-skin" defence: a muscular, sensory or vocal means of holding the personality together externally which develops from early infancy in the absence of any internally secure psychic holding (see Chapter 4). In John's case the mode seemed to be a muscular one. He was a brilliant sportsman, as his father had been, but in no other area of his life did he excel. The requirement of any response beyond the most clichéd and conventional provoked intense anxiety.

The following dream epitomizes his predicament and focuses his aversion to exposing himself to the painful process of growing up, with the attendant anguish of separation and the risk of change. In the dream,

> he was a child, gazing at a Harley Davidson motorcycle (with associations closely linked to his father) which stood on the summit of a mountain, outlined against the gorgeous hues of the evening sky. Between him and the bike, which he desperately wanted to reach, lay a dark mountainside. He would have to ascend a steep, drizzly and foreboding road, winding its way towards the top. He had a powerful sense of wanting to be "raised up" so that he could simply "be" the motorcycle.

John longed, in other words, just to *be* his father, to be grown-up like him, having eliminated the alarming and hazardous adolescent process. He wished to evade the risky business of separation which he would have to undergo in order to become himself. His adhesive mode of identifying had put in abeyance any genuine growing-up. His unconscious desire was to bypass the problems of adolescence, or rather, perhaps, to deny the adolescent state of mind in favour of a pseudo-adult one; to deny, that is, the function of adolescence in the process of maturing into one's own, as opposed to a borrowed, identity (see Chapter 10). The fact that in the dream he was still a child suggests that the nature of his learning processes had, from early on, blocked the path to becoming himself as opposed to being a look-alike version of his father. While outwardly nearly a "grown-up", inwardly he had hardly begun.

The second patient, Simon, brought to his first therapy session a dream which also perfectly described his life's predicament: the major disparity between his external academic success and his internal unhappiness and sense of emotional emptiness.

He encountered a large pink, fleshy snail in the corridor of the Obstetrics and Gynaecology Department of a hospital in which he was currently doing a psychology placement. Inside the hollow of the articulated tail was a huge cavity in which fellow students were cavorting with a perverse, sacrilegious, orgiastic air. "Come on in" they cried, "it's fun in here". He joined in, but swiftly became overwhelmed by the sexually-charged atmosphere and rushed out again. He fled along a corridor, finally tunnelling his way into a lecture theatre and taking up a position where the professors usually stood, on the podium behind the projector.

The dream signalled the unconscious anxieties which turned out to underlie Simon's sense of unhappiness: anxieties about female sexuality, about homosexuality, about intimacy and intellectual fraudulence. In an attempt to avoid these anxieties he tunnelled his way into a place—"behind the projector"—where he could be in identification with his clever, academically and hierarchically superior professors, in order to evade the more dangerous and threatening awareness of his own immature self. His adoption of a projective mode in order to fend off painful experiences had hitherto stood him in good stead in terms of external success, but internally it had left him lacking any genuinely supportive structure.

The third patient, Tom, had, in the course of a long analysis, begun to move from the kind of adhesive mental state that John was in, through the over-projective mode which characterized Simon's learning and functioning, and beyond, to a more "mature" capacity to form intimate and loving relationships with others. As with Simon, the first dream of Tom's analysis eloquently described his internal predicament.

He was trying to play tennis on an indoor court of which one of the walls was missing. Every time he threw the ball up to serve, it hit an unnaturally low ceiling and bounced back at him prematurely, making it impossible to set the ball in play.

This dream seemed to evoke the frustrated experience of a baby of a depressed mother, who, as it was later learned, was to become schizophrenic when her son was two. It suggested a very early experience of lack of containment on Tom's part (the missing wall), and of the hopelessness of his attempts to communicate. His projections were felt to be prematurely pushed back at him (the unnaturally low ceiling), as if bouncing off the surface of his mother's unreceptive mind. This made it impossible for him to set in train the normal processes of projection and introjection in the game of life.

A much later dream of this same patient gave evidence of the third kind of identification under discussion—introjective. It described an internal situation which was very different from the frustrations and insecurities of his early indoor-tennis-court-self. The dream gave some indication that a process had imperceptibly been occurring in which Tom was able to take in, and make use of, a thinking and holding quality in his relationships—a process that had previously been impossible for him. He had started to progress from his initial adhesive and projective tendencies towards a more even balance between projective and introjective modes. He had begun to engage with, and suffer, his own experience rather than fleeing to his old habits of premature certainty, or to any of the readily available forms of mindlessness in which he had been inclined to indulge. In the dream,

> he was in a house that was solid, well-built and rather beautiful (unlike the shaky and chaotic dream-structures of earlier times). He seemed to be staying with a group of friends, not his old drinking companions but college friends whom he did not yet know very well but whom he liked and who seemed serious about what they were doing. Among them was a particular woman who had a name similar to that of his analyst and who had often, in terms of looks, attitudes and qualities, been identified with her. The atmosphere was relaxed. He found that he was unusually unstressed, able to talk, to be himself. He spent the night in the house alone, his companions seemed to have gone elsewhere. In the morning he discovered that the young woman had also spent the night in the house, but without his knowledge. He wished that he had known that she had stayed, but he also felt very good that she was somehow there with him, there whether he knew it or not.

Tom acknowledged that the containing house seemed much more solid than those of previous dreams and that he was at ease with the figures within. But most important and illuminating of all was the description of the young woman/analyst figure who was somehow there with him, whether he was aware of her or not; present internally as a companion and a resource "in the mind". He described her as having qualities to which he aspired and in the light of which he felt humble: ones of integrity, loyalty, helpfulness and friendship. The dream suggested that, at least some of the time, he could feel that he possessed these qualities himself, that within his now more solid house/mind, there was a very different structure from the tennis-court area where he had previously been trying to "play out" his life, in the absence of any obvious source of containment.

These three dreams have been drawn on as representing, schematically, the different modes of identification under discussion. Although each may indicate the predominance of one particular state of mind, there is always a certain fluidity and a person may be constantly shifting between one or the other mode. They offer evidence of very distinct types of learning: with John and Simon ones that had been in place from early times; with Tom one that he was able to develop in the course of his analytic experience. In external terms, we are familiar with the ways in which emotional factors may adversely affect a child's capacity to take things in and to learn, whether in the most general sense or in specific cognitive ways. Less familiar is the complexity of the interaction between what might be called a learning ability and a learning capacity, that between "thinking in the mind alone" and "thinking in a marrow bone". As we have seen, an individual may show ability in the acquisition of particular skills, be it with figures, words, computers, sports, exam-passing, but the difficult question always remains that of whether, in simple terms, these abilities, over time, contribute to the personality as a whole—to the singing of the "lasting song"—or whether they are developed either as distinct from, or at the expense of, other parts of the self.

A shy, latency child whose mathematical ability has served her well, in terms of gaining her status and supporting her fragile self-esteem, may find, in adolescence, that that particular defensive armouring or carapace begins to limit her emotional development. The turbulent and imaginative flowering of her inner-self may be inhibited by an understandable tendency to hang on to what wins approval and makes her feel safe. Indeed, as we shall see, it may be often only during adolescence that the degree to which an early use of intelligence as a defence against genuine thinking becomes apparent. As at any age, work may become a way of avoiding intimacy and evading engagement with painful and conflictual emotional reality.

*   *   *

Psychoanalysts, along with some progressive educationalists, have long striven to define and encourage the child's capacity to learn in a way which is associated less with narrow educational attainment and socially visible qualities and more with the enrichment of a person's creative potential. Conventional success and inner development need not be at odds with one another, but it is important to determine for whom, and for what, the success is sought before welcoming it with any special acclaim. Historically, psychoanalysis has always concerned itself with matters of learning and thinking, but the focus has changed considerably over the decades to the point where theories of thinking have now become central to our present ways of understanding the individual as a whole person.

With Freud, thought, or the ability to think was, roughly speaking, regarded as a way of bridging the frustrating gap between the moment a need is felt and the point at which the appropriate action satisfies it (1911). By contrast, Klein's early concerns centred on much broader and more personal matters of a child's education: on intellectual inhibition and emotional blocks to learning. She was interested in how psychoanalysis and education might together contribute to the blossoming of the personality in all its dimensions. She and her friend and colleague Susan Isaacs (who founded and, for several years, ran the progressive Malting House School in Granchester) wrote about the way in which intellectual and creative capacities are inhibited, in particular by anxiety and also, quite specifically by the repression of sexual curiosity (Klein, 1921, 1923b, 1931; Isaacs, 1948). Their view was that the child can only learn from his own real experiences and that the educator should seek to support those experiences rather than to stand in the way of them.

Underlying these views was a notion that the child's need to know and understand the truth about himself and his experience of the world (initially represented by the mother's body), was an impulse so fundamental that it almost amounted to an "instinct". Klein called it the "epistemophilic" impulse or instinct (1928, 1931, p. 262). She thought of it as originating in the infant's desire to fathom the contents of the mother's body, and she introduced a central distinction which later acquired significant dimensions: a distinction between intrusive curiosity, stimulated by a voyeuristic need to "know" in order to master and control, and a more enlightened desire to understand; something more akin to a thirst for knowledge, in the interests of growth rather than of mastery.

These ideas raised questions as to the degree to which learning and finding-out would encourage, or inhibit, the developing self; whether learning would be in the service of the genuine growth of the mind, or would function as a defensive prop for the more timid self; whether or not, at root, learning was an emotional experience. Such questions became fundamental to Bion's way of conceptualizing these matters. His theory of thinking (1962a) put emotionality at the psychoanalytic heart of things. Learning of the kind that properly contributed to development (by contrast with mere cognition) occurred primarily through experience and not through increasing the stock of knowledge. He pointed out that in certain states of mind "having" knowledge can become a substitute for learning. It may often be the case that a kind of mental law of "unequal development" occurs in which there is an inverse relationship between "brains" and a deeper kind of thinking; between an intellectual ability to manipulate concepts of, say, truth, meaning, or virtue, and the emotional capacity genuinely to espouse these things. If knowledge is acquired in the interests of potency rather than of insight, it may function in the psychic economy rather like a material possession. Wherever this happens, knowledge will run counter to any genuine quest for understanding. Much rests on the motive—what is being sought in the process of acquiring knowledge, and what is being avoided.

Bion designates the distinction between these different modes of mental functioning as that between K, a thirst for knowledge, and −K, the mental state in which experience is stripped of its true meaning and knowledge is treated as a commodity—it is superficially attractive but has no lasting or transformative influence. The model Bion draws on as a prototype for learning is the feeding relationship between mother and baby, taking into account both the disposition of the baby and the mother's state of mind, or capacity for "reverie". These issues reach back to earliest times. They relate to the way in which anxiety has been registered and responded to from the first. They relate to the kinds of identificatory mode which have been established. The dominant emphases of these modes may be significantly altered in the light of later experience, and in relation to a range of environmental factors, but important patterns are laid down in these early days, patterns which, in simple terms, may be defined as stemming from the nature and quality of the relationship between baby and carer.

Bion proposed the term the "K link" to signify a relationship of mutual dependency and benefit whereby both mother and baby could grow emotionally. Just as the baby who has been talked to by his mother is better able to begin talking himself, so too with complex mental processes: the baby's capacity for taking in sense impressions develops in relation to those same capacities in the mother, and with that capacity comes an awareness of the nature of the outside world and of his own experience of it. "Learning depends on the capacity for [the growing container] to remain integrated and yet lose rigidity. This is the foundation of the state of mind of the individual who can retain his knowledge and experience and yet be prepared to reconstrue past experiences in a manner that enables him to be receptive of a new idea" (1962b, p. 93). Bion saw this "container/contained" relationship between mother and baby as representing an emotional realization of a learning experience which becomes progressively more complex as it constantly recurs in different forms throughout mental development, finally encompassing the possibility of whole hierarchies of hypotheses, and scientific deductive systems (1962b, p. 86).

As we saw in Chapter 3, the mother's capacity to contain the projected infantile fears (the contained) renders the original anxieties more manageable. When something interferes with this early linking, or mutually communicative capacity between mother and baby, a quite different process is set in train which, if it occurs too often or too extensively, is ultimately in the service less of understanding than of misunderstanding, as represented by –K. This active misunderstanding is the product of the experience described in Chapter 4. At times the emotion to be projected is felt to be too toxic, or the projection itself too forceful, and/or the mother is, for whatever reason, unreceptive. At these times the projection is not understood by her and the content of it is experienced by the infant as being forced back into him, together with that non-understanding aspect of the "breast" (Bion, 1962b, p. 96).

The emotion which brings about this "denuding" of meaning is thought of as a primitive form of envy. The baby has hostile and destructive feelings towards the object/breast which is felt to have what he lacks. For example, the breast is felt to be feeding itself, and leaving him hungry; or the breast is felt to be the source of good feelings, but these feelings are being withheld rather than freely given (see Chapter 5). This emotion of envy is incompatible with growth and learning. It is the source of particular problems subsequently manifested (especially, perhaps, during adolescence) for example, in assertions of superiority, or in finding fault with everything, or in hating any "new development in the personality, as if the new development were a rival to be destroyed" (1962b, p. 98). The effect of this kind of process, which may *look like* learning is, in fact, to inhibit rather than to promote knowledge. The process is often tinged with moral superiority, one of the characteristics, Bion thought, of *UN*learning (1962b, p. 98).

The degree of the toxicity and of the intensity of the projections relates to the baby's response to frustration, the frustration that naturally belongs to any experience in which need is not immediately gratified. If the baby/learner is intolerant, there will be a tendency to try to evade the pain of absence, of uncertainty, or of not knowing. One way of doing this is to project all the more massively and insistently, to the point where so much of the self is felt to be in the other that an illusion arises that there is actually no difference between the two, that is between the self and the other. As we saw in Chapter 5, when there is no experience of twoness, neither separation nor envy need be felt, but, equally, no learning can occur. Bion suggests that an alternative way of avoiding the pain of frustration is to turn to phantasies of omniscience and omnipotence, as substitutes for the dreaded experience of being starved of food for thought. "Knowing" thus becomes something which consists of "having" some "piece of knowledge" (a misunderstanding frequently echoed in political debates on educa- tion, and sustained by the "mastermind" model of educatedness). This is quite different from what is meant by K, a capacity which resides in the more complex and arduous process of "getting to know" something, supported by being able to tolerate both the sense of infinity (that there is always more to know) and of doubt (that is, of being able not to know).

A characteristic of a particular kind of omniscience, one which stems from the lack of a sufficiently holding and integrating experience between baby and mother, is that there is a tendency to substitute for the complex ethical discrimination between truth and falsehood a dictatorial affirmation that one thing is morally right and another is wrong. A potential conflict then arises between the assertion of truth and the assertion of moral ascendancy. In such a case there is an attempt to avoid the painful business of moral conflict and uncertainty by the unthinking imposition of moral certitude, always a hindrance to genuine learning.

The infant who is capable of tolerating frustration is able, in the absence of the needed breast, to draw on his own resources, if only very temporarily. He substitutes for what Bion calls the "no-breast" something which amounts to an embryonic thought. That is, he draws on something of his own to tide him over, thus, in Bion's view, initiating a very early kind of thinking and learning apparatus. These resources result from having had an experience of a mother who is herself, at least some of the time, able to bear anxiety and frustration; from the opportunity, that is, to take in, from the first, that particular function of her personality. If he has neither a dispositional capacity to bear frustration, nor the experience of adequate maternal reverie, the baby will attempt, all the more forcefully, to get rid of whatever it is that the physical/emotional system feels unable to digest or metabolize.

A further hindrance to learning at this early stage, and one that is also a feature of the −K link, stems from the fact that, in difficult circumstances, the baby's predicament will be one of having to take back inside him not only his own feelings left unmodified, but also that part of his mother's mental state which was incapable of receiving those projections. The baby thus has lodged within him not an understanding object, but a "wilfully misunderstanding one" with which he is identified (1962a, p. 117).

These early interactions were offered by Bion as "models" for thinking and learning processes. As such they enable a fundamental differentiation to be established, whether for individuals or for groups, between the kind of learning and thinking which is in the service of the growth of the personality and the kind which is opposed to growth, favouring instead aspects of character which obstruct development—superiority, for example, or dishonesty, or moralism. Aspects of the group component will be discussed in the following chapter on "the family", but a few broad distinctions may be made here. When the "K" mentality predominates, the group is enhanced by the introduction of new ideas or people, and the atmosphere is, as Bion says, "conducive to mental health" (1962b, p. 99). By contrast, under the sway of the −K mentality, a quite different kind of functioning emerges, that which Bion would refer to as the "lying group", who are dominated by envy. In such a group new ideas and new people are stripped of their meaning. The group feels devalued by any source of interest or significance which is not generated from within its members. As a consequence, it becomes no longer viable as a group. The essential die-hard obstinacy of many group processes rests on an inherent resistance to change. Change is felt to threaten the group's survival. Change puts the group under pressure to integrate aspects of character and functioning which are felt to be more comfortably kept elsewhere, held off in the other person, or in the other group.

K and −K connote fundamentally different kinds of linkage between self and other, whether in individual or in group relationships. The individual's capacity to learn is determined both by the kinds of internal dynamic already discussed and by the modes of learning dominant in a particular family and culture at any specific time. Indeed, in any situation, qualities of learning will be significantly influenced by the attitudes of the teaching group, that is, by whether that group promotes or discourages honesty in the individual. Especially in an educational setting, creative thought may be undermined by the stirring of feelings of inferiority and defensiveness, by the push towards certainty which obscures further penetration into the area of the unknown. Perhaps not surprisingly, very little has changed in this respect over the centuries, as we can see in George Eliot's description of Daniel Deronda's disillusionment when he first went to Cambridge:

But here came the old check which had been growing with his growth. He found the inward bent towards comprehension and thoroughness diverging more and more from the track marked out by the standards of examination: he felt a heightening discontent with the wearing futility and enfeebling strain of a demand for excessive retention and dexterity without any insight into the principles which form the vital connections of knowledge. [*Daniel Deronda*, p. 220]

As we have seen, the kind of thinking that will be going on in any one learning-situation is based in processes for which the mother/ infant relationship offers the prototype. The degree to which an individual can retain his own capacity for thinking rests, to a great extent, on the nature of the learning that has been possible from the first. It rests on those earliest defences against psychic pain, defences which are inevitable in the experience of life at whatever stage or age. It also rests, as already suggested, on the predominant identificatory modes which will have developed in the attempt to resolve the central conflict between need and frustration and, ultimately, between love and hate. We return to the original question: does the baby in pain try to expel that pain, seeking to rid the self of it by projecting it into a containing object, or does he have the capacity, and the opportunity, to introject an experience which can ameliorate the pain internally? The third kind of identification, the adhesive one already outlined, is particularly visible when it comes to describing different learning processes. As we have noted, this mode of being tends to occur defensively when the three-dimensionality of a containing experience is lacking and instead a two-dimensional sticking-of-the-self-onto-the-other develops. In the absence of an internal structure, an external one is felt to be essential to survival. The result is that as little feeling of separation as possible is suffered, and very little learning can take place. In-so-far as learning does occur, it tends to be based in the memorizing, and rote-methods which characterized John's educational experience.

It is perhaps becoming clearer just how complex is the relationship between cognitive and emotional learning and their underlying mental states. The issue is not simply that emotional factors affect the individual's capacity to think, to learn and to understand, but rather that the capacity genuinely to take things in, and to use them to develop a truer picture of the-self-in-the-world, is rooted in very early experiences.

This question of the types of learning which contribute to

development, and those which undermine it, links the Kleinian picture of the instinct for knowledge to Bion's conviction that every individual has an unconscious desire to seek truthful experiences in order to know the self; a belief that people are fundamentally truth-seeking. Truthful experiences are, in his view, food for the mind. Lying experiences are its poison. In some ways, the positive and negative aspects of Klein's "epistemophilic instinct" look very similar to Bion's formulation of K and −K. Klein traced a close connection between the early acquisition of knowledge, and sadism and anxiety. She suggested that the epistemophilic instinct initially arose in the context of the child's anxious desire to explore the nature of his immediate world, represented, in these earliest times, by the inside of the mother's body. When the baby was feeling frustrated and needy this exploratory desire was motivated, in phantasy, by negative impulses, envious ones perhaps, to destroy, to control, or to take possession by eliminating feared rivals. The main stimulus was thought to be one of anxiety-driven voyeuristic curiosity. Slightly later, in her view, the baby begins to harbour a curiosity which is more akin to a thirst for knowledge than to a compulsion to "know about" things. The desire is to understand both the self and the other, to explore the self in the mother's mind. Such an exploration takes place through the kinds of projective processes which are in the interests of understanding rather than of disavowal. The discoveries made can be re-introjected and drawn on for knowledge of the self and for further understanding of the outside world. The first kind of investigation is profoundly inimical to genuine learning. It encourages a mentality which regards knowledge as a thing to be "had", to be possessed, usually for ambitious, rivalrous, competitive and self-serving purposes. As we saw with Simon, it carries with it many pitfalls, in that it stirs fears of fraudulence and provokes crises at moments of success when, for example, internal qualifications are feared to fall short of the external acclaim.

*   *   *

Several brief examples may convey a sense of the importance of discerning both the quality of the learning that is really going on, and its precise function for the personality, in relation to the motives and goals which underlie it. The examples each have their own particularity, but they are not age-specific in any precise way. They may be taken to represent recognizable aspects of the different kinds of learning under discussion, whatever the actual developmental stage of the children and young people described.

Susan was two-and-a-half. She had been struggling hard to come to terms with the existence of her little brother, Roy. By temperament she had always been rather brittle and nervous, by contrast to Roy's easy and relaxed disposition. Her relationship with her mother became unsettled, indeed stormy, after Roy's birth and she drew markedly closer to her rather bookish father, who, in turn, delighted in his daughter's precocious intellect and her new-found fondness for him. On this particular occasion, Susan was finding it especially difficult not to interfere with, and obstruct, whatever it was that Roy was trying to do. She would insistently "upstage" him with her superior abilities, especially her manual dexterity. Undaunted in the face of her contemptuous comments, Roy would doggedly pursue his projects. Observing, with growing frustration, Susan's repeated sabotage of Roy's attempts to fit different-shaped wooden blocks into their respective holes, their mother fiercely remonstrated: if Susan continued to behave like that she would have no jelly for tea. Only momentarily crestfallen, Susan immediately turned to her father and asked if they could "play schools". She sat, as if at a pretend-desk, while her father asked her a series of questions. To a casual observer the questions seemed startlingly sophisticated for such a young child: "What is the name of the Prime Minister?". "What is the flag of Great Britain?" etc. Susan answered most of the questions perfectly, much to her father's delight. But when she made a mistake she became excessively aggrieved and vociferously challenged his probity.

This simple sequence describes with great clarity the way in which Susan needed to acquire intellectual skills to help her to combat the sense of being displaced by her charming little brother. She turned to factual knowledge to boost her confidence and to enable her, in phantasy, to win her father over to his clever-little-girl, and in so doing, perhaps, to persuade herself that being daddy's favourite intellectual companion was somehow preferable to her mother's attention to "baby" things. The greedy gathering-of-facts-and-information was being drawn on to assuage her longing for the special position which she had occupied as her mummy's only baby. Ultimately, sucking up to clever-daddy, though perhaps temporarily effective, could function as but a flimsy protection against the painful feelings of her wounded and displaced self. There was a discernible risk that her parents would derive amusement and intellectual gratification from Susan's big-girl-self and that her baby-self would be overlooked rather than understood in such a way as to help her to integrate these infantile feelings into a sense of herself as a true, rather than as a performing, person (as we saw with Nick in Chapter 5).

*   *   *

Mental performance is very often mistaken for mental health and the desperate feelings behind the cognitive functioning are often lost in social and educational acclaim. Two highly-achieving adolescent girls were referred for psychotherapy: Sandra was capable and brilliant but anorexic and mute; Claire had won a scholarship to Cambridge but was prone to frequent bouts of tears and inexplicable distress. It emerged that both of these clever and troubled girls had suffered serious losses at around the age of five: Sandra's parents had separated and Claire's little brother had died of meningitis. Both sets of parents described how wonderfully the girls had behaved at the time and what a shock it was to discover that they now seemed so distressed. Not surprisingly, it soon became clear that both Sandra and Claire had taken refuge in academic prowess in order not to engage with their intolerable sadness. Each had sought to spare her parents further anguish by "managing" her own grief, through intellectual success. Their unconscious anger, guilt and rage, possibly even triumph, were "taken care of" in the socially acceptable realm of competitiveness and achievement. This turned out to be at the expense of an integration into their personalities of aspects of themselves which, at the time, they couldn't bear. Each found it necessary to disown and attribute elsewhere (in both cases, as it happened, into a troublesome and recalcitrant younger sibling) these dangerously disruptive emotions.

*   *   *

The contrast between the different states of mind under discussion is well caught in George Eliot's description of the difference between being egotistically enclosed within a set mental attitude and being able to form a sense of connectedness with all ordinary human existence:

> It is an uneasy lot at best to be what we call highly taught and yet not to enjoy: to be present at this great spectacle of life and never to be liberated from a small, hungry shivering self—never to be fully possessed by the glory we behold, never to have our consciousness rapturously transformed into the vividness of a thought, the ardour of a passion, the energy of an action, but always to be scholarly and uninspired, ambitious and timid, scrupulous and dim-sighted. [*Middlemarch*, p. 314]

The kind of learning which contributes to the growth of the personality is that which engages with life passionately and honestly, if painfully. It is a learning which encourages change, one which inspires growth and supports a person in thinking for himself and thereby becoming more genuinely himself.

The capacity to pursue such learning may waver or feel only sporadically possible. It is rooted in the nature of the identificatory mode which has predominated from the earliest days, but it is also sensitive thereafter to the complex relationships between internal motivation and social expectation. As the foregoing examples have shown, shifts may constantly occur between the kind of learning which remains "scholarly but uninspired, ambitious and timid", and the kind which stirs aspiration and further endeavour.

CHAPTER EIGHT

The family

"Psychoanalytical experience shows that character is deeply etched by the preferred mode of learning and these preferred modes are in turn deeply influenced by the modes current in the nurturing family group and its state of organization"

Donald Meltzer

I n the previous chapter considerable emphasis was placed on the nature of the mother/baby relationship as the prototype of a particular quality of thinking and learning, or the failure to achieve this experience. As the child grows up the containment first offered by the mother will extend to both parents, to the family, the school, peer relationships, to the wider community and eventually to professional and work settings. The way in which the family group functions can now be viewed in terms similar to those discussed in relation to the mother and infant: that is, how does the group foster or hinder the development of its individual members?

The "family" is loosely conceived here as a normative category, connoting the nurturing group, or groups, within which the child is being reared. The family may be a group of two, a single parent and child, or it may comprise a multiplicity of relationships between new partners, half and step siblings. What is at issue is how to describe the predominant ways of relating in any one group, whether a complex or a simple one. An attempt will be made to characterize a range of possible types of family in terms of how each may help or hinder the emotional growth of those who belong to it. The question is always one of whether the grouping contains and supports, or whether it inhibits developmental potential and the child's move towards being separate. Naturally states of enlightenment or of oppression in the broader social and political setting have a significant bearing on how any one family develops. Questions of race, class, economics, health, housing, isolation, jobs, friends, school etc. play an important part in the family's capacity to maintain equilibrium amidst the tangled and ever-changing interrelationships of its members. Yet whatever the pressures of the external circumstances, the way in which they are engaged with is significantly determined by how the family itself functions internally. It is a matter, for example, of the family's tendency to organize itself around the intolerance of pain and adversity on the one hand, and on the other, to organize itself around the enjoyment and promotion of hope and well-being, whatever the external circumstances.

The latter part of the chapter will draw on a particular conceptual framework which has thrown light on the complexity of the psychoanalytic picture of family life, in preference to the sociological. The emphasis will be on the internal dynamics which inform, and importantly determine, the quality of family relationships. These are dynamics which stem from the predominant emotional functions performed by the person, or persons, who carry the main parental responsibilities. Such functions include "generating love; promulgating hate; promoting hope; sowing despair; containing depressive pain; emanating persecutory anxiety; thinking; creating lies and confusion" (Harris and Meltzer, 1977, p. 154).

These emotional categories are not exhaustive, but they do furnish helpful models for speculation and, between them, they encompass a broad spectrum of the kinds of family culture within which the individual child will be trying to grow up. Without going into the descriptive details of each category, it is possible to make some links with the different kinds of learning already described.

The determining issues will be seen to be very similar ones to those previously discussed. They are ones which relate primarily to the relationship between adult and infantile states of mind, to the degree of containment available, and to the kinds of identifications which have been going on from early times. As before, flux is a constant factor and will have to be allowed for in any schematic description of these life processes.

A general account of family dynamics may offer a more specific set of links between emotional functions and learning modes. An individual enters the institution of the family by birth. Since the terms of the following discussion are primarily those of the two-parent family, it should, perhaps, be emphasized that whether or not two biological parents are present at the time of birth, two parents did originally come together at the baby's conception. Whatever the complexities of that actual event, the mother continues to relate internally, if not externally, to the paternal element in her baby's origin and being.

In the conventional situation it is at the point of birth that what had previously been primarily the dynamics of a couple relationship (though itself influenced by the respective internal parental figures) becomes part of an external reality. This institution is thus already the composite of several others, the mother and her internal and external family, the father and his internal and external family. This is a simple enough statement, yet in terms of the forming and maturing of a family, the birth of the baby has to be seen as a particular kind of event, in the sense that it marks the beginning of dynamics that will be bringing about continuing and quite specific patterns of relationship in the future of that family. With the birth, or indeed, perhaps, with conception, a triangle comes into being which may already be part of an internal triangle or shared phantasy between the couple. It now becomes a visible triangle, rather than simply an internal one, and thus introduces into the newly-shared joys and bonds of parenthood a range of possible problems: problems of exclusion, for example, of marginalization, of jealousy, and of competition. There may be a sense of loss as well as of immeasurable gain.

The change from couple to family is likely to bring into play aspects of relating between the parents which they will not have experienced before. Their baby's birth may evoke in each not only caring, devoted, protective, deeply loving feelings, but also quite infantile, possibly hostile and dependent ones. The apparent asymmetries between physically strong adult and helplessly weak baby may feel less simple than they appear. For together with the infant's actual helplessness is the enormously powerful impact of his emotional states. Together with the mother's mature and sensitive responsiveness lie other feelings of newly stirred uncertainty and ambivalence. Early and quite complex reactions may be aroused, ones which are embedded in her relationship to her own mother. Such emotions may be experienced with an intensity that causes her to feel, at times, like a powerless infant herself.[1]

As time goes on, particular aspects of these interactions, both between the parents and between each parent and the baby, may acquire special significance. The degree of anxiety, for example, which infantile emotions and behaviour arouse, will vary from parent to parent. Mothers have different abilities to contain distress and anxiety and to be aware of the areas of similarity and difference between their own needs and their baby's. Likewise, fathers have different capacities to contain the baby's mental state, and their own ability to support the intensity of the relationship between mother and child will be being tested for the first time. Feelings of exclusion may be re-evoked, sensed or actual, resentment about being left out of what has now become, if only temporarily, the primary couple. Responses to this situation on the part of either parent will be deeply affected by past dynamics in their own families, by present ones being set in train, and, later, by others still to come, the roots of which are being established in these early days of family life.

It may be some time, even years, before an unresolved difficulty in these early relationships makes its appearance in the family, usually under the impact of some kind of renewed stress. In the following example the stress was that of the onset of adolescence. The Willis family became increasingly troubled by violent acting-out on the part of their only child, Andrew, aged fourteen. The family came to discuss their concerns about Andrew's excessively aggressive behaviour towards his mother. There were also conflicts in the marital relationship, further stirred by the disparity between the hostility between mother and son, and the strikingly close and affectionate bond between father and son.

It was discovered that at the time of the pregnancy and birth of her child, Mrs Willis's self-image and confidence had been extremely low. Her distress was reinforced by two major factors: not only had her sexual relationship with her husband been physically painful to her over a long period of time, but shortly before she became pregnant she had had an unusual form of cyst removed (a dermatoid cyst), the nature of which, containing as it did, bits of hair, gland and nail, she had found repulsive. When her baby was born, she experienced him as a mixture of the horrible and the perfect. She could not allow herself to believe that her son was really an ordinarily beautiful little boy and not the monster which she had convinced herself that she was about to give birth to. She wished to give the "good baby" to her husband for "safe-keeping", and indeed to a large extent she did hand Andrew over to his father's care. The "nasty baby" she "kept for herself". Not surprisingly, the relationship between baby and mother became very troubled, constantly undermined, it seemed, by Mrs Willis's fears about her own badness and self-disgust, fears which she could not keep separate from her feelings for her baby.

The extent to which the monster/saint split, which originated in Mrs Willis's anxieties and in the marital problems, was later expressed in the boy's actual personality and behaviour was very striking and became the focus for the therapeutic work. The course that Andrew's development was taking both resonated with, and contributed to, the family difficulties, particularly his mother's fears of having a deformed child—the "deformity" now being expressed in Andrew's disturbed and disturbing behaviour (see Chapter 2).

This painful and rather dramatic example offers an extreme representation of a dynamic that is easily recognizable in more ordinary family interactions. That is, the way in which a family member may experience himself, and may indeed behave, is intricately related to the internal state, either of another family member, or of the parental couple, or even of the group as a whole. At times, it appears that one person may take on certain character traits that have been in some sense unconsciously assigned, fixed and colluded with within the group from very early on.

The family itself may, on one level, be quite conscious of, and troubled by, the manifestations of these "assignments", but may not be aware of their sources. Indeed, with families seen in treatment, these manifest roles are often brought, in one form or another, as presenting symptoms, especially if located in one of the children. In other words, what is felt to be the family "problem" is taken to therapy to be removed or cured: for example, the underachieving child, the phobic adolescent, the crying baby. Polarized and over-simple perceptions are common: "She is the quiet one, he is the noisy rascal". "He is doing brilliantly, she won't lift a finger." Such perceptions often describe firmly held views about a child's personality, but may turn out to represent differences and divisions which lie hidden in the fabric of the family relationships. For individual and group functioning are not separable in any simple sense. What has become clarified by psychoanalytic work with families is the way in which troubled aspects of the individual find expression in the family group, and how troubled aspects of the family group can find expression in the individual member. By treating the family itself as a kind of psychic entity, the unconscious processes underlying this complex tangle of enactment and attribution may become somewhat clearer.

We have seen how, from earliest days, in anxious states of mind a person will experience both himself and the other (originally the feeding mother) in extreme ways, either as very good or as very bad. In early states of mind, this splitting is felt to be necessary in order to preserve a sense of the unity, or integrity of the self and of the other. That is, the aspects of each which are felt, for whatever reason, to be unacceptable have to be kept out of conscious awareness. In the same way in the family, a sense of unity, either that of the individual or that of the marriage, or of the group, may be preserved by attributing the good qualities to one family member and the bad to another. In order to experience themselves as, for example, tolerant and responsible, the parental couple, or the group, may have to split off their angry and delinquent impulses into one of the family members, who then becomes designated the prob-lematic one. In some cases a lot of blaming, however unpleasant and potentially damaging, may be quite explicit and conscious. But it also often happens that one child becomes the embodiment of certain parental characteristics and/or family conflicts that are *not* overtly expressed; only covertly, and often unconsciously, through that hapless child. This is a process which is explored in Edward Albee's play, *Who's Afraid of Virginia Woolf?* Here the couple's grievances, hatred, bitterness and inadequacy are split off and projected into a child who does not even exist. If, by looking at such splits in the therapy situation, the underlying anxiety, be it about separation, failure, hostility, fear, or even, perhaps madness, can be stated and understood in comparative safety, the projections may be acknowledged and responsibility can be taken for them. They can then be kept where they properly belong, rather than having to be lodged in the other, be it group or individual.[2]

It is inevitable in a family that more or less benign or malign attributions will constantly be being made, largely on the basis of these kinds of unconscious identifications. The ways in which they are played out in any single family are naturally extremely complex. But generally it is clear that the more insistent and forceful the projections from the parents, the more danger there is that the child will take on and become introjectively identified with their version of him at the expense of his true identity. Similarly, a parent, or parents, if subjected by the child to constant and unremitting charges of, for example, ignorance or inadequacy, begin to identify themselves with those charges, to lose faith in their actual parental capacities or even to behave in ignorant and inadequate ways.

*   *   *

These processes can function both in quite immediate and short-lived ways, often as expressions of temporary anxiety, challenge and experimentation as much as anything else. But they can also function in more long-term and disruptive ways, ones in which the individuals concerned become limited by the attribution of characteristics which can seriously affect and distort their development. In the Chiltern family, for example, Mrs Chiltern had an intensely close and loving relationship with her son, Peter, whose frequently surly and unco-operative behaviour was a source of constant battles with his father, especially over his poor school performance. Though overtly belligerent, Peter felt demoralized by being the butt of constant criticism, and was rapidly losing any sense of self-esteem. While consciously disapproving of, and upset by, the tensions between Peter and his father, it emerged that Mrs Chiltern was also somewhat gratified by them. Through her rebellious son, her frustrated desires to take issue with her husband were being satisfied, and, through her husband, scores were being settled with her own father. For in her choice of husband, with whom Mrs Chiltern had had a coolly hostile relationship for many years, she had found a man who was in important ways similar to her father. To neither of them was she able to express any overt aggression. To address the problems where they belonged, that is in the marital relationship, was unconsciously felt to be too potentially explosive.

In the case of the Dean family, it was also possible to see the mechanisms operating across generations as well as within the same generation. The family was one in which one child, Mary, was experienced as attractive, successful, popular, kind, and the other, Christopher, as difficult, socially isolated, bad-tempered and under-achieving. Over time, contrasts which had, in covert ways, become established early on, had been reinforced: all good qualities being invested in Mary, who shone; all bad ones in Christopher, who failed. The process was to the detriment of each child, for in neither case was the other side of the picture acknowledged, so that Mary might own her deficiencies and Christopher his merits.

In both the Dean and the Chiltern families problems occurred when these mechanisms of splitting and projection, which had been unconsciously adopted to maintain a kind of uneasy family equilibrium, themselves began to fail. Not only destructive feelings and impulses, but also more positive, indeed exaggeratedly good ones, were parcelled off into individual members of the families, in such a way that characteristics became either over- or under-represented in a single individual. In these cases the function of the projective identification was clearly primarily defensive and concealed unworked-through anxieties, needs and repressed feelings on the part of the parents. As the years went on, each of these children's experience of themselves was a complex combination: of the ways in which their parents had perceived and treated them; of aspects of each child's disposition, impulses and anxieties, and of the different circumstances of their childhoods.

The ways in which problems which are internal to a family group may become internal to the individual, and ones which are internal to the individual may be played out in the group, can be traced with some clarity in the family background and early experiences of Mary and Christopher. Their parents had married just as the last war began. Mrs Dean had had a miserable childhood and had been passive in the face of the emotional deprivation forced upon her by a mother who, perhaps as a result of her own deeply unhappy past, had become somewhat envious and bullying. Mrs Dean was committed to trying not to reproduce the same situation with her own children. Her husband had also had a financially and emotionally deprived childhood but was less cowed by it, having compensated for lack of attention from his well-meaning but overworked parents by becoming a scholarship boy and separating himself early on from expectations of familial intimacy and peer group culture alike.

Christopher was their first child and was born during the Blitz. Mr Dean was by this time away fighting, and his new wife was left alone with a small baby as the bombs fell on central London. At the end of the war a second child, Mary, was born. During the confinement Christopher was sent away to a hitherto unfamiliar nursery and returned ten days later, a ball of tempestuous and jealous fury, never to forgive his sister for being born at all, nor his parents, in particular his mother, for the betrayal. His anger raged unabated until, in despair of controlling his persistent bullying and delinquent enterprises, and worried about his incapacity to learn or to take things in, his parents, despite financial impoverishment, sent him away to school at seven. They believed that institutional England would provide the disciplinary setting he needed. They had little notion of the relationship between containment and constraint, between structures of understanding and structures of repression. Nor were they aware of the renewed and ever more ferocious attacks on their young daughter during the school holidays. They later discovered that she had been terrorized into silence and had submitted to the bullying, in thrall to Christopher and his local gang of fellow-persecutors. As far as her parents knew, Mary was happy, highly achieving and surrounded by friends; her brother unhappy, isolated, troublesome and no good at anything. Both children married bullies. Both marriages failed.

Some interesting elements emerge from this outline. Christopher's problems did not begin when his sister was born. His mother later described to Mary what a difficult baby he had been from the first, and how ill-equipped she had felt to handle him, her first child, alone in war-torn London, with little experience of babies and no support. She recounted how he had never seemed to seek any emotional contact, even as a little boy; had never wanted to be hugged or cuddled; had never seemed to miss her, and was always "fiercely independent", as she saw it. There was such a contrast with her, Mary, who seemed a perfect baby from the beginning. "He was an alien little creature, but I felt at home with you from the moment I set eyes on you", Mary reported her mother as having told her.

In the Dean family, aspects of the parents' difficulties, however valiantly struggled against, were nonetheless expressed in their polarized attitudes to their children. For circumstantial as well as for emotional reasons, neither parent had had much opportunity to resolve their own difficulties, caricatured versions of which subsequently found expression in Christopher and Mary's lives. Much depends on the fate, from the very beginning, of the frustrated, angry, aggressive, sadistic and frightened feelings inevitable, to some degree, in any child's upbringing. In a family where the parent, or parents, can neither endure mental pain of an anxious and fearful kind, nor the way it is usually expressed, that is, in anger, the infant or child may be left struggling with his own feelings not only unmodified but perhaps, worse still, augmented, if the parents' feelings of rage and inadequacy are pushed back into that frightened young person (see Chapter 4).

In this predicament there are all sorts of options open to the child: to cut off from relationships and develop a pseudo-independence, too fearful to risk seeking, and failing to find, the needed response; to try to project all the more forcefully, as if banging the head against what is felt to be a mental brick wall; or to split his feelings, keeping good ones for one relationship and putting bad ones elsewhere. This latter process becomes recognizable when, for example, the "good-as-gold" child at home becomes the terror at school, or the one child remains the "goodie" at the expense of the other "baddie", as was the case with Mary and Christopher. The child who consistently projects bad and destructive feelings towards, or into, an adult (be it a parent or later, perhaps, a teacher), who cannot contain them and thereby modify them, often believes that person to have become the embodiment of the aggressive impulses. Subsequently this child internalizes a persecutory and guilt-inducing figure, who is felt constantly to challenge and undermine any good intentions or finer feelings. The child may then seek to get rid of this figure again, by trying to make someone else harbour it, or to feel what it feels like to be left with it. This is a source of the impulse to bully.[3]

Depending on the quality of the internal and external models of parenting in the family, the kinds of splitting and projection just described will be balanced by other processes, ones in which parental capacities of the kind that can hold mental states, digest pain and render difficult feelings more manageable to the child, may be sustained. Parental functions, at whatever stage of the evolving family unit, remain those which characterize the early state of mind of the mother "in reverie": a particular quality of unconscious, as well as conscious, receptiveness which involves the capacity to be "continent and cognizant" of one's own infantile feelings, and to relate to one's own particular child in his own particular context (see Chapter 3).

The parental couple, as a consequence of being able to hold generational boundaries and to contain the needy and dependent aspects of each other as well as of the children, may, between them, develop joint capacities to encourage those same strengths in their children. With the opportunity to internalize these kinds of adult parental functions, the children too can find the freedom to become themselves, without being excessively intruded on by the aspirations and anxieties of others. Thus they may be able to have their own experience and to learn from that, rather than to be the recipients of projected thoughts and feelings which would otherwise interfere with the process of "growing up". The capacities for generosity and restraint on the parent, or parents' part, will safeguard the ordinary communicative projections of mental and emotional states from acquiring too pernicious a force, of the sort which made life so difficult in the families described here.

In exploring the kind of family which can sustain and support the emotional growth and development of its members, the emphasis has been on qualities, attributes and functions rather than on stereotypical roles. In this sense it may well be that a single parent can encompass and combine within the self the various aspects of character, resilience, strength and integrity which carry the ethos of a benignly functioning family couple. It is the combination of such qualities, whether shared between parents or held within a single parent, which most fully lends itself to the encouragement of learning processes, be they emotional or cognitive, of a kind which are most likely to be able to meet internal and external demands. Learning of this kind is rooted, as we have seen, in a family culture in which the parent, or parents, are able to generate love, promote hope, contain pain and to think. Such a culture offers to the child the jointly creative capacities of maternal and paternal inner functions, whether or not both parents are actually present.

In externally visible terms, it may be hard to distinguish between this way of being, which so clearly fosters a child's development, and what can be called "the doll's house family". Here, in caricatured terms, the aims of respectability, security and conformity may be too highly valued by the parents. Such aims often stem from the observation and imitation of parental roles before there is an internal readiness to take on the responsibilities of genuine parenthood. Probably all parents are somewhat concerned about the external pressures of social position, achievement etc. The real problem arises either when those issues are the only ones which are felt to matter, or when the fact that they matter is denied. In either case the parents may be blind to who their child actually is. For being able to tolerate the degree to which their children may, in fact, be different from their aspirations for them is always difficult. Being sensitive to the children's independent needs and hopes is based in the mature capacity to bear loss and separation rather than to be locked into a more child-like imitation of what is taken to be "being a parent".

Families in which social position and "getting-on" are over-valued often gain a considerable measure of economic and social success. But there may be hidden personal costs to the children. There may, for example, be excessive pressure on them to fit in with the family ethos, to do well, to be good, to become accomplished and not to cause trouble. There may be a constant hidden threat that set-backs will be experienced as catastrophes, that minor failure will spell disaster. Properly engaging with the World of Circumstances is not an easy option for children of this kind of family, unless they find some external support to help them break free and attempt to do things in their own way, rather than in their parents' way.

Any one of the other broad and more negative emotional functions (sowing despair, promulgating hate, emanating anxiety, creating lies and confusion) will be likely to underlie the cultures of families in which the dominant mode tends to be that of the splitting and projection described earlier. Of the many possible types of "structural" splitting, a few may briefly be delineated here: stereotypical splits in gender roles may result in the predominance either of a matriarchal or of a patriarchal group, each issuing invitations to the children to gang up with, or to submit to the authority of, one parent at the expense of the other. Alternatively, the splitting may be *between* generations, for example where child-rearing is founded on criticism and rejection on the parents' part of their own parents. In this situation parenting tends to be based on ideas about how to bring up children in general, rather than on an understanding of each child's particular needs and anxieties.

A split may also occur between the family and the outside world, a split in which, for reasons of perversity, persecution or grievance, the family becomes pitted against the neighbours, or the community, and an air of predatory, scavenging, advantage-taking and triumphing-over-others prevails. There is often a deep suspicion of others' motives, especially those of the so-called caring professions, whether in terms of welfare services or educational provision. The introjective functions of thinking, planning, nurturing and containing pain tend to be minimal in this kind of group. Stirring up hate and sowing despair by projective methods often characterize the family's way of functioning, with the consequence that action is likely to take precedence over thought. The action takes place primarily between the family and the outside world, but it may also take on quite vicious proportions within the family. The next one down in the pecking order becomes persecuted by the next one up.

In any one of these scenarios of adversity the issue is not usually one of the conscious intentions of the parents, but rather of the fragility of their unconscious internal capacities. The "best-intentioned" parents may, nonetheless, find that, to their distress and consternation, their children are either re-enacting aspects of their own past or hidden selves, or are suffering in ways which mysteriously link to scarcely-known, but recognizable, patterns of their experience. These may be ones which it seems impossible to escape from, or to change.

These are somewhat sweeping characterizations, but they may convey some sense of the force which these broad family cultures can exert in terms of binding the child to a way of being which limits, rather than fosters, his creative potential. There are many

more: there are families for whom attention to "what the neighbours will say" prevails over questions of principle, or obstructs a
sufficiently sensitive registering of pleasure or of distress; there are
families whose "I don't mind as long as you're happy" attitude is
belied by covert competitiveness and concern with ambition which
is not lost on the children; there are families whose fears of
inadequacy pervade, in the guise of apparently unyielding and
undentable superiority, always knowing best; or there are those
who cannot recover from economic or physical set-backs and
remain chronically beaten or aggrieved.

Most families will, at times, function in any one, or all of the
above ways. But the emphasis here is on the predominant
underlying types described by Harris and Meltzer rather than on
temporary characteristics. Each type of family attitude attests to a
shared difficulty in integrating different facets of experience, both
good and bad, in tolerating them and processing them in such a
way that, on the whole, honesty and integrity can inform relationships both within the group and outside it. Difficult family circumstances will, to some extent, inhibit, but not necessarily determine, a
child's development. For the child's own resilience and disposition
may, especially with outside support, find a way of keeping the
kinds of qualities alive in the self which may enable him to survive
familial adversity and not so much to reject as be able to detach
himself, when necessary, from the more malign family influences.

More fortunate are those who belong to families where there is a
parental capacity to acknowledge and hold a balance between
constructive and destructive forces: to sustain hope, to allow the
children to suffer only what is within their compass, and to know
that a degree of anxiety is necessary as a spur to growth. The
children may then develop courage, confidence and respect for
themselves and their parents, from which qualities derive vitality
and a thirst for knowledge, truthfulness and understanding.

Notes

1.   The original Oedipal myth described in the Appendix lays out, with
     great clarity, the nature of internal family dynamics as they are played
     out (if left unmodified) from one generation to the next.

2. For further clarification of these processes, see Graham, R. (1998) "In the Heat of the Moment: Psychoanalytic work with families", in Anderson, R. and Dartington, A. (eds), *Facing it Out: Clinical perspectives on adolescent disturbance*, London: Duckworth.

3. For further clarification of these processes, see Waddell, M. (1998) "The Scapegoat", in Anderson, R. and Dartington, *op. cit.*

CHAPTER NINE

Puberty and early adolescence

"In time, who knows, the agitation
of inexperience would have passed ..."

Pushkin

P uberty is a time when bodily changes occur more rapidly than during any other period of life, except in the womb. This rapidity of change naturally brings with it enormous psychological upheaval. And yet the distinction between the states of mind associated with the latter part of latency (ten or eleven) and those associated with the early part of puberty (twelve or thirteen) is a complex one; and one which is not necessarily as closely linked to biological changes as is sometimes supposed. The physiological changes of puberty tend to occur earlier than the emotional ones, especially in girls—many of whom are beginning to menstruate and develop secondary sexual characteristics by the age of ten, or even nine. Traditionally the physiological and the emotional were felt to coincide. But now a discrimination is made between the kinds of bodily changes which would seem to herald the onset of puberty and the mental and emotional shifts in states of mind which psychologically mark the transition from one phase of life to another. The physical ability to have a baby is wholly distinct from the emotional readiness to have a boyfriend. Thus although the statistically and chronologically recognized years of puberty may generally fall roughly between the ages of twelve and fourteen or fifteen, an understanding of where the "psychic" part of this psycho–sexual change finds its place in the overall development of the personality, or fails to find it, is a different matter. For, as usual, it is a question of states of mind as well as of stages of development.

It is even harder to make a clear or general distinction between puberty and adolescence proper. For in essential ways they are inextricable—the nature of adolescence and its course are organized around responses to the upheaval of puberty. Adolescence can be described, in narrow terms, as a complex adjustment on the child's part to these major physical and emotional changes. This adjustment entails finding a new, and often hard-won, sense of oneself-in-the-world, in the wake of the disturbing of latency attitudes and ways of functioning. The means by which this altered relationship to the self may be achieved vary across an enormously wide range of behaviour, of different modes of defence and adaptation, from being the "conforming", "pseudo-adult", "good" boy or girl, to being the "tear-away", the "drug-addict", the "suicide-risk", "bad" boy or girl. It may take several years, or even decades, for the turmoil to settle. For adolescents the psychic agenda is a demanding one: the negotiation of the relationship between adult and infantile structures; the transition from life in the family to life in the world; the finding and establishing of an identity, especially in sexual terms; in short, the capacity to manage separation, loss, choice, independence, and perhaps disillusionment with life on the outside.

This chapter focuses on the physiological facts of puberty and on the emotional responses to it. Adolescence encompasses a particular mental and emotional orientation to life, one that is usually epitomized by the teenage years but is by no means limited to them. For, as I have said already (see Chapter 1), adolescent states of mind may be found in an eight, eighteen, or eighty-year-old. The mental or psychological period between childhood and maturity does not necessarily occur at the time traditionally defined as "youth".

Adolescents have been described as "that happy/unhappy multitude caught betwixt the 'unsettling' of their latency period and their 'settling' into adult life" (Meltzer, 1973, p. 51). What does negotiating adolescence mean in the life cycle of the individual? What is its function? What is its place, or task, in the psycho–social process of maturing?

In very general terms, adolescence is now regarded as highly important in a person's development, a crucial period of time during which essential aspects of the personality become shaped, and eventually organized, into a more coherent and stable sense of self. A notion of adolescence as providing a necessary period for the re-structuring of the personality is a comparatively recent way of understanding this troubled and exciting time. The view stems largely from the work of Klein, who had always been interested in a person's emotional and intellectual potential as well as in his presenting symptoms. Before Freud, adolescence had had special significance simply because it was thought of as constituting the beginning of a person's sexual life. But after Freud claimed to have discovered infantile sexuality, adolescence was, in a sense, demoted. In Freud's classic formulation in the "Three Essays on Sexuality" (1905), adolescence came to be defined as the time during which particular changes took place, ones which entailed a re-working of the infantile sexual impulses, in order that they might be integrated into the more intimate and loving aspects of sexual relationships. Freud regarded this integration as involving essentially three things: the crystallization of sexual identity; the finding of a sexual partner; and the bringing together of the two main stems of sexuality, the sensual and the tender. In these early days there was little mention of the emotional growth of the personality as a whole, and enormous importance was attached to the very early developmental stages of childhood, which were thought to be more or less complete by the age of five (the oral, anal and phallic stages). Anna Freud (1958) described adolescence as a "neglected period", a "step-child where analytic thinking is concerned" (p. 255).

Now, however, the challenges of adolescence and its resolution are generally viewed as making a central contribution to a person's future life, in terms of his character and the growth of his personality. Although versions of the pressures and complications which often erupt in early adolescence may have been rumbling about for some years, their stark and extreme expression will usually begin with puberty. At this point a reactivation takes place of the emotional and impulsive states which were, in a general sense, suspended, or "hidden", during the latency period. As the latency child begins to mature sexually, his reactions, phantasies, thoughts and passionate urges become caught up in a maelstrom of unresolved, and often seemingly unresolvable conflicts. Anatomical, physiological and endocrinological changes are occurring. The rising levels of sexual and growth hormones lead not only to the development of sexual organs and secondary sexual characteristics, but also to greatly increased, though highly variable, sexual and aggressive drives, often with powerful accompanying fantasies. The bodily changes already referred to involve fundamental alterations to the known self, alterations of shape, of smell, of texture, of size. Menstruation begins. Semen is produced. Bodily and facial hair appears. Voices start to alter. Genital excitability often becomes insistent. Renewed conflict arises, for example between the conscious thoughts and the unconscious impulses attached to these new physical sensations. This conflict is partly emotionally and partly chemically fuelled.

Whether or not such disturbances are felt to be manageable, and whether or not they can be thought about, will depend on several things: for example, on the quality of the original containment of infantile impulses and feelings; on the degree of stability achieved during the latency years and on the internal and external pressures which the young person has to contend with. Very often the conflicts are experienced as "too much", as having to be got rid of, or extruded from conscious awareness. Delinquent behaviour is felt to be a way of "letting off steam", at its peak, according to the statistics, at the age of fourteen. Such behaviour is frequently felt to ease the tension of the aggressive and sexual impulses. Moreover, in that such behaviour is likely to invite punishment, it may also be the means of assuaging internal unconscious guilt, if only temporarily. Delinquent enterprises test the boundaries of external authority, whether that of actual parents, or of those who may be felt to represent them—of teachers, or police, for example. But they also test the internal versions of those parents, ones which may be felt to be much more harsh and critical than the figures they represent. As we have seen (Chapter 5), these figures may, at times, assume monstrous powers, quite out of proportion to the external "reality", but a fair reflection of the acuteness of unconscious fears relating to internal reality—fears about phantasized destructiveness, whether in wish or in deed. As aspects of the young person's superego, such figures may need to be appeased, and punishment for external acts is often looked to to relieve the pressure of the internal situation.

In his classic paper on "Some problems of adolescence" Ernest Jones (1922) described the way in which during puberty

> a regression takes place in the direction of infancy... and the person lives over again, though on another plane, the development he passed through in the first five years of life ... it signifies that the individual *recapitulates and expands* in the second decennium of life the development he passed through in the first five years of life ... [pp. 39–40]

In other words, old conflicts, especially those of infancy and of Oedipal struggles, are being reworked (in the context of new genital drives), conflicts which test the quality of early containment and internalization.

The re-emergence of the kinds of sexual and aggressive urges which characterized earlier Oedipal feelings arouses the impulses and desires which the latency child has, in the intervening years, been trying, with greater or lesser success, to manage or to defend himself against. The important difference is that the genital changes of puberty mean that these desires can actually be carried out. The boy's wish to impregnate his mother, and the girl's to conceive a baby from her father, need no longer be in the realm of phantasy but can now move into a more frightening one of being physically possible. Moreover, the increased physical strength of the child also poses a new order of threat to his parent, as well as to himself. The child is faced with an alarming situation: he can actually enact his genital desires and destructive feelings rather than seek to satisfy those lusts and hatreds merely in phantasy, whether conscious or unconscious.

The physical ability itself may stir anxiety to such an extent that renewed splitting and repression set in. In early adolescence, sexual anxiety naturally propels the young person into a preference for friends of the same sex, but the tendency may be strongly reinforced by the underlying Oedipal fears and dangerous possibilities. The homosexual attractions and mutual explorations, so common at this stage, are usually a bid for reassurance rather than indicators of any more significant sexual inclination. The detachment from parents and the hostility towards them on the part of the early adolescent arise from many sources, but an important one is often an unconscious fear that continuing intimacy with parents brings parent and child too close to one another for Oedipal comfort.

Intimations of this alarming situation can be inferred from the fears and difficulties of Joe and Annie (Chapter 6), each approaching puberty and each exhibiting anxieties which, if they had not been gathered up and understood at the time, could well have erupted later, with even more disturbing force. With each child fear of death seemed related to their own unconscious, murderous wishes and to anxieties about separation and about feelings of abandonment. Joe's incapacity to engage with these feelings, or even to be aware of having them, suggests his need to keep certain areas of emotional conflict completely outside consciousness, particularly, in his case, murderous impulses towards a father. During latency Joe was struggling, by means of increasingly obsessional defences, to hold these anxieties at bay. When desires and fears that are already strong become intensified by the biological changes of puberty, a child such as Joe might, if he had no help or support, find himself having to contend with unmanageable feelings. His fear of dying, and/or of being trapped inside a coffin-like object, could be interpreted as evidence of anxiety about guilt and punishment for having sought to enter into, and to possess, what he most wanted, namely his mother. He was terrified that, once inside, he would be trapped and consigned to a living death. Indeed this was a fairly accurate representation both of what Joe felt his state of mind to be and of how he was experienced by others.

Similarly, it could be conjectured that Annie's self-destructive predicament suggested intense anxiety, not so much about the stated fear (lest her parents separate in her absence, and in so doing leave her outcast and abandoned) as about an unconscious, and not yet knowable wish, the wish that the desired separation should indeed occur. Her primitive terror and rage about being excluded from the parental couple may have originally stirred in her a particularly intense need to displace and possess. There were hints of the degree of her destructiveness, and of her struggle to overcome it, in the way in which she described her anger, and, more seriously, in her impulse to mete out to herself (by dying) what she was guiltily wishing to do to the other. Her major worry was in relation to losing her mother, a worry which very possibly also incorporated a wish to oust her. Such a wish was accompanied by fear and anxiety about what these desires, both to separate her parents and to separate from them, might really entail.

As the child develops, his or her anxiety about the kinds of separation which may now be quite appropriate to their age, naturally re-evokes these earlier fears. Such fears, if they were not sufficiently contained and understood at the time, will now be kept in check only by extreme measures. Similar sorts of underlying impulses in Joe and Annie were, as we have seen, expressed very differently by each of them and were met by each with quite different defensive strategies. Annie's anxiety burst traumatically across an apparently successful and accommodating path through latency. Joe's had begun more insidiously to undermine his confidence, his faith in himself and in his relations to others, draining him of his previously lively and intelligent self. In each case it was clear that the earlier uncontained anxieties could not be sufficiently held or kept in proportion, even by the rigid splitting, projection and repression that are characteristic of latency.

With children like Joe and Annie, already troubled by unresolved Oedipal problems, it is easy to see how the revival of the original feelings, now intensified by biological changes, could, in early adolescence, demand ever more radical forms of psychic defence. But even when life has been reasonably steady in the preceding years, the changes of puberty can set in train what seem like major personality alterations, often to the consternation of all, and not least to the child himself. These test the quality of early internalizations. They test how well the child is able to contain his emotions. They are highly variable in relation to intensities of hormonal change and to social and familial pressures. For when the strength of internal structures is being so severely challenged, the external environmental ones acquire enormous significance. Are they supportive or further undermining? The degree of coherence and harmony in peer groups, in school life or in the family, is crucial to the availability, or absence, of some kind of broader containing structure within which these confusing and troubling dynamics may be confronted and thought about. Adolescence may be compliant or rebellious—it is a process, not a state.

In general terms, this process may be said to represent an extraordinary range of different ways of processing the mental pain, confusion, and conflict which are initially stirred up by the physical changes taking place. There is often a bias towards the expulsion of the pain rather than the containing of it, so evident in the adolescent's tendency to enact, or to "act out" internal conflict, in preference to trying to resolve it. Indeed, technically, "acting out" means precisely this, the replacement of thought by action in order to reduce internal conflict. The general propensity to rely on extreme projective mechanisms rather than on introjective ones as a mode of functioning, and the constant tension between the two, could be said to typify the adolescent's approach to his difficulties.

Many aspects of this kind of behaviour constitute different versions of a non-thinking process by which the young person attempts to stave off, or to hold in abeyance, any kind of engagement with his actual feelings, in his actual circumstances. The aim is to avoid internal conflict, if at all possible, by adopting a range of defensive measures to protect the self from what are felt to be excessively disturbing, confusing or disruptive states of mind. The impulse tends to be to act rather than to think; to move in groups, sometimes gangs, rather than to risk being an individual; to become ill physically rather than to suffer emotionally (to "somatize"); to experience the world, the self and other people in extreme terms, of good and bad ("splitting"); to take drugs, alcohol or abusive substances in an attempt, literally, to become mindless. Another, less easily detectable way of evading the turbulence of these years is to become pseudo-mature, thus being only apparently mindful, in the sense that ideas and information may be acquired for the purpose of self-protection rather than for the love of knowledge (see Chapter 7). For many in this age group use intelligence itself as a defence against real thinking, or as a way of avoiding intimacy and the risk of being disturbed by emotional reality.

Characteristically, the adolescent draws on projective mechanisms in his desire to get rid of uncomfortable feelings. This unconscious process of attributing to others what are really aspects of the self means that somebody else can then become the problem if it is the "bad" parts that are being projected, or indeed the favoured one if it is the "good" parts which are now felt to reside in the other and not in the self. This latter experience of being depleted of lively and imaginative qualities and left with only dull and ordinary ones may become a basis for self-doubt, depression and lack of confidence.

Yet it may also be that the great tendency of this age group toward depression, to loneliness, to the sense of being stuck or of being different from everyone else represents, in part, the failure of projection—an absence of the questing and experimentation which, despite being painful and confusing, need, at this point, to be embraced. Though much less likely to attract attention to himself, the withdrawn or isolated young person may be suffering from a kind of internal impasse. Such an impasse is often related to not being able to participate in the to-and-fro of the sorts of projection and re-introjection which are a necessary part of establishing a sense of self at any age, but particularly during the unstable flux of early adolescence.

Thus, in some respects, during adolescence projective tendencies, if moderate, can in a more positive way ease the conflicts. For if there is a certain flexibility and fluidity in terms of the aspects of the self that are being projected, and then re-introjected, a degree of self-exploration can occur. Parts of the self can be related to in the other, and can then be owned or further disowned by the self. The projective mode, if not too extreme, may at this stage stem from curiosity about the self as well as from anxiety, and may thus enable someone to investigate and engage with emotional possibilities which are not yet experienced as integrateable into his sense of who he is. The adolescent's frequent changes of style of dress, of music and of taste may, especially in the early teenage years, betoken precisely this exploratory uncertainty—the need temporarily to "be" someone else, in order to sort out "whether the cap fits".

In the most general terms, the developmental progress that may be hoped for in the course of adolescence, if things go well, can be characterized as epitomizing a fundamental aspect of life's endeavour: the move from a state of mind dominated by selfish and narcissistic interests, to one in which there is a genuine concern for the feelings and experiences of others—a more "object-related" state of mind. As we have seen, George Eliot much less aridly described the move as marking the difference between the tendency to experience the world "as an udder to feed our supreme selves" and the capacity to recognize and relate to another as having a separate centre of self, "whence the lights and shadows must always fall with a certain difference". More technically, adolescence can be thought of as requiring a re-working and re-establishing, however reluctantly, of the earlier emotional gains of the depressive position, in the face of renewed paranoid–schizoid splits. The reluctance is evident in the way the adolescent characteristically attempts to bypass the complex and painful task of working through depressive anxieties. For to do so, at whatever age, is no easy task, in that what is meant by "working through" involves a re-engagement with the sense of guilt and responsibility for damage done, with fears of loss, with gratitude and sensitivity to others. Such a process is prerequisite to the feeling that there is an internal sense of self of some strength and coherence.

Early adolescence is a crucial time of inevitable turmoil and confused identity. The emphasis here is on "crucial", since the undergoing of turmoil and confusion is an important and necessary aspect of the adolescent process. It is also the case that the very stress of undergoing this degree of psychic disruption and dislocation may often propel the adolescent into various behavioural and emotional states which can be disturbing and a worry to others. For many "normal" manifestations of adolescent confusions are hard to tell apart from what may dramatically, or insidiously, become "pathological" ones.

The kinds of attitude and behaviour which arouse concern are often attempts to avoid suffering by "refusing" to engage with what is really going on, with that which Beta Copley (1993) explores in "the agitation of inexperience" (p. 57). This latter tendency to avoidance often functions as a defence against the full impact of confused and painful feelings, as a protective, though fragile, carapace within which the more vulnerable aspects of the personality may shelter for a time. ("I don't know why I cut myself", said one fifteen-year-old. "Maybe I just couldn't face the music. I mean my own music.") But such a carapace is all too prone to fissure or breakage. The precipitating forces may be from external circumstances: bereavement, broken friendships and relationships, ill health, exam stress, leaving home, even the impact of success which is felt to be unmerited. Or they may occur as a result of internal circumstances: the eruption of buried impulses, tormenting and insistent thoughts, inexplicable obsessions, perverse desires, aggression, alienation, despair. In adolescence it is usual for the external and the internal to become confused. What we are often witnessing in the crises and tumults is the failure of the systems of defence, or of the modes of functioning, which have more or less worked so far. The protective mechanisms of latency which have offered temporary camouflage for, or refuge from, the more troublesome elements in the personality, no longer suffice. Many adolescents belatedly discover that the containing (as well as restraining) structure of the family and of school life provided a lot more security than the often tempestuous relationships with either, or both, had suggested at the time.

There may be a good as well as a bad side to the various defensive strategies which are drawn on, although sources of optimism often feel all too remote. The taking of drugs and alcohol, for example, may represent a preference for insistently mindless states, that is, ones in which there is little capacity to engage with the properly "thinking" self, a self who is able to exercise a measure of restraint and to make sense of what he is doing. But such activities may, as already suggested, also include a degree of self-exploration. However risky, this kind of behaviour can also be helpful in discovering different aspects of the self, just as we have seen with some projective tendencies. The main question is one of "too much" and of "too little". When does self-exploration become abuse or addiction; when do care and restraint become obsessionality; when does a degree of masochism become self-mutilation? ("I can't bear mental pain", was the opening remark of a waif-like adolescent presenting herself for a first assessment, her arm a scarred patchwork of stitched-up lacerations.) When does the supportive group become the subversive gang in which the individual personality becomes subsumed under group values of a destructive rather than constructive kind? When does withdrawal from the characteristic adolescent mêlée turn into a worrying degree of boredom, listlessness and apathy? When does anxiety about sexual identity become fear and hatred of homosexuality? When do slightly controlling food fads, particularly around body image, become serious eating disorders? When does a tendency to hard work turn into an inability to enjoy oneself? When does ebullience become mania, or caution become depression? In each case there may be very fine lines between ordinary adolescent processes and worrying indications of pathology. To make discriminations between the two is a problem, as much for the adolescent himself as for those concerned with his welfare.

Clearly at this point of sexual development and character formation, the various ways in which that interrelation itself links to the different identifications with which the adolescent is experimenting are inextricable. At puberty an attempt is made to break out of the constrictions on sexuality imposed during latency. The child now seeks to achieve sexual potency. In the early days, this attempt may feel compelling yet it may also feel alarming. It may result in anxieties about potency being expressed in a whole variety of different ways: by the behaviour typical of what may be called a "phallic swagger", for example; or by a kind of know-all, pseudo-maturity; or by withdrawal from the threat of intimacy altogether. Such withdrawal may involve an intensification of the caution and unadventurousness characteristic of latency—behaviour which often borders on the obsessional. Splitting takes place but of a rather different kind from that encountered earlier. At puberty, a splitting occurs between different parts of the self. It is not so much that the internal world as a whole is being externalized and played out, as in the structured games and hierarchical pecking-order of the previous phase. It is rather that the general certainty, however precariously upheld, of that earlier period dissolves into confusion about good and bad, adult and infantile, male and female etc.

The much more insistent and confusing splitting of the self which results has characteristics, as we have seen, of a paranoid–schizoid state of mind: not only does the other come to be experienced in extreme terms of love and hate, the polarities of which are felt to be irreconcilable, but the self also comes to be experienced in equally extreme terms. The "teenager" may be co-operative one moment, recalcitrant the next, unable easily to acknowledge that he who undertook the task and he who failed to deliver was one and the same, namely himself. All this is taking place in a parental setting which is not felt to be "holding" in the same way as before. The result is that excessive splitting is often directed towards, and indeed actually threatens, what had previously been felt to be the secure boundaries of life in the family. The latency period, perhaps never as stable as the epithet suggests, is decisively unsettled and the young adolescent becomes

attached to a group-orientated subculture in which peer relationships acquire enormous significance. For at this time of stress and
change, the adolescent group often begins to perform an extremely
important holding function. As family bonds start to loosen, social
life to extend, and feelings of uncertainty and confusion to intensify,
the company of friends may be sought to enable the young person
to sustain some kind of relationship with the different aspects of his
personality. He may temporarily be having difficulty in integrating
these different aspects into his previously known childhood self—
feelings, fears and impulses which are dimly recognizable, but also
frighteningly unfamiliar.

Group members often come together in flexible and changing
combinations in which the various individuals represent different
aspects of each others' personalities, whether attributes or deficiencies, ones that are desired or repudiated. When these different
aspects of self are located in the group, the adolescent can remain in
touch with them, as somehow pertaining to himself, and yet not be
excessively troubled by them. Thus groups can become safe places
in which different parts of the personality may be played out,
especially the parts which, for some reason, are felt either to be
difficult to experience as belonging to the known-self, or to reinforce
the known-self. When benign, group life can provide these young
people with social ways of sorting out who they are. The seemingly
inexhaustible appetite for conversations (especially on the tele-
phone) about each other's feelings, reactions and activities offer
possibilities of "trying out", or experimenting with, different
versions of themselves and others' reactions to them. As such, they
are endlessly fascinating to those concerned, and often involve the
invaluable ingredient of humour as a bulwark against taking
themselves too seriously.

When feelings are particularly intense, adolescent groups take
on an almost tribal significance of passion and attachment towards
each other and hostility or indifference towards adults, or towards
other groups. The negativity is often difficult for parents to
understand or to tolerate. And yet these powerful, fluctuating
relationships, at times fickle, at times trusting, often represent the
only flight from family intimacy yet available or appropriate. It is
too soon for the pairing intimacy of later years. The group provides
a form of containment, so that some of these deeper questions of

identity can be struggled with. The individual feelings of distress and anxiety may be masked by the day-to-day joys and crises of group membership. Thus adolescent group life, which is often so troublesome to adults, may offer something of a haven for the confused young person, extending both a challenge and a respite until he is able to hold disparate feelings together within a single self. This is only possible as the sense of identity becomes increasingly coherent. If the group is relatively fluid and well-intentioned, it can support the developing personality through these turbulent adolescent years.

If it is malign, however, the grouping can take on rather sinister, gang-like characteristics, co-opting the more negative and destructive aspects of the personality to sign up for the role of being partners in crime. All groups at times exert pressures on their members to do things which those members would not have ventured as individuals. But that kind of group activity is a different matter from falling in with others *because* they seem to represent the more timid or vicious parts of the personality. It is a different matter from falling in with others in order to reproduce an atmosphere of fear and oppression that is attractive if one has oneself been intimidated and oppressed. Just as the baby can be felt to explode with the hatred and fury of unmet need if he feels uncontained, so too does the adolescent who is contending with his own versions of those same infantile struggles. The gang-like mentality invites a kind of group sanction for the expression of destructive feelings and attitudes which cannot individually be kept in check.

It is the dynamics of these early adolescent groupings, or gangings-up, which illustrate particularly clearly the relationship between the binding effect of thought and the evacuatory significance of action. Indeed it is adolescence, above all, which defines the difference between the two. This is especially the case at this early stage when the emotional responses to puberty are so raw, so unexpected, and so untried. But they may reappear at any point across the life-span when internal or external pressures again propel the individual into modes of acting rather than thinking, into seeking illicit sexual gratification rather than loyalty and commitment, into evading responsibility rather than shouldering it, into identifying with infantile states rather than seeking to contain them from a more parental position.

*   *   *

The dilemmas and difficulties of a fourteen-year-old, Christine, will give some sense of the problems of coming to terms with, and processing, many of the typical conflicts faced by her age group. Christine was referred for assessment as a result of pressure from Social Services, from her school and from her mother (her father had left when she was a baby). She had been stealing. The objects stolen belonged to the family, that is, to her mother and grandmother: a wedding ring, earrings, a watch and, in the last incident, a large sum of money. Christine had spent the money on grown-up, sexually-alluring clothes which she had ostentatiously worn in what seemed like a clear invitation to be found out.

On first meeting in the waiting room, Christine was indistinguishable from the six friends who accompanied her. They were all dressed in the currently fashionable 501 black jeans and heavy Doc Marten boots. "My friends come with me everywhere", were Christine's first words in the consulting room, after she had shyly and smilingly identified herself and reluctantly come up the corridor. Her second comment was that she was only there because there was a worry that the police would have to be involved. She said that she had stopped stealing so there was really no longer any problem. Again she smiled winningly.

The account that followed made it clear that what was being "acted out" by the stealing constituted a constellation of characteristically early adolescent issues. Christine described how she had been accused of causing arguments between her mother and her mother's boyfriend of three years, Paul, who had recently moved in unexpectedly. The arguments were about Christine's habits around the house, particularly her tendency to wander around in a state of semi-undress, to which her mother objected; "totally unreasonably", Christine thought. "She's probably jealous because she's becoming a fat old bag" (her mother was a trim thirty-four-year-old at the time). Christine outlined her plans to move out, to get a flat of her own, to do it up and to have a baby. But, she added, suddenly tearful, she would have to have her Mum behind her if she did something like that, "I couldn't do it alone". It was as if she was suddenly aware of how practically and emotionally unrealistic her plans really were.

Her mother was described as alternately in tears about "losing my daughter, my little girl", and furious about her daughter's indiscipline and moodiness. The Oedipal issues, perhaps starkly present for the first time now that Paul had moved in, were fully apparent. Each member of the family was having difficulty in adjusting to the new situation and in recognizing what was really going on, and why. The struggles were made worse for Christine, in particular, by fears of growing up, of separating, of becoming a woman, finding a job, hoping for a partner. She was clearly worried about leaving her childhood behind at a time when she was suddenly having to relinquish the exclusive relationship that she had enjoyed with her mother for so many years. Not only was the containing function of the family being threatened, but also the more loosely containing structure of the group, for the friends who had accompanied Christine to the waiting room were a year older than her and were about to leave school.

Christine did not feel that *she* herself was a problem ("I don't know what the fuss is all about"), but rather that she had been "fielded" as the difficult one because of her mother's unhappiness and Paul's anger: "We'll have to throw you out if it goes on like this," he was reputed to have said to her.

These rather selective sequences and comments were part of a bare fifty minute session. On the surface it was an ordinary sort of discussion with a rather likeable, but troubled, young adolescent. Yet it represents many of the problems, preoccupations, reactions and defences, which are so characteristic of this age. It encompasses, for example, the experience of renewed Oedipal anxieties, centring on jealousy, exclusion and competitiveness. It focuses on a particular presenting symptom, "delinquency". It relates to worries about separation. It clarifies enmeshment in the all-girl group, one which probably went along with the delinquent enterprises, yet which also seemed to provide a still much-needed supportive structure. It highlights the oscillations between infantile and adult attitudes. It points out the splitting of the same figure (the mother) into good and bad. It reveals typically unrealistic fantasies ("I want to buy and decorate my own flat and have a baby"). It emphasizes the anxiety about sexuality, and so on.

It is striking that Christine started stealing soon after her mother's boyfriend moved in. At puberty stealing is one of the most common manifestations of "acting out". It may represent any one of a range of meanings: perhaps of restoring what is felt to have been lost, here a mother/daughter relationship. It may be aggressive, that is, to deprive someone else of a treasured possession out of primitive envy and rage; or of precious things (her mother?) of which the person him or herself feels deprived, and consequently impoverished. In Christine's case there may well have been feelings of guilt and a desire for punishment in relation to her attitude to Paul. Was this, in other words, a protest? Or was it a statement about something having been stolen from her to which she had a right (the commitment symbolized by the wedding ring was something which she now felt she lacked)? Was the problem one of anxiety about her own attractiveness (it was feminine things that were stolen—a ring, a necklace, a purse, clothes, watch)? Was there also a jealous attack on her mother and a desire to take her partner away from her, a desire enacted by the flaunting of her own sexuality? Whatever the specific reasons, there was clearly a general anxiety about change and growing up, about losing relationships on which she was currently counting.

Christine was worried about being excluded from the newly-formed family and about having to leave the safety of school (despite the fact that this was, in her case, still a year away). She told her therapist that going into the Army had seemed a rather good option for her, in that it entailed a tight, disciplined organization and "something interesting to do all the time". It was evident that she idealized this potential structure just as she idealized the alternative and equally unrealistic goal, namely to have her own flat and family. Perhaps the unconscious idea behind this latter plan was that she could continue to have her infantile needs met by entrusting her own baby (self) to her mother. She wanted her mother to remain her mother and not be a sexual partner to Paul. Thus she set herself up in competition (no underwear beneath the tracksuit). Christine was terrified of rejection and therefore behaved in ways that would provoke it ("We will have to put you in care"). She was both fiercely independent ("I want to leave home and get my own flat"), and at the same time childishly dependent ("I want my mum behind me and to bring up my baby at home").

Christine was trying to cope, in early adolescence, with a number of problems which aroused in her (though not consciously) feelings and anxieties about abandonment, exclusion, separation, and about being surpassed and relegated to second place. She was unable to contain either the implications and threats of her present predicament or the echoes of the past which those threats conjured up. She did not have a family setting within which her feelings might easily be registered and understood, nor was she herself, at this point, able to communicate her distress in ways that might be heard. She could not understand that there might be other emotional priorities in the family besides her own. She feared that she could not count on her mother's continued emotional support for her daughter's growing feminine independence and need to establish a secure heterosexual relationship of her own. Christine felt impoverished and uncertain about such loving resources and her insecurity led her to steal the symbols of commitment and femininity—i.e., concrete representations of feared emotional deficit.

At this early stage an extraordinary range and diversity can be recorded of adolescents' responses to the predicament in which they find themselves. But it is not so much the details of these various strategies for evading mental pain, or, less commonly, for actively seeking it out, that are of primary interest here. Rather, the question is one of the overall picture of the adolescent situation and its function for the developing personality. Whilst the description of Christine's difficulties in coming to terms with the pressures described are especially typical of her age group, they may also make their appearance at any subsequent stage in life, when the prevailing state of mind favours action rather than thought, and provokes infantile rather than adult responses. For adolescence is indeed a process, and its outcome, at whatever stage, fundamentally affects any future capacity to engage with what Rosalind, in *As You Like It*, described as "the full stream of the world" (III, iii, l. 410).

CHAPTER TEN

Mid-adolescence: a clinical example

"Both in nature and in metaphor, identity is the
vanishing point of resemblance"

Wallace Stevens

This chapter offers some further thoughts on the nature and implications of the different kinds of identification to which a person may be drawn in their mid- to late adolescent years. The main emphasis will be on the projective processes, to be followed in Chapter 11 by an exploration of the more introjective ones. An account is given of the character development of one particular patient, Simon. The description of aspects of Simon's treatment may serve as a useful way of making clearer the links between Kleinian notions of identification and more recent ideas about the role of different kinds of learning in a person's progress towards self-knowledge. At the core of these matters lies the familiar and important distinction (or, more accurately, conflict, where adolescents are concerned) between the kind of identification which is in the service of growth and development on the one hand, and on the other, the kind which may oppose development, encouraging instead an avoidance of anxieties rather than an engagement with them.

The central question, now as previously, is that of how the personality is structured. This question depends first of all on the primary relationship between mother and baby, and subsequently on the factors, internal and external, which may affect that early structuring, and help or hinder the realization of a person's creative capacities. Freud (1933) put the issue of structure very clearly:

> If we throw a crystal to the floor, it breaks; but not into haphazard pieces. It comes apart along its lines of cleavage into fragments whose boundaries, though they were invisible, were pre-determined by the crystal's structure. [p. 59]

The notion of planes of cleavage affords a way of thinking about the underlying operation of forces which often only become evident in puberty or late adolescence. The concern throughout has been with elucidating a number of aspects of these underlying forces—primarily those of early identifications. As we have seen (Chapter 7), the predominance of one kind of identification over another arises from the complex relationships between matters of temperament and disposition in the baby (the capacity to tolerate frustration, for example) and matters of circumstance and setting. The most intimate aspect of setting, at the earliest stage, will be that of the mother's state of mind. Much, as we know, depends on a baby's early experience of having his mental states held and understood, an experience which is not just a function of the mother's personality but also of what the baby is trying to communicate and the intensity with which he is doing so.

The nature of the impact which these early experiences may have had often becomes particularly clear as the young person makes his way through adolescence. The following account of aspects of eighteen-year-old Simon's therapy outlines the effect on his personality of having tried to live out, from early times, an identity which was not entirely his own. It describes the movement towards his gaining a better sense of his real identity. Simon manifested neither gross disturbances nor obvious developmental failures. Rather, he presented himself as riven with characteristically adolescent uncertainties and conflicts, unable to sort out who he really was or, despite apparent successes, to move beyond his problems into a more secure sense of himself-in-the-world. Although, chronologically, nearly an adult, the nature of his problems belonged to mid-adolescence. He is discussed here because his difficulties help to make clear, in detailed clinical terms, the ordinary developmental processes taking place at this difficult age, their complexities and their possible resolutions.

Simon was looking for something. It was with intense earnestness and courage that he undertook to explore and sought to understand aspects of himself which many would prefer, at this age, not to look at or to know about. He came from an unhappy, lower-middle class family. They lived in a small Scottish town. He described his mother as over-worked, often depressed and excessively concerned with domestic matters, and his father as rather remote, but at times quite sadistic and tyrannical. His academic achievements, probably defensively related to the pain of his home background, began to cut him off from family and community at an early age. He chose to go to university in the south of England and referred himself for psychotherapy just as he was embarking on a psychology degree. His ambition was both poignant and unusual in someone of his age. He wanted, ultimately, to do research into the predisposing factors of developmental arrest. (One of his younger brothers had been diagnozed as autistic and Simon, with characteristic, if excessive meticulousness, had already sought out, and immersed himself in, the current developmental and psychoanalytic theories on the subject.)

He was worried about being depressed and emotionally cut off. He often felt sexually confused, panicky, and at times irrationally angry, especially with his male, intellectual superiors, whom he experienced as clever but often elitist and verbally sadistic. He felt that his own academic achievements were in inverse proportion to his emotional development. It was Simon who had brought the "snail dream" to his first session (see Chapter 7), a dream in which, sexually threatened by engulfment within the hermaphroditic body of a snail, he had fled the situation and taken up a position "behind the projector", where the professors normally stood. In so doing, he had dispensed with his first-year-student-self and "tunnelled" his way into an identification with his superiors. This tendency to assume an inappropriately senior and clever persona turned out to be Simon's characteristic mode of evading the more dangerous and threatening experiences of his adolescent self.

In the course of his therapy he found it possible to begin to relinquish this somewhat fraudulent persona in favour of an engagement with his small-child-self, a self who feared intimacy and who had never really found a way of relating to his parents, either outwardly or inwardly. It seemed that he had cut himself off from any very passionate or dependent feelings towards them in the wake of the birth of his many younger siblings—first twins, then the autistic brother, and lastly a baby sister. Resistantly, he began to risk emerging from behind the projector and to fight his impulse to bypass the adolescent struggle, an impulse which had threatened shutting down his authentic self in favour of an acquired identity. The expansiveness, humour and generosity, which his therapist could only occasionally glimpse in the early days, became far more evident, warming up his previously rather chilly self.

In terms of personality structure, it became possible to think about the difficulties Simon ran into in adolescence as based in, though not determined by, the tendency from early on to lose touch with the qualities of his actual external parents, and instead to relate to a distorted internal representation of them, and to live in a kind of defensive imitation of, and identification with, competitive, superior and clever people. This tendency was at the expense of being able to take in and assimilate parental qualities of ordinary care and concern, and to bear being a not-knowing child rather than an all-knowing pseudo-adult. Bion (1962a) identified the baby's crucial dilemma as being about whether to evade the frustration of early needs and wants or to find the resources to tolerate it (pp. 111–112). Until now Simon had, on the whole, sought to evade it. In mid- to late adolescence, however, the disparity between the external version of himself and the internal fears and doubts about his real capacities, was becoming a source of increasing anxiety.

The focus here is on the notion of "unretrieved projections" and on how, in the course of treatment, it slowly became possible for Simon to begin to take his projections "back", thus freeing him to become more truly himself, with the attendant enriching and deepening of his personality. The question for any age, but particularly perhaps for adolescence, is how does one reach stability and at the same time retain flexibility? It is the internal relationship which requires stability but the changes in identification, in primary terms with maternal or paternal figures, internal and external, have to be freely mobile. Thus constant psychic work is required if a person is to continue to develop. In the months following the snail-dream, it had become increasingly evident that Simon was inclined to retreat to a particular kind of intellectuality as a defence against engaging with his more genital desires, ones which might put him in touch with unresolved inner conflicts, in particular with his problems of sexual orientation. This intellectuality was of a greedy-incorporation-of-facts-and-skills sort, one which had a distinctly oral quality of wanting to gobble up, to swallow down and later to regurgitate, his knowledge and experiences rather than to digest them psychically and to metabolize them.

His very polarized relationship with his internal parents, in terms of the extreme disparity between "maternal" and "paternal" characteristics (usually along quite caricatured or stereotypical lines) was very clearly expressed in the transference to his therapist. In fantasy the therapist would be, at times, intellectually belittled. Alternatively, what might be construed as her maternal capacities would be overlooked. In Simon's mind she would often become identified with some excessively clever theoretician, displaying male intellectual (meaning sadistic and tyrannical) characteristics. At other times her actual and ordinary capacities would be cast into shadow ("weak", "masochistic"), by comparing her with the brilliance of the Melanie Klein, Wilfred Bion or Hanna Segal sort of analyst-figures who frequently appeared in his dreams.

In important respects, Simon's serial academic achievements were a burden to him. They further distanced him from his more authentic self, and were reminiscent of the particular adolescent difficulties which tend to emerge on the eve of success rather than at the moment of failure: the crisis when exams are passed, for example, or the entrance scholarship won, or the job offered; that is, when fear about absence of internal qualification threatens the security of the external role. He even "knew about" Bion's "theory of thinking". But, paradoxically, the way in which he used his own mind epitomized, at least in the early days, the $-K$ mode, the inverse of a truthful desire to know, represented by the K link.

The account of Simon's therapy that follows clarifies the developmental significance of Bion's discrimination between different types of knowledge (see Chapter 7): the distinction between a thirst for knowledge and understanding (K), and its converse, the kind of intrusive curiosity which stems from defensive desires, those which seek to control, to triumph, to exercise power or deny littleness etc. (−K).

Simon's characteristic mode of mental functioning is well illustrated by the following dream: having, in reality, seen his therapist in the street talking to a male colleague, he dreamt that

> he came to his session at the usual time. But his therapist was not available to see him because she was in another part of the building with her husband and child. He waited in the consulting room, thinking out a "grid" system, along the lines theorized by Bion, which could describe what Keats called "The Language of Achievement". He thought that the "grid" would constitute an abstract representation of a literary reference which would be far too esoteric for his therapist to understand.

This dream very clearly marked what, at this point, Simon's knowledge was in the service of: a defence against feeling depressed and left out, against the realization that he could not have "mummy" all to himself because she already had a husband, and that these parents were busy caring for another child. In order not to engage with these painful emotions of jealousy and need, he turned to intellectual over-valuation, competitiveness and contempt. He used his mind to master his feelings rather than to experience them, demonstrating the pseudo-mature nature of his prodigious knowledge. Indeed the dream provided a rather clever commentary on his precise problem: had he really understood, from within, what Keats meant by the notion of a "Man of Achievement", perhaps he would not have been stuck in the way that he was. For Keats described the Language of Achievement as characterizing the genius of Shakespeare. It is brought about by what Keats (1817) called "Negative Capability", that is, the capacity to be "in Mysteries uncertainties and doubts, without any irritable reaching after fact and reason" (*Letters*, p. 43).[1]

Simon had sought, in the dream, mentally to triumph over his therapist/mother and to deny his need for her. The "grid" system referred to a particularly obscure aspect of Bion's theory, and the reference to Keats's *Letters* turned out to be one which Simon thought his therapist might be familiar with. In other words, he was intrusively trying to enter an area of her mind and to take it over with his superior understanding. The dream thus became less an expression than a caricature of knowledge.

His difficulties with the Oedipal constellation, so clear in this dream, as in the initial snail-dream, seemed to have undermined his capacity to establish lasting intimate relationships. Indications of his tendency to attempt intellectually to overcome his deeper anxieties were replicated in many subsequent dreams and sessions, in each of which, some considerable time later, the same conflicts were still manifest. He eventually achieved a first-class undergraduate degree and won a scholarship to do research. Not surprisingly, however, his external success was not yet matched by any very significant internal shifts. In one dream, for example, which he had soon after graduation, there featured a ghastly spider-couple, locked in oral intercourse (seemingly a "combined" parental symbol in continuous sexual coitus[2]) from which, in great anxiety, he fled to thoughts about homosexual comfort. (It should be made clear here that the discussion is not about homosexuality as pathology, but focuses rather on the nature of Simon's internal relationships, on his anxieties about gender identity so common at this stage of adolescence, and on the impact that those confusions may have on identity as a whole.) Although they had never been acted upon, homosexual anxieties, so common in early adolescence, still lingered in Simon's inner world, as did the related and rather rigid and polarized internal configurations in which male and female elements were still kept stereotyped and separate. As a consequence, his capacities to form warm and loving external relationships were depleted, as indeed was his feeling that he could "live" in any full sense at all.

For a long time Simon remained somewhat depressed and withdrawn, although outwardly as successful as ever. He could allow little flexibility in his internal relationships and, as a consequence, his external relationships continued to suffer. As far as intimacy was concerned, homosexual fantasies, though disturbing to him, were a preferable option to the dangers of actual heterosexual experience. For the time being he was neither able to install internally, and identify with, parental figures in any kind of creative combination, nor was he able to relate to them as having qualities to which the child-like self might aspire, rather than believe a superior version of them already to be in his possession. It was as if the successive births of his younger siblings were felt not only to have deprived him of the parental care which he still so badly needed, but were felt also to have inflicted on him, time and again, the painful evidence of his parents' sexual relationship with one another. In seeking to protect himself from these unwelcome internal realities he had continued to identify with a powerful intellectual elite, often with unpleasantly authoritarian overtones. He wanted little to do with any softer or more nurturing aspects of himself. These aspects were ones which he tended, at this point, to locate in much-despised female figures.

Some much later material will demonstrate the process of Simon's emergence from the half-life of his existence hitherto and his entry into a much more full-bodied and rich sense of himself, "daring to fly", "to shed a skin", as he himself put it on different occasions. The process seemed to involve real character strength and large-heartedness, by contrast with the brittle quality of his earlier big-headedness. The shift began to have significant implications for his sense of his sexual self, his work and his relationships generally. It seemed that the change may have been linked to a realization on his therapist's part that her way of responding to Simon sometimes tended to take the form of a rather unhelpful engagement with his pseudo-thinking self, rather than with his feeling-self. In a series of sessions soon after he won his scholarship, his dreams clearly indicated that a mode of relating which suggested greedy incorporation was predominating. More significantly, his therapist found herself responding in such a way as further to entrench that mode, rather than to understand and to modify it. Patient and therapist became collusively drawn into a series of interactions which involved using knowledge of psychoanalytic theory to defend against feeling rather than to experience it.

One session, in particular, shows how, in the patient/therapist relationship, there was a misjoining of thinking going on, of a −K type. The possibility of genuine learning was put into abeyance in favour of an anxious desire to defend against pain by means of intellectualization at the expense of real engagement. At this time, some of Simon's deeper anxieties were stirring and he was worried about his therapist's ability to hold, and to tolerate, his more destructive impulses and attitudes. Possibly in response to some such anxiety, he dreamt that:

as a result of a "technical" mistake on his therapist's part, in which she revealed something personal about herself, he had had to go into treatment with a psychoanalyst, someone extremely eminent. In his first session he had protested to this analyst that he was really committed to his previous therapist but had had to change his treatment at her insistence.

He sadly recognized the import of the final "at her insistence". It described an insistent part of himself, the existence of which was confirmed by an immediate, troubled aside, "I suppose that that is my model for human relationships, use people up and move on".

Shortly after this, in the first meeting after a Christmas break, Simon recounted a dream which he had had on the night of his last session two weeks previously. He began this post-break session with no allusion to the pain of separation, but by forcefully refuting an interpretation which had been made on the earlier occasion. He said that he had *not* felt that his therapist might not hold him in mind during the break, as she had suggested, but that he had felt completely "dropped", as though he was "falling apart". After a pause he went on to say that he was worried about his skin: it seemed to be "breaking out all over the place". He then recounted the following dream:

> he was in a seaside resort which was "peopled" by giant ants, mutations of some sort, as a result of poisoned or polluted air. He came to a fence-like structure where he was told by the ants to dig a six-inch square in the sandy road. As he looked at the road, the six-inch square section dropped down in sudden jerks. [He likened the action to that of a young child who lacked fine motor control, and was trying to hammer a peg into a hole.] Unexpectedly, the square of earth rose up and broke through the road surface, at which point Simon could see down inside. There were many parents and children there, smothered with ants which were biting, stinging and crawling all over them. The people were screaming in agony as they were injected with the formic acid. There was a woman there too, who resembled his therapist and who seemed immune—the bites appeared not to be affecting her. Simon said, "We must steal her away to a laboratory, find out how she has become immune and get the inoculation".

This dream reminded Simon of a waking thought which he had had shortly before this Christmas break: if he were stranded in the Amazon forest and starving to death, with only his mother nearby, would he eat her? In the course of the session the therapist spoke of a possible link between this comment, the way Simon had been talking about "being dropped" and his "skin breaking out", and the contents of the dream. She suggested that at the beginning of the session he seemed to have Esther Bick's theories in mind (she knew that he was familiar with her work). Was he, perhaps, both defending himself from the pain of the holiday break by theorizing his experience in the light of Bick's paper on "second-skin" formation? And was he, at the same time, being superior to his therapist by mentally, though not explicitly, dismissing her interpretation about maternal containment? If so, he was, perhaps, doubly distancing himself, both from the actual experience of the separation and from the fact that that separation mattered to him. His therapist then linked this possibility to the dream: feeling like a very young child in a threatening environment, frightened and abandoned at the boundary/beginning of the break (the fence), Simon had experienced his internal world as being utterly at risk. He felt persecuted by vicious, biting, stinging, oral-sadistic attacks of the kind that had been unconsciously levelled at his therapist in the "eminent psychoanalyst" dream. He managed, nonetheless, to retain what he initially described as the "good" internal figure; "good" in that she was able to be immune from these damaging assaults. But his only way of relating to this figure's life-saving qualities was to subject her to scientific tests, to seek to learn her secrets. His idea was to do this mechanically, in a clever-laboratory-part-of-his-mind, and then physically to put those secrets into his own body, by means of inoculation—a process which seemed tantamount to a kind of pseudo-introjection. He thus sought to inject himself with the essence of his therapist's immunity. There was a sense, Simon thought, that the immunity had been acquired by the therapist/woman in the course of the very different process of having undergone, and survived, the pain of the persecutory attacks.

Simon's caricature of learning emphasized the difficulty of being able to take in the qualities of this therapist/person psychically rather than physically, so that her capacities might then function internally as a genuine source of strength for him. The real predicament was that of how he was to survive the dangers of the "Amazon forest" aspect of his internal world, without either feeding off his therapist in a "devouring" sort of way, or intrusively having to become identified with her stolen qualities. How was he to allow himself to experience, and to cope with, some of the real pain of separation and loss? Instead of suffering the pain, he had sought an inoculation against it by becoming a pseudo-therapist.

Simon came to the next session in a frenzy of envy of what he thought were his therapist's "clever", but technical interpretations, and seething with verbal aggression towards her. Furiously he described what he felt about the way in which she had "so effortlessly" dismissed his desire for a simple antidote, and had suggested that he believed that he could just "make off with" a painless solution, in preference to engaging with the actual pain of his experience. With a slight edge of contempt, but also with a tone of despair, he said how little, despite his extensive psychoanalytic reading, he really understood of anything—"projective, introjective identification, internal objects, all these fancy concepts". His therapist realized how far, in the previous session, she had joined in with his system of intellectualization. As a consequence, she had not only strengthened his defences against feelings of littleness and abandonment, but also her own defences against susceptibility to the noxious mental substances which he directed towards her when he felt so let down by her and so unimportant. It may be that this kind of tendency on his therapist's part to draw on aspects of herself which Simon associated with his father, in extreme contrast to what he needed from his mother, had made it harder for him to relinquish his polarized view of intimate relationships.

In retrospect, it seemed that the "error" of technique in the "eminent psychoanalyst" dream was precisely this tendency to participate in Simon's projective system, as a result of which he had had "to move on" to a famous analyst. He now had to face, without defensive protection, the idea that, in psychic reality, his position was that in order to survive he would have to eat his own mother ("to use people up and move on"). In the session described, his therapist was all too easily identifiable with the dreaded professors. In effect, in giving him a "lecture" about psychoanalytic theory, she revealed the way in which she sought to protect herself from his denial and hostility: that is, by the use of her own mind, in intellectualizing mode, to get away from the pain of what was actually happening. The temptation defensively to fall back on theory in this way thus doubly reinforced the problem, leaving the patient with no real food for thought but rather an arousal of envy. The envy understandably provoked yet more intense verbal attacks on the links of intimacy between patient and therapist, and on Simon's trust in a securely good source of strength and insight.

Understanding these sessions brought about a kind of watershed in the way of working. Hitherto it had been very difficult to diminish the attractiveness of his habitual "incorporative mode", in which anything thought to be good would be "swallowed up", and "taken over" as if it were his own. Now it seemed more possible to recognize, and to appreciate, the distinctive value of the other, not as something immediately to be possessed by him, but as something of which the genuine qualities could be taken in and assimilated as loved and trusted resources. This latter introjective process is always hard to describe because it is so gradual and happens almost imperceptibly (see Chapter 11), but indications of an internal shift began to become clear in Simon's dreams and in changes of other kinds which were slowly becoming evident in the rest of his life.

One of the final dreams of his therapy clarified the shift between his previous and his current states of mind.

> He arrived home to find that a large bag had been left outside his door by the postman. He began unpacking what seemed to be rather bizarre bits and pieces, associated with particular forms of extremely advanced technical knowledge, relating to his more omnipotent states of mind of days gone by. As he continued to explore, the pieces took the form of a railway-track with bridges, tunnels etc. and he realized that the bag contained a train-set—the sort which he had possessed between the ages of about three and seven, he thought.

The way he recounted the dream was striking. There was a strongly Oedipal flavour in the description of his memories of playing with this train-set, in the details of the train's progress under the bridges and into the tunnels. It was as if the internal world/bag now contained not so much fragmentary bits and pieces of split-off skill and expertise, but rather a genuine mother and father who could be tolerated as having a relationship with each other and could be internalized in a way that had clearly been impossible when Simon had confronted this situation as a little boy.

Many other dreams had led up to this last one, each of them, in different ways, representing a coming-out-of-projective-identification, and, in the process, indicating the acquisition of a much fuller sense of himself. He described feeling that he was no longer living "in role", and could sense that he did have internal qualities which were beginning to match his external achievements. He no longer merely resembled a successful student, but felt himself to be becoming one. Another of his final dreams seemed to indicate a "decision" to relinquish his projective self and to support a much more genuine alternative:

> he was setting out along the road of his original departure from his small home town to the big city. [En route, he had a series of significant experiences which, in the dream work, undid, as it were, the state of mind which he had been in on that original journey some years before.] He passed a shop displaying shoes—"Hush Puppies", he thought, the sort of thing that professors might wear. At that moment there was a blackout and it occurred to Simon that he could steal a pair of shoes and put them on and no-one would know. He decided against that, however, and at the same moment the lights went on again and he realized that his estimation of the shoes was quite erroneous; they were nothing like as attractive as he had thought. They looked entirely different now, rather "tacky" and pretentious. The next shop was a basement selling records, cassettes and CDs [a world of popular culture which he had much frequented in dreams and in reality, and which had come to represent a projective mode in which he became identified with rather mindless groupings, devoid of any individuality or enduring qualities.] Again he passed by. Next he came across his little brother in a bath with one of Simon's colleagues [whom Simon believed to be homosexual.] He gently lifted his brother out of the bath.

This little brother/self had featured prominently in fantasized situations in which homosexual desires had confused and tormented Simon. The dream expressed the possibility of relinquishing these various confusions, projective possibilities and temptations, but in favour of what was not yet clear. In another dream that same week, feeling upset at the prospect of leaving his research post and of terminating therapy in the near future,

> he found himself as a four-year-old boy, sitting at the kitchen table. One of his professors came in, in a daddy's-just-back-from-work way, and greeted him with the tickling, cuddling warmth of a loving, paternal and non-erotic kind.

This dream put Simon more closely in touch with a deep sadness, a sense both of loss and of responsibility for the quality of his past relationships (rather than blaming his parents as in days gone by). He also began thinking about his father's very real paternal capacities, ones of gentleness, attention and affection, which he had hitherto so resolutely denied. He had tended, as we have seen, to identify instead with somewhat tyrannical, cold and occasionally eroticized male figures, with the consequent problems of identity which had characterized his essentially joyless teenage years. The superior, verbally sadistic professors became recognizable as aspects of himself, the type of persona with whom he became identified when he felt threatened and ignorant. As he acquired more confidence, the power of his love/hate relationship with this side of himself began to diminish.

An important factor in this process of coming-out-of-projective-identification seemed to be the genuine mourning which he was able to undergo in relation to the ending of his therapy and to the completion of his research. In the past, at times of separation, he would seek to protect himself from anxiety in a variety of ways: by a kind of defensive mental omnipotence and denial of pain, for example, or by homosexual fantasies, or by the rigid separation of his internal male and female figures. He now described intense grief, the pain of leaving real and warm relationships, the experience of "missing", and of pining. He had an urge to give generously and warmly to others. He described his ambitions as those of becoming a genuinely helpful person rather than merely a successful one. "Leaving" no longer meant "using up and moving on", but involved a powerful sense of loss, tinged with expectation. It seemed that his way of knowing had all but ceased to constitute a defence against depressive pain and Oedipal conflict, and that his mind could now be employed less in mastering his feelings than in experiencing them. In Oedipal terms, a change seemed to have occurred, one that was particularly clear in his relationship to his therapist. The male/female, masculine/feminine characteristics of those to whom he was close were no longer confused, as in the snail and spider dreams, nor did they have to be kept out of contact with one another. Instead, they could be allowed to come together in the idea of an attentive and caring couple in intimate relationship.

Qualities of love, concern, gratitude, dependence, co-operation, began to appear in his daily life, and with them dreams which were less often about being a famous psychoanalyst, as in the past, and more likely to focus on such activities as visiting his grandmother in hospital, or buying plants for his mother. He exhibited a certain humility, a playfulness, a pleasure in ordinary things, and, consonant with that, his body seemed to fill out, finally appearing to be more in proportion to his head. With a new-found confidence in a sense of wholeness and integration in his personality, he began, for the first time, to express a genuine interest in forming an intimate relationship. On one occasion, with no hint of boastfulness but with rather disarming surprise, he said that he felt that he sometimes had a positive impact on other people. He started to realize that he was likeable; that he could be experienced as friendly, "without trying"; that he was emerging from "being an ugly duckling", not unfearful, but certainly more resolute. With considerable difficulty he was becoming aware of the changes in himself. His identity was acquiring new boundaries, new but also, of course, untried. He remarked, at one point, that he had started to believe in happy endings. He was daunted, however, by beginning the rest of his life, and was worried lest the really interesting bit of the story was not what happened afterwards but rather the complexity and uncertainty of what had led up to that point.

Simon had had the courage to involve himself in the painful struggle to become "real" which is the point at which he left therapy, about to embark on his future life. For him this entailed a diminution of his powerful, aggressive impulses, most manifest in the way he used his mind, and a capacity, as a consequence, to bring the various split-off elements together, both in the transference to his therapist and in life. The rigidity of his projective tendencies, ones which had been strengthened by how well they suited him to the academic world to which he was attracted, could then give way to a different kind of identification, now with true and differentiated functions of maternal and paternal figures, both separately and in relation to each other. The shift was a fundamental one. He became much more able to form genuine relationships with others and with the different parts of himself. The change marked the shift from "resemblance to identity". He finally looked as though he might be able to emerge from his turbulent teenage years into a more genuine and loving grown-up self. Ernest Jones (1922) commented that in the course of adolescence it will be found that "the capacity to love has grown stronger at the expense of the desire to be loved" (p. 39). This seemed very true of the change in Simon.

In describing these aspects of Simon's therapy it has been possible to trace a number of congruencies between the evolution of a particular therapeutic treatment and a person's capacity to go on developing, the capacity to grow up internally, as well as chronologically. Being a late-developer emotionally, Simon had found it very difficult to move from early-adolescent confusion to a state of mind in which he might confidently be poised to progress into adulthood. His eventual tentative steps to do so were importantly related both to what he was able to work through in his relation to his therapist, and also to having to endure endings in the external world. It was something embedded in his experience of these events which enabled him, internally, to begin to relinquish outworn and restrictive states of mind and to become more receptive to qualities which might really assist his development rather than hinder it. Of particular interest were the changes in the relationship between Simon and his therapist. For what these changes draw attention to is the necessity, especially where adolescents are concerned, for continuing flexibility on the part of the container, whether that be parent or therapist, in order to offer the young person the freedom to be himself or herself.

Out of feelings of need and uncertainty, Simon had tended to live within an insistently projective mode, at the expense of his real self. But slowly, as we have seen, he became less inclined to disown aspects of his personality, both good and bad. He had been attributing to his version of others those characteristics which he was not yet ready to own as belonging to himself. Instead, he began to be able to take in and internally to benefit from the actual qualities of those to whom he was emotionally close. As he did so he could at least begin to imagine forming a genuinely intimate relationship, though perhaps in practice not for some time to come. In finding a more authentic sense of himself, Simon began to discover a truer estimation of himself-in-the-world—a process described by Keats (1818):

> The difference of high Sensations with and without knowledge appears to me this—in the latter case we are falling continually ten thousand fathoms deep and being blown up again without wings and with all [the] horror of a bare-shouldered Creature—in the former case, our shoulders are fledge, and we go thro" the same air and space without fear. [*Letters*, p. 92]

Notes

1. Bion (1970) drew on the notion of Negative Capability (pp. 125–129). It may be that there was a particular reason for Keats's interest beyond the plea for openness and receptivity which the words themselves imply. Stephen Coote (1995) writes: "the choice of the word 'negative' almost certainly derives from Keats's chemistry lectures, where negativity implied not a rejection, a minus or an absence, but rather a sympathetic receptive intensity. Just as, for Bailey, Keats had compared the action of great minds to catalysts, so, for his brothers, he could imply that the 'negative capability' of the true poet was like an electrical negative: passive but, in its receptive power, quite the equal of the positive current" (p. 115). Keats also knew that the "influential Bishop Butler" held that a man may have religious belief even though his mind remained "in great doubts and uncertainties about both its evidence and nature" (*ibid.*).

2. Klein (1929) described the perception of parental sexuality, in a paranoid–schizoid state of mind, as being that of a frightening, even horrific, combined figure. Such a phantasy figure is formed by the projection of the infant's oral, anal and genital desires into an idea of parents' destructive intercourse, which is felt to be continuous and beastly—Shakespeare's "two-backed" monster (p. 213). This primitive "combined object" is quite different from a perception, possible in the later depressive state of mind, of the parents' relationship as being one of creative intercourse. This benign "combined object" is one which Simon became able increasingly to relate to and to appreciate as involving creative figures in his own internal world.

CHAPTER ELEVEN

Late adolescence: fictional lives

"certain books like certain works of art, rouse powerful feelings and stimulate growth willy nilly"

W. Bion

During the adolescent years there is a likelihood, as we have seen, that to both good and bad ends, the projective tendencies will predominate over the introjective. The anxiety involved in a young person's attempts to discover who he is, or who she is, and to define more clearly their sense-of-themselves-in-the-world, often arouses extremes of defensive splitting and projection. But in the course of this quest for self-definition other more moderate and exploratory ways of establishing a better understanding of themselves are also in play. These other ways involve less intense and extreme degrees of projection and include the capacity to value and to take in the kinds of mental and emotional qualities which can help to support their developing selves. In the consideration of so crucial an aspect of growing up as the transition from adolescence to adulthood, more detailed emphasis now needs to be given to the nature of introjective processes

—those which were so integral to Simon's being able to change.

Intrinsic to the introjective process is the capacity to relinquish external figures of dependence and attachment and to install a version of them within, as resources which inspire and encourage the independent development of the personality. Such processes, as we have seen, involve the capacity to mourn what is being let go, or what is felt to have been lost. Strengthened by such an undertaking, it may be felt to be possible to move on. The process occurs over time. The changes may be akin to those internal shifts in Dorothea, so subtly described by George Eliot in *Middlemarch*:

> That new, real future which was replacing the imaginary drew its material from the endless minutiae, by which her view was gradually changing with the secret motion of a watch-hand from what it had been in her maiden dream. [p. 226]

We are familiar with Freud's view that central to the achievement of adolescence is the satisfactory fulfilment of the task of crystallizing sexual identity, of finding a sexual partner, and of bringing together the two main stems of sexuality, the sensual and the tender (see Chapter 9). The struggle towards an internal capacity for intimacy is what, in important ways, adolescence has been working towards all along. Developing such a capacity may, for some, take many more years and possibly several different attempts. And, indeed, the pairing-off which does occur at this stage of young adulthood may, despite appearances, have little to do with a genuine transition from adolescent to adult states of mind. It may have little relation, of any real kind, to the internal capacity which is now being described. Indeed such couplings can constitute precisely the opposite: that is, a defensive bonding in the face of anxiety about what stepping into adulthood might really entail.

As already noted, one of the main undertakings of adolescence is that of establishing a mind of one's own, a mind which is rooted in, and yet also distinct from, the sources and models of identification that are visible within one's family, or in the wider school and community setting. In late adolescence the struggle for separation, one which is fundamental to this capacity to be one's own person, tends to take on certain characteristics which differ from the early teenage years. Usually the young person will, by this time, be emerging from the often addictive complexities of group-life and of the multifold and shifting relationships which have hitherto been part of the process of separating from parents and family. He or she will be facing a different and more extreme separation: that of leaving school and home, of having to be independent as never before. It is a time of hope and expectation, but for many, also of extreme sadness and distress, and even of breakdown for the few who find themselves unequal to the task.

The success or failure of this challenge will, as we have seen in successive age groups, importantly depend on how experiences of love and loss have been negotiated in the past, indeed from the very beginning. The nature of the negotiation, as repeatedly stated, is deeply affected by the extent to which the parent, or parents, can bear to relinquish their children and to help them on their way. The pain of so doing often carries with it an intensity and a poignancy which tests the bravest of hearts. Intrinsic to this stage in the separation process is the seeking of an intimate partnership outside the family. The capacity to establish a deep and lasting relationship is dependent on the outcome of a number of complex internal processes which will, almost always, have been problematic as well as rewarding during the adolescent years. At the heart of the matter lies the degree of a person's capacity to experience loss, a loss especially stark as childhood is definitively left behind and engagement with the adult world becomes a necessity.

For the task of becoming oneself, now and always, involves relinquishing the denigrated and idealized versions of the self, of other people and of relationships, in favour of the real. It involves re-negotiating dreams, choices and hopes, whether self-generated or imposed from without. It involves tolerating opportunities lost, and roads not taken. Painful conflicts are aroused as the young person has to set forth and simultaneously to let go. Such difficulties confront a person at every stage of life, but they are perhaps most demanding and intransigent at major points of transition, whether it be first going to school, or finally retiring from work, or, as in this case, embarking on the rest of one's life. These sorts of losses test the capacity to mourn, to feel remorse, to take responsibility, to experience guilt and also gratitude. All such capacities are fundamentally involved in a person's being able to love and all are intimately linked to the nature of the balance between the projective and introjective processes which have been established from the very first.

It would take a whole book about a patient's life to describe the introjective processes taking place in the course of an analysis. In fact it is the book-length accounts of a character's development that *do* encompass the extensive chronology of the capacity to grow. The scale of the nineteenth-century novel particularly lends itself to such an enterprise. For in the course of the narrative what is so often established is precisely the late-adolescent process under discussion: the gradual development of a character's internal capacity for intimacy. The external event of "marriage" functions as a symbolic representation of the point of emergence into adulthood, of the culmination of late-adolescent struggles towards establishing a place of their own, by contrast with that which is conventionally assigned to them. Thus marriage marks the realization of internal capacities which have been developing in the course of the narrative, promoted by the impact on one another of the characters concerned. In many nineteenth-century novels a shift can be described as having taken place from an initial *idea* of marriage, often culturally and contractually framed, to a final *capacity* for marriage. The shift is effected by the gradual yielding of the temptation towards splitting and projection in favour of a more introjective capacity, or, perhaps, by a gradual re-balancing of the two tendencies, with all the problems that that re-balancing entails.

The nature of these inner developments will be explored in Jane Austen's *Emma* and, very briefly, in Charlotte Brontë's *Jane Eyre*. The developments are characteristic of, but by no means exclusive to, late adolescence. In these novels the institution of marriage is naturally, in terms of social and cultural setting, very differently underpinned from marriage today. But there is a shared developmental thrust, one that still informs the process of late adolescence albeit often in much less obviously conventional form. This thrust is towards encountering, or recognizing, a true partner and developing the capacities to be committed to a life-long relationship.

The capacity for marriage must not be confused with the contractual relationship of marriage. In nineteenth-century novels, as in life, people continue to get married to each other. But they do not all do so on the basis of what is being described here as an "internal capacity for marriage". Nor indeed do they have the capacity *not* to be married. For contractual marriage, as already suggested, often functions either as a defence against separation, loss and intimacy, or as a perpetuation of an unresolved Oedipal problem. Jane Austen's novels, in particular, both wittily and painfully depict any number of bad marriages. These unions are wholly distinct from the kind of central progression in which development proceeds as the protagonists engage ever more deeply with their lives and loves.

A compelling aspect of each book is the nature of the internal odyssey which is embarked upon. The central characters suffer, endure, weather self-deception and, perhaps most importantly, face and survive the experience of loss. At one point Emma exclaims: "I seem to have been doomed to blindness, I have been a fool." Whence does Emma derive the capacity to learn from her mistakes and her erroneous perceptions? How is it that one person embraces and another evades the possibility of growth, settling instead for a less disturbing conformity, or a reinforcing of the defensive fastnesses? These narratives are explorations of how a young woman joins the adult world, not only the constricted world of the writer's youth, but the contemporary world of any young person's struggle towards maturity. Whether or not the actual texts are familiar, the psychic predicaments described "speak" for themselves.

Emma Woodhouse was, as the opening paragraph of the book establishes:

> handsome, clever and rich, with a comfortable home and a happy disposition [she] seemed to unite some of the best blessings of existence and had lived nearly twenty-one years in the world with very little to distress or vex her. [p. 37]

In the few densely packed pages of the first chapter, the subject of marriage is immediately introduced. Indeed, the beginning, middle and end of the book are marked by marriages. Emma's part in these different unions charts the shift in her from child-like omnipotence, through defensive manipulation (typical of the projective mode), to some degree of self-knowledge and a more mature sense both of gratitude and unworthiness, which is characteristic of the introjective mode. The key factor in this shift is the changing relationship between Emma and Mr Knightley—a figure in whom Emma, the arch-matchmaker, finally meets her match and her "maker".[1] It is the oscillating progress of a capacity to recognize Mr Knightley as her "match", as the embodiment of qualities which were becoming internal to herself, which provides a sustaining source of fascination and instruction in the course of the book. From the beginning, the reader has no doubt but that Mr Knightley (a local landowner and the most gentlemanly and eligible figure in the community) is the man for Emma. But Emma turns a blind eye, only slowly and with great difficulty relinquishing her projective and narcissistic defences against "seeing" what to others has long been so clear.

On the first page of the book the marriage takes place between Mr Weston and Miss Taylor, Emma's governess since her mother's death sixteen years previously. "It was Miss Taylor's loss which first brought grief. It was on the wedding day of this beloved friend that Emma first sat in mournful thought of any continuance" (p. 37). But Emma's disposition soon saves her from any protracted continuance of mournfulness. To experience herself as architect of what might otherwise have been felt to be a kind of Oedipal reverse, protects her from too lasting or severe a pain.

> "And have you forgotten one matter of joy to me", Emma said, "and a very considerable one—that I made the match myself. I made the match, you know, four years ago; and to have it take place and be proved in the right, when so many people said Mr Weston would never marry again, may comfort me for anything".
>
> Mr Knightley shook his head at her. Her father fondly replied, "Ah! My dear, I wish you would not make these matches and foretell things, for whatever you say always comes to pass. Pray do not make any more matches". [Mr Woodhouse, "a valetudinarian all his life" (p. 38), is the archetypal killjoy, opposed to anything on the side of life or relationship and thus, especially to marriage.]
>
> "I promise you to make none for myself, Papa; but I must, indeed, for other people. It is the greatest amusement in the world! And after such success you know!" ...
>
> "I do not understand what you mean by 'success'"; said Mr Knightley. "Success supposes endeavour ... where is your merit? What are you proud of?—You made a lucky guess; and *that* is all that can be said". [pp. 43–44]

This relatively light-hearted exchange is very suggestive. We immediately understand that Emma's matchmaking constitutes a defensive procedure against awareness of any desire for intimacy on her own part, as well as a way of trying out what intimacy might feel like. Protected by the self-imposed duty of having to stay at home to look after her child-like father, she can perpetuate the pseudo-adult role ("having been mistress of his house from a very early period"), and keep at bay any risk of actually feeling dependent herself. She had been used to "doing just what she liked; highly esteeming Miss Taylor's judgement, but directed chiefly by her own" (p. 37).

Not at all consciously preoccupied with pursuing a man *she* might care for, Emma concerns herself, either fancifully or actually, with these issues on behalf of others, primarily on behalf of her friend Harriet Smith, through whom she can indulge her notions of matchmaking without any risk of engaging her own feelings. There is a kind of excitement and energy about Emma. She generates interest. As Mr Knightley says: "There is an anxiety, a curiosity in what one feels for Emma. I wonder what will become of her?" The reader is caught up in what will occur to her next ("At this moment, an ingenious and animating suspicion was entering Emma's brain"). Much of the novel is concerned with Emma making matches, or assuming the existence of matches, only fleetingly allowing herself into any of the complex equations. One reading would be that her addiction to matchmaking is a way of protecting herself from being vulnerable to experiences of love and loss, and that her inability to relinquish her loyalty to the care of her father is based on an anxiety about exposing herself to the emotional turbulence of a different kind of intimate relationship. The central movement of the novel describes the extremely elaborate entanglement and disentanglement of projective possibilities for intimacy, an intimacy which cannot, initially, be worked on in any more direct or immediate a way. A central question becomes, what is it that enables Emma eventually to begin to be able to take in and to appreciate the qualities and functions represented by Mr Knightley? What is it that emboldens her to risk engaging with her own sincere feelings rather than "managing" those of others.

Initially, Harriet Smith suits Emma's defensive purposes perfectly—both as a much-needed companion and as a vehicle for her projective schemes. Emma's incapacity to distinguish in whose interests her imagined attachments really are, is a measure of her unconscious denial of the ordinary adolescent need for fantasy and experimentation, before she can recognize or develop any readiness for a lasting partner for herself. The description of her artistic talents offers a marvellous encapsulation of an adolescent's shifting tastes and enthusiasms and of Emma's narcissistic investment in admiration.

> Her many beginnings were displayed. Miniatures, half-lengths, whole-lengths, pencil, crayon and watercolours had all been tried in turn. She had always wanted to do everything ... she played and sang; and drew in almost every style; but steadiness had always been wanting ... She was not much deceived as to her own skill either as an artist or as a musician, but she was not unwilling to have others deceived, or sorry to know her reputation for accomplishment often higher than it deserved ... A likeness pleases everybody; and Miss Woodhouse's performances must be capital. [p. 72]

However, her portrait of Mr John Knightley does not please. "I put it away in a pet, and vowed I would never take another likeness" (p. 73).

This passage describes a more positive aspect of the projective mode, the now familiar process by which, during adolescence in particular, individuals may investigate who they are by projecting aspects of themselves into others and relating to them there, whether with acceptance or rejection. With Emma, the issue is more complicated, for instead of experimenting with possibilities herself, Harriet is proposed and promoted, with endless confusions, self-deceptions and mistaken perceptions, and with the constant imposition of a great deal of disappointment and needless suffering. To begin with, Harriet is so malleable that Emma can more or less elicit in her what she will. Emma is an arrant projector, but she is also, as we have seen, knowingly and not unwillingly, the subject of other people's projections—at times far beyond her deserts. It is Mr Knightley who remains the touchstone of the relationship between Emma's illusory and actual ability. He retains throughout the capacity for judgement, duty, moral values, selflessness and right-mindedness—a true gentleman, a true knight. "Mr Knightley, in fact, was one of a few people who could see faults in Emma Woodhouse, and the only one who ever told her them" (p. 42). He recognizes that she would never submit to anything requiring industry and patience and a subjection of fancy to understanding.

He has, we are told, an exquisite manner, and good manners in Jane Austen, tend, on the whole, to be an authentic index of people's moral qualities.

When Mr Knightley questions Emma's claims to success in bringing about Miss Taylor's marriage, he is, with an honesty, straightforwardness, and, as the reader soon discovers, deep concern, trying to encourage Emma to think about the meaning and consequences of her actions. One of the problems he clearly perceives is Emma's difficulty in feeling that there is anything *to* learn: "How can Emma imagine she has anything to learn herself, while Harriet is presenting such delightful inferiorities?" (Better, he says elsewhere, "to be without sense than to misapply it as you do".) Mr Knightley's easy access to Emma's household, outside any formal calling hours, conveys the sense that he is somehow continuously in her house/mind. Ronald Blythe describes the clever dichotomy whereby the reader "sees everything with Emma's eyes but has to judge it by Mr Knightley's standards" (1966, p. 14). It is this very dichotomy that enables the reader to trace the evolving relationship between self and other in Emma, to follow the gradual decrease of her narcissistic projective mode in favour of a greater capacity for a realistic perception of herself and of the external world. The relationship between Mr Knightley and Emma has much in common with that of Bion's "container/contained". As we have seen, the prototype is the relationship between mother and baby, analogous in important ways to that between analyst and analysand. The prerequisites for thinking and learning lie in the availability of a mind capable of introjecting the baby's projective communications and evacuations, whether they be in love or in hate. Thus a person can investigate his or her own feelings in another personality, one which is felt to be resilient enough to contain them. In late adolescence what becomes particularly evident is the way in which normal development is dependent on the mechanism for satisfying curiosity about the self (that is projective identification) being introjected in such a way as to foster an increase in thinking and in understanding. If this can happen in relation to figures in the external world, it can, as a result, also gradually happen with figures in the internal world.

As a consequence of Mr Knightley's availability as a containing object, Emma's insistently projective mode begins to diminish to more "normal" proportions and her introjective capacities to increase. The observation of Mr Knightley's growing influence on Emma involves the reader in an experience of the process of the growth of the mind under the influence of a benign internal figure. At first Emma tends to deny any weight to Mr Knightley's admonitions. She shelters from her disquiet in the claim that they are jokes: "Mr Knightley loves to find fault with me you know—in a joke—it is all a joke. We always say what we like to one another" (p. 42). But, despite her rationalizations and self-justifications, she is troubled: "Emma made no answer, and tried to look cheerfully unconcerned, but was feeling uncomfortable and was wanting him very much to be gone."

So absolute is Emma's emotional blindness, and so insistent her misrepresentations, that it is only much later that she can, with horror, recognize the extent of her self-deception. Yet the recognition carries with it a sense that something had been working within her for a long time—something of which she was scarcely conscious and which finally, in the face of the fear that she has lost the absolute centre of her affections, threatens internal collapse. The decisive turning point is Emma's intense remorse and the desire for reparation for her cruel snub of the elderly Miss Bates, during a picnic expedition to Box Hill. Mr Knightley rounds on Emma. She mentally turns to her father for comfort and has to recognize his emotional inadequacy (as an internal figure), and his dependency on *her* (as an external one). Her blindness hitherto to her father's limitations has allowed for the perpetuation of a pseudo-mature sense of herself, offering artificial gratification because built only on idealization and denial. The reader now observes Emma herself beginning to recognize the shift which has slowly been occurring within, a shift of which we, the readers, have long been aware. She discovers the truth of her own feelings. There is nothing indulgent in this anguished account of self-recognition. It carries with it the acute sense of shame and the biting edge of remorse and responsibility—the poised uncertainty of the turbulence of catastrophic change.

> The rest of the day, the following night, were hardly enough for her thoughts.—She was bewildered amidst the confusion of all that had rushed on her within the last few hours. Every moment had brought

a fresh surprise; and every surprise must be a matter of humiliation to her.—How to understand it all! How to understand the deceptions she had been thus practising on herself, and living under!—The blunders, the blindness of her own head and heart!—she sat still, she walked about, she tried her own room, she tried the shrubbery—in every place, every posture, she perceived that she had acted most weakly; that she had been imposed upon by others in a most mortifying degree; that she been imposing on herself in a degree yet more mortifying; that she was wretched, and should probably find this day but the beginning of wretchedness.

To understand, thoroughly understand her own heart, was the first endeavour. To that point went every leisure moment which her father's claims on her allowed, and every moment of involuntary absence of mind ...

With insufferable vanity had she believed herself in the secret of everybody's feelings; with unpardonable arrogance proposed to arrange everybody's destiny. She was proved to have been universally mistaken; and she had not quite done nothing—for she had done mischief. She had brought evil on Harriet, on herself, and she too much feared, on Mr Knightley. [pp. 401–402]

Yet there is also a sense that whether or not her worst fears are realized in the loss of Mr Knightley to Harriet, Emma has the strength emotionally to survive.

When it came to such a pitch as this [that it had all been her own work], she was not able to refrain from a start, or a heavy sigh, or even from walking about the room for a few seconds—and the only source whence anything like consolation or composure could be drawn, was in the resolution of her own better conduct, and the hope that, however inferior in spirit and gaiety might be the following and every future winter of her life to the past, it would yet find her more rational, more acquainted with herself, and leave her less to regret when it were gone. [p. 411]

The relationship which allows Emma to become "more acquainted with herself" is one in which another change has also imperceptibly been occurring. It is profoundly true that when a person is able to grow as a result of learning from the inner capacities of another, that other is also deeply affected. "Those who can trust us, educate us."[2] Just as the analyst learns from the patient and the parent from the child, so Mr Knightley learned from Emma, and he too developed. The change here is a subtle but important one. He observes of Emma early on that, "in her mother she lost the only person able to cope with her". Clearly Mr Knightley assumes the parental mantle. It is his jealous but, as ever, selfless conviction of Emma's affection for a feared rival, Frank Churchill, which awakens him to the realization that his love for Emma is not merely parental but is rooted in the desire that she should be his wife. He too, in other words, finds an internal capacity for marriage, one which had been lacking at the opening of the book. He stumbles upon the truth about himself; not so much the early expression of his disinterested interest in Emma's declarations that she will never marry ("I wonder what will become of her"), but in his passionate longing for her—finally and so movingly understated: "If I loved you less, I might be able to talk about it more" (p. 417).

It had been Emma's belief that she had lost Mr Knightley to another. That belief revealed to her the nature of her true feelings for him. When her jealousy was fired, she discovered that in Mr Knightley she had slowly begun to invest not merely parental qualities, albeit deeply significant ones, but also, without her knowing it, aspirational ones of hope and renewal, qualities which were now represented by the idea of marriage. "It darted through her, with the speed of an arrow, that Mr Knightley must marry no one but herself!" (p. 398) It was, moreover, the internal development which had been imperceptibly occurring that enabled her, despite her conviction that the object of her love was now lost, to sustain the notion of a possible future alone. Thus the reader has a sense of how Emma's development is initiated and assisted by the internal changing quality of the one to whom she is deeply attached, before she herself has any awareness of what is happening. Emma gradually moves from wishful fantasizing to the beginning of a capacity for growth and change.

The final description of her inner state defines the significance of the character shift. The key-notes have become those of self-knowledge and of sincerity, qualities on which the internal capacity for marriage is based—on the recognition of an internal presence which combines parental capacities, standards and aspirations with sexual longing. On the recognition of the meaning for her of someone who bears such qualities depends the move which we have followed in Emma from a vain and self-centred, albeit charming, adolescent, to a young woman who is beginning to be able to occupy a more adult sense of identity. This adult state of mind is characterized by feelings of humility, of gratitude, and of concern for the other, feelings which make mature intimacy a possibility; if, in Emma's case, still far from realized.

> What had she to wish for? Nothing, but to grow more worthy of him, whose intentions and judgement had been ever so superior to her own. Nothing, but that the lessons of her past folly might teach her humility and circumspection in future. [p. 456]

Further developmental possibilities for Emma and Mr Knightley, and for the relationship between them, remain yet to be known, and, at the end of the novel, the question of her capacity genuinely to separate hangs very much in the air. She does not, for the time being at least, leave her family home and establish one elsewhere with her husband. For a condition of the marriage is that she remain with her father, to be joined there by Mr Knightley. Much is yet to be resolved.

The absence, in the novel, of a convincing internal resolution in the main characters of this central problem, both of physical separation and of psychic separateness, is also true of *Jane Eyre*. Charlotte Brontë's novel offers a wonderful and intensely poetic rendering of a courageous thirst for a "real knowledge of Life". It is an extraordinary moral and psychological investigation of Jane Eyre's childhood, her girlhood, and her emergence from adolescence into maturity. Charlotte Brontë describes the process of protracted truth-seeking at its most painful and most resolute. Mr Rochester (the other central protagonist and the man whom she loves) has often been compared to Mr Knightley in terms both of his combination of tenderness and strength, and of the Oedipal overtones of his part in the central relationship. This Oedipal aspect is especially pronounced in the much more explicitly sexual and passionate attachment between Jane and her rather Byronic "Master", and importantly relates to the nature of the final marriage.

Jane has been much criticized for leaving Rochester and Thornfield Hall after the devastating discovery, on the day of her proposed marriage to him, that he already has a wife—the mad woman locked up on the third floor, Bertha. Jane's suffering and mental devastation are described with a depth and poignancy which are scarcely bearable. When she falls into fitful sleep on the night of her departure, she dreams of one of her earliest traumatic experiences, that of being shut in the "red room" in her then home, Gateshead. Here, as a child, her terror, her sense of abandonment and the loss of any shred of sustaining goodness in her life, had driven her to near madness. It is clear from the text that this early episode had significantly Oedipal connotations. The voice she hears now, in her wakeful dreaming, as a white human form emerges mysteriously from the moon is, "My daughter, flee temptation!". "Mother, I will", she replies. What this passage, and the last part of the book, imply is that in order to achieve a genuine capacity for intimacy (in this case with Rochester), Jane still has to resolve some inner ties. She has to relinquish the ideals of infant/adolescent romance. Both she herself and he to whom she is devoted have yet more to learn about themselves. Jane has both to experience the impact of loss through renunciation, and to recognize the nature of her own attachment to subjugating herself to the needs of another (St. John Rivers) rather than being able to establish a relationship of equality and reciprocity.

Rochester's accident in the fire symbolizes his becoming a changed man, with seared vision and crippled hand. In the flames he lost the "sinister" ("left" hand) part of himself and, as a result, he began to be able to own his needs and dependency, relinquishing his proud omnipotence. Hitherto, as Jane says, he had disdained every part but that of giver and protector. Now he acknowledges how he, "can begin to experience remorse, repentance, the wish for reconcilement to my Maker" (p. 495). As a consequence of his loss, anguish and sorrow, Rochester's thoughts become directed inwards and his *mind's* eye sees much more clearly than he was able to before becoming blind. He experiences humility, unworthiness, gratitude and now, deep joy.

Charlotte Brontë seeks to establish, in this last part of the book, the basis for the internal capacity for marriage which Jane and Rochester, through their respective suffering, might finally achieve. As with Emma, that capacity seems to be essentially rooted in the *internal* presence of the loved one, an internal presence which is able to sustain the failure, absence or fallibility of the *external*. Yet Jane and Rochester's is a singular kind of marriage. The setting is profoundly reclusive. Ferndeane, their home, is at first sight scarcely distinguishable from the trees, "so dark and green were its decaying walls ... it was as still as a church on a weekday; the pattering rain on the forest leaves was the only sound audible in the vicinage, 'Can there be life here?', I asked" (p. 479). Their relationship is described as almost symbiotic:

> No woman was ever nearer to her mate than I am: ever more absolutely bone of his bone and flesh of his flesh. I know no weariness of my Edward's society: he knows none of mine, any more than we each do of the pulsation of the heart that beats in our separate bosoms. Consequently, we are ever together. To be together is for us to be at once as free as in solitude, as gay as in company. We talk, I believe, all day long: to talk to each other is but a more animated and audible thinking. All my confidence is bestowed on him, all his confidence is devoted to me; we are precisely suited in character—perfect concord is the result.[3] [p. 500]

With the ending of *Jane Eyre* and *Emma*, as with many nineteenth-century novels, notably those of George Eliot, the reader is left with qualms. The dimensions of the internal voyage into true adulthood seem so much more extensive than the suggested potential of the married states through which the stories find resolution. When George Eliot, towards the end of her life, said that she had never been happy with her endings, she was perhaps reflecting on a crisis of genre. The novel can observe and describe a process of becoming which formally requires an ending but cannot really have one. Yet possibly she was also recognizing a different kind of issue—that the achievement of a committed partnership only represents a port of re-embarkation. It simultaneously marks the distance already travelled and the distance yet to go. And so it may be that it is the very imperfection of these unions that could be said to represent not so much arrival as potential for further development. The final unease, at the end of these and other novels, poses questions of whether, and how, individuals can go on growing up within a partnership; how they can achieve or attain independence of mind; how they can come to experience and to tolerate the chosen other as they really are, as opposed to how they may have been wished to be. This latter process will very likely continue to involve its own kinds of loss, whether they be conscious or unconscious ones, as well as the unquestionable gains. But that is a different story, the nature of which is deeply affected by the distinction under discussion: that between the external fact of marriage or partnership, and the internal "capacity" for it; that is, by the basis on which the original relationship has been founded.

The two novels discussed describe development as being rooted in a delicate balance between introjective and projective processes. Maturity is slowly acquired through the experience of having the more infantile and insistent projections received and rendered both bearable and meaningful. When this is the case, not only the content of the projections themselves but also that very capacity to process them can become part of the personality. A coming-out-of-projective-identification then becomes possible, the foundation, as we have seen, for adult identity and for intimacy.

The central emotional development that takes place in these narratives represents a process to be found in much drama and fiction, one that is epitomized, perhaps, in the great nineteenth-century novels.[4] That development, as argued in this chapter, clarifies a particular way of relating which later became known as the introjective mode, or as introjective identification. But what, precisely, that "something" really is, is often unclear, or missed, in the various theoretical expositions of the process. The point about Bion's idea of learning as being a capacity based in introjection, is that he is suggesting a process which is more complex than Klein's notion of the internalization of a good experience "which supports and protects the self". Learning in Bion's sense, and in the sense realized in the fictional characters described here, is based on the capacity to *have* emotional experiences, ones, that is, which can be felt to be meaningful. These then become the basis for further thoughts and higher levels of abstraction. Such experiences tend to be of the moment, ones that have not been excessively interfered with by other considerations: by, for example, "having an eye to the future"; or by a "sentimental attachment to the past"; or by too immediate an "awareness of consequences"; or by too nostalgic "a bond to the familiar".

Meltzer (1978, 1994) suggests that Bion's recommendation to the clinician of a temporary suspension of "memory and desire" is related to this internal situation, to Bion's awareness of the way in which a consciousness of the past and a hope for the future may disrupt, or co-opt, the experience of the present (p. 463). Being able genuinely to engage with a present emotional experience then becomes an achievement—one that is essential to the conflict and turbulence of growth and development, and one that is, for that very reason, so often resisted.

In each of the novels discussed here, the decisive developmental steps taken are the result of intense emotional experiences which force those characters who have the capacity to undergo them, to "think"; to think in the fundamental sense of allowing themselves to "have" their experience. These steps take place in relation to a potential partner who is also impelled to "think", to suffer and to learn in similar ways. It is the characters' capacity genuinely to engage with emotional experience, to learn from it, and to change as a consequence, that makes these ordinarily limited and flawed people into "heroes" or "heroines". It is not because they are ideally beautiful or virtuous that they achieve heroic status, but because, unlike other characters, they are prepared to struggle to become themselves in the immediacy of the anguish of their emotional engagements.

Meltzer (1978, 1994) draws attention to how evident it is in the history of our patients,

> that they have often been broken in their development by bad, painful experiences—weaning, birth of the next sibling, the primal scene, death of a love object. But it is equally apparent from the histories of great men—Keats, for example—that they have been "made" by the acceptance and assimilation of these same events. Equally, we see patients who have been broken by "good" experiences, where [those experiences] have inflamed megalomania, or, conversely, stirred intolerable feelings of gratitude and indebtedness. Freud's "character types met within analysis" could be seen to fall into this category. [pp. 466–467]

Recent psychoanalytic views based in the work of Bion correspond more closely to this developmental picture than to those of Freud or Klein. For this picture of "character" is one in which a person can begin to learn to take responsibility for him or herself, and to build their personality, by eventually acquiring the capacity to learn, both from good and from bad experience.

These novels describe the conditions in which such growth of character can take place, by implicit contrast with all those in whom little or no development occurs. At the heart of the process lie the central challenges of the depressive position: the realistic estimation of the actual qualities of the other, and an acceptance of what is found there; the capacity to bear the loss of the external presence but nonetheless to retain that presence internally in the face of absence, of doubt and uncertainty, of loss of trust, and even of fear of betrayal by the loved one. The defining element lies not in the fact of "good" and "bad" as such, but in the different capacities to relate to, and to make sense of experience, whether that be in itself good or bad.

Emma and *Jane Eyre* encompass some of the major themes of this book generally, and some of the issues which belong to late adolescence in particular. The personality can grow in-so-far as it is able to survive psychically the disturbing experience of change and the losses that that entails. It also has to be able to establish an identification with an internal thinking figure, a focus of love and attachment, which can eventually function independently of its external origin and representation. Psychic change and survival depend on the fledgling self being contained and guided, whether in the course of its own intimate relationships in the family and in life, or by the artist's internal world being given symbolic form for the reader, or by some such process in the therapist/patient setting. Each re-evokes, as they must ever do, the infant's earliest experiences. The late-adolescent is struggling with his psychically emergent self. An intimate relationship may be looked to, or even grasped at, to assuage the anxieties about separation and the move into adult life. Depending on the internal capacity for intimacy, such a relationship may either further bind the personality to its unseparated self, or may free it to go on discovering its own potential. How the subsequent lives of Emma and Jane will unfold is uncertain. Their choices and commitments carry no guarantees. But these choices and commitments were made with a kind of honesty and integrity which leave the reader somewhat hopeful.

Notes

1. Tony Tanner (1986) *Jane Austen*, London: Macmillan, p. 176. Tanner's emphasis is one of identity: "Emma is a matchmaker who meets her

match and, in a sense, her 'maker': the conflated words have to be properly separated (and morally monitored) so that Emma can become most properly—Emma".

2. This is how George Eliot (1876) describes the impact of Gwendolen on Daniel Deronda. *Daniel Deronda*, London: Blackwood; (repr. Harmondsworth, Penguin, 1967), p. 485.

3. For an extended argument of similar points, see Blum, M. (1995) "An exploration of the inner world as expressed in two novels", unpublished M.A. Dissertation, City University.

4. The development of Dorothea in George Eliot's *Middlemarch* and of Gwendolen in *Daniel Deronda* are particularly fine examples of this same process.

CHAPTER TWELVE

The adult world

"The presence of a noble nature, generous in its wishes, ardent in its charity, changes the lights for us: we begin to see things again in their larger, quieter masses, and to believe that we too can be seen and judged in the wholeness of our character"

George Eliot

"When I grow up I want to be a 'dult'" was how one small six-year-old described his life's ambition. In the mind of the latency child there exists a distinct and centrally important "world" in relation to which he defines and organizes his own: that of the "grown-ups". At the age of seven, or even eleven, it is impossible to imagine that the "grown-ups" are themselves still struggling with what being a "dult" means; that throughout their lives many of them remain significantly engaged in the process of "growing up". And yet that ongoing engagement is a necessary one, for the belief that maturity has been attained may be a seriously infantile delusion. What is an adult identity? How are we to define maturity? Bion (1961) suggested we should not "assume too easily that the label on the box is a good description of the contents" (p. 37). The fact that somebody superficially looks grown-up (whether by attaining the age of twenty-one, servicing a mortgage, wearing a white coat or a pin-striped suit, or rearing children) may have little to do with the childish or infantile states which underlie the socially defining exterior. The burden of inauthenticity is often immense. Many would share Margaret Atwood's sense that as an adult she was "in disguise".

Over the years psychoanalysts have defined maturity in a number of ways. Freud thought about it in terms of being able to work and to love; Klein, as an increased capacity to live in the depressive position; Bion, as being able to go on developing. Just as much Romantic poetry was preoccupied with how to become a poet, so Bion (1970) saw his many years as a psychoanalyst as a process of learning how to become one. He concerned himself with how to further an individual's endeavour to move from knowing about reality to becoming real (pp. 26–40).

When it comes to notions of adulthood and maturity it makes more sense than ever to think in terms of states of mind and not of stages of development. For we again find ourselves faced with the necessity of making distinctions, ones which are similar to those discussed in relation to infancy, and indeed to all subsequent phases and stages. The difference between maturity and immaturity hinges not on the fact of chronological years but on a person's capacity to bear intense emotional states; on the extent to which it is possible to think about, and reflect on, psychic pain as a consequence of having found, and sustained, a relationship with external and internal figures who are able so to do.

The contrasting response is to adopt all sorts of means to avoid engaging with painful matters. Those means often seem more exciting and compelling than their alternatives. And in many ways it is easier to define maturity in terms of what it is not, than to find a way of expressing the contrapuntal intricacies of anguish and joy, action and thought, fire and calm which underlie the capacity fully to engage with experience. Wisdom would seem to be more to do with living and feeling than with acquiring knowledge. It is not a case of believing oneself to have grown out of infantile impulses and longings, but rather one of knowing and understanding those undeveloped aspects of the self and, as a consequence, being alert to their potential effects, particularly their destructiveness. Keats's "Soul-making" emphasis in the experience of life belongs to the capacity to tolerate the perception that "the World is full of Misery and Heartbreak, Pain, Sickness and oppression" (*Letters*, p. 95). It lies in the capacity to engage with internal conflict, beginning with the explorations and gropings of foetal life. In a world of Circumstances, he writes to his brother and sister-in-law, it is the Heart which is "the teat from which the Mind or intelligence sucks its identity" (*Letters*, p. 250). The distinction between learning about things and learning from experience was never more clearly put.

Although the strands which run through these pages have, for the sake of clarity, been broadly chronological, between them they have been making up a picture of different states of mind, whether infantile, latency, adolescent or adult, states that constantly shift and oscillate in relation to one another, whatever the age under discussion. In adulthood all those various strands are no less present, though some may be better concealed, and others may have become so much part of the personality that they begin to be described as "how someone is". Klein writes with great clarity about the way in which the so-called "adult world" is permeated by the infantile. The question is not so much how to get rid of those states as how to accommodate them within the personality, and to reduce their potentially destructive effects, both on the self and on others. Central to the adult state is the capacity to recognize and to integrate the other aspects of the self without excessive disruption of the psychic equilibrium; to integrate them rather than to seek to disown them by ridding the self of them and projecting them elsewhere. As Klein (1959) put it: "we are [in certain states in mind] inclined to attribute to other people—in a sense, to put into them— some of our own emotions and thoughts; and it is obvious that it will depend on how balanced or how persecuted we are whether this projection is of a friendly or hostile nature" (p. 252).

A sense of mature adulthood may be achieved, at least some of the time, not by disclaiming, ignoring or enacting whatever infantile impulse may arise, but by recognizing such impulses for what they are and managing them appropriately; not by eliminating the playful, adventurous, even tempestuous parts of the self, but by finding some measure of balance and integration for them. This has been the task for the growing personality all along but, like each previous age, adulthood has its own special character, a central part of which is engagement with the outside world of work, of community and of society at large; with responsibilities and freedoms hitherto scarcely tried or tested. It is at this point in life that it becomes particularly tempting to mistake a sense of status for a sense of identity, though the danger may long have threatened. The thoughtful adult will still be struggling with the familiar adolescent imperative to try to move "from resemblance to identity", but the world of Circumstances does not make that easy for anyone at the age with which we are now concerned. In a society organized around status and hierarchy, one which "knows the price of everything and the value of nothing" (Wilde, 1891), there is a cruel and insistent pressure to conform to the dominant ethos. Such conformity may, however, be at the expense of the individual. If so, the achievement of having a sense of one's own personality is swiftly traduced. Its rival and enemy is the culture of "personalities".

Martha Harris was particularly aware of the complexity of the relationship between the individual and institutional and societal groupings. Gnomically she wrote, "It is difficult enough to become the person one is without positive encouragement from the establishment towards conformity and deception" (1981, p. 327). She described the tension between "man as a social animal dependent upon, and with obligations to, society; and man as a developing individual with a mind that grows through introjecting experiences of himself in the world, impelled to think in order to retain internally relationships with needed and valued objects in their absence" (p. 322).

The nature of the struggle involved at this adult stage will depend on the patterns of engagement, or defence, which have been developing from the first. These patterns are now tested with particular severity and the extent to which they have become ingrained make the possibility of functioning in a different mode all the harder, especially if there have been early traumas and setbacks. For some, early difficulties may be constantly re-experienced and repeated in one form or another. For some they may be denied. And for some it may have been possible to understand those difficulties, to integrate them into the personality, and to move on.

The problems and pitfalls of the whole project of growing up are beautifully described in seven-year-old Carol's story, dictated to her mother who, when asked "how do I grow up mummy?" had invited her daughter to relate her own thoughts on the matter:

> There was once a little girl and she wanted to grow up but she didn't know how. She tried putting on high heels but that didn't work. She just tripped down the stairs. She tried eating but that didn't work. That just made her have a tummy ache. She tried putting on make-up but that didn't work either.
> And then she saw her grandma and she said:
> "How do I grow up?"
> "Have you tried waiting?" asked her grandma.
> "No", said the little girl.
> She waited and waited and waited. And when she grew up she wanted to be little again because when you are little you get all the nice things.

In its delightfully simple terms Carol's story is suggestive of a number of important and complex insights. She knew, whether consciously or unconsciously, that imitating the adult world did not constitute "growing up". It may be that she was already acquainted with some "grown-ups" who suffered precisely this illusion. They thought that looking like a grown-up was tantamount to being one. She described both a projective kind of identification (getting into someone else's shoes) and an adhesive or second-skin type: the desire to feel psychically held together by physically holding, or sticking, onto something (perhaps the make-up). Carol had a sense that growth cannot be forced, "by eating more", for example. Development occurs in its own way in relation to its own conditions, certainly unevenly. Allowing a child to develop in relation to what is properly within his or her compass, rather than to what is required by the exigencies of others' expectations, is often an uncomfortable test of adults' aspirations and capacities for restraint. It involves waiting on the part of both parent and child. Time, different degrees of time, is required, as Carol rightly pointed out, to discover how to make one's own way and to encourage others to make theirs.

Carol had also realized that the impulse to shun the pains of adult responsibility forever threatens. She had the intimation that being grown-up is hard, and that the lure towards "nice things" remains great. It was, perhaps, "nice" to be pseudo-grown-up and, in "dressing up", to imitate the adult world. It was "nice" to be able to divide the world into goodies and baddies; to believe that your parents knew all the answers or, when parents didn't come up to scratch, that you were an orphan, and that you were really the long-lost son or daughter of the King and Queen of the world; or that by thinking something you could make it so; or that bad deeds need not have bad consequences because there's always someone there to make things better. "Nice" things involve not only sweets and birthday parties, but being made a fuss of, being forgiven. Carol intuitively knew that these "childish" things were quite different from the difficulty of acquiring a sense of self-esteem and a capacity to embark on the hard road to genuine self-forgiveness: quite different from having continually to engage with "Reality's dark dream".[1]

The "dressing up", the day-dreaming, the fantasies or treats all belong to a desirable, even a necessary, part of a child's world—they are a way of negotiating some kind of place both in the culture which is temporarily theirs and in that to come. They are an essential part of the continuous testing of internal and external reality which needs to go on during childhood. Carol was, in effect, commenting on the distinction between the time when such involvements express those relationships (both fantasied and real) which appropriately belong to a child's world, and those which, less appropriately, may continue to be lived-out in what is supposed to be an adult's world.

Perhaps few children will have shared Carol's good fortune in having available a thinking mother who could enable her daughter also to think, or a kindly grandmother who offered the wisdom of her years. For those who have little opportunity in childhood to sort out and bear, somewhat at least, the experience of being one of the "little ones" and not yet one of the "big ones", properly becoming an adult will be all the harder. For having an adult sense of identity involves the capacity to make a differentiation between role and function. To be grown-up "in role" only, is brought about by the sorts of projective and imitative modes which Carol described—ones belonging to the happy-ever-after picture of adult life which imbues romantic fantasies at whatever age. But intuitively Carol knew better. There is a suggestion in her story of the realization that allowing time for growing up, without leaping prematurely into what superficially *looks* grown-up, may have something to do with a particular quality of learning: the realization that learning concerns the internalizing of adult functions; the knowledge that those functions may be burdensome as well as desirable. The truthfulness of that perception has a certain beauty to it.

In disregarding chronology and thinking metapsychologically, in terms, that is, of pervasive states of mind, it is possible to recognize the infantile structures which are present in the adult, and the adult structures which are present in the infant, if only momentarily. Broad differentiations between the two will be similar to those between the paranoid–schizoid and the depressive positions. In designating maturity as an increased capacity to live in the depressive position, Klein was stressing the importance of the infantile structures giving way to a more generous and integrated set of mental attitudes. The infantile states are propelled mostly by the vital need for protection against psychic collapse, in the face of powerfully conflicting internal forces.

By contrast, the depressive position, as we have seen, involves the capacity to experience the other as genuinely other: that is, as an "other" who has independent needs and priorities; and the capacity to suffer grief and concern for damage felt to have been inflicted on that other by anxiety-driven greed and tyrannical demands. It involves carrying the burdens of being grown-up as well as claiming the rights and privileges. It involves being able to experience gratitude for care received, being able to spare, to repair. Ultimately, perhaps, it involves the capacity to identify with parental concern, a concern which will include a preparedness to take up the particular responsibility entailed, whether or not in relation to actual babies. It involves a shift from a narcissistic frame of mind to one that is able properly to take others into account. Such a shift is related to the capacity, and the opportunity, at least some of the time, to take in figures who can function as benign inner resources.

*   *   *

The following account by a young mother offers a vivid description of a situation in which the ever-shifting relationship between infantile states and adult capacities is particularly clear:

I was driving home with Carl [two years old] and Lucy [fourteen months]. We'd spent the day with friends in Luton. Fifteen minutes from home they started arguing and within seconds it had escalated into full-scale war. They hit, they shouted, they called for me to get involved. I could feel my exhaustion growing and my rage building up. I completely lost control. I slammed on the brakes and started banging on the steering wheel and shouting at them to go away and to shut up, and to leave me alone. Awful shocked silence followed. Then someone started stroking me and Carl said, "It's all right Mummy, it's all right". That precipitated me straight back into adulthood and motherhood. I feel so guilty at the moments when I become the child and sort of force them to parent me.[2]

The internal capacities which Carl, in a crisis, was able to draw on are observable in even younger children. One baby can wait for a feed, sparing the stressed mother, another may scream, first with frustration and then, perhaps, with fear. Yet another will withdraw into his own world, trying to find comfort in his bodily sensations, or perhaps in sensuous attachments to material objects. But in this example one can see with particular clarity how little Carl was able, temporarily, to encourage his harassed mother with precisely those enlivening reassurances with which he had himself clearly been sustained on so many previous occasions.

Eighteen-month-old Peter displayed a similarly mature capacity for care and concern for his mother; a readiness to spare her his own neediness when perceiving her distress, and to offer her his thoughtful attention. On this particular occasion Peter had been looked after all day by his aunt, while his mother was at work. His mother was unusually late home and in the last hour or so Peter had turned anxiously and expectantly towards any sound which might signal her return. When she came in she was clearly upset and in a state of some excitement. It turned out that she had just had a row with a neighbour who had been very abusive to her.

Usually Peter was rather clingy when his mother came home, but on this occasion, although running after her to keep her in sight while she hung up her coat, he then sat quietly on the floor and listened while she recounted the incident to her sister. His mother noticed Peter's quietness and picked up a book, as if to read to him. But she was immediately distracted by what had happened and continued animatedly talking. She told her sister that she should have stayed at home that day, since she still had an awful cold. At this point Peter got up. He went to fetch his medical kit and handed it to his mother. While she held the little plastic container he got out the stethoscope and first of all put it to his own ears. Then he gestured to his mother to wear the stethoscope herself. She put it on and made as if to listen to Peter's chest. But he shook his head firmly and pointed to her own chest. Realizing that this was an attempt to look after *her*, his mother smiled and lovingly gathered him into her arms.

This identification on Peter and Carl's part with a capacity to bear frustration and to care, cheer and encourage in the face of hardship goes to the heart of the adult sense of identity. It derives from the kind of introjective identification already described, one with internal, benign and supportive, parental figures. This was certainly Freud's view and has been extensively elaborated ever since. The work of the Oedipal process, at whatever age one locates its inception, is, as we have seen, to do with relinquishing the libidinal attachment to external parents, whether in love or in hate, taking them into the internal world, and identifying with them there, where they will be experienced as mixed figures, being both loving and encouraging, and also censorious and punitive. Which of the two it will be depends on the degree of persecution with which the parents have already been experienced by the child, as well as on their actual qualities. It should again be noticed that at the heart of the Oedipal constellation lies the capacity to allow for growth through relinquishment. The sense of separateness, so intrinsic to an adult state of mind, is premissed on the experience of loss, or fear of loss, being felt to be bearable, to be painful but not catastrophic. Whether that experience turns out to be painful or catastrophic depends on how separation and loss have been experienced and endured from the first; on how secure, or fragile, internal resources are felt to be.

The distinction between different kinds of identification in determining prevailing states of mind, and the importance of the possible reasons for those identifications, is well caught in a few short extracts from an infant observation:

Charlie (sixteen months) walked steadily across the room. He found a little plastic figure of a man wearing a three-cornered hat. He took the hat off and fixed it on again. Looking at me [the observer], he put the hat that he had taken off into his mouth. He soon took it out again, with a serious expression on his face. He dropped the hat and picked up his mother's ruler from the table [his mother teaches Maths in a secondary school]. Holding the ruler he walked into the living room where his brother Frank (three years old) was watching television. Frank mumbled "naughty baby" in a slightly superior tone, and went on watching his programme. Charlie sought out his mother in the kitchen. "Careful with that ruler", she said "you'll have an accident". She suggested that he put it safely back on the table; which he did.

Later on both boys were tussling on their mother's lap, fighting each other for space. As Charlie definitively possessed the field by managing to get his arm round his mother's neck and to oust his brother, Frank got down, boldly announcing that he was going in search of his hat. While he was away Charlie and his mum enjoyed an intimate few moments, playing and singing "Row, row, row your boat" in perfect accord and well within Frank's earshot.

Frank returned with a fireman's hat on his head. With an air of importance he climbed onto his plastic bicycle. His mum said admiringly, "Oh good. We shall need a fireman because we might have a flood. The washing machine is full and I can't open the door. If there *is* a flood I shall definitely have to call for a fireman". (There was a shared implication that the machine was stuck because Charlie had fiddled with the buttons.) Frank looked pleased and important.

Without wishing to infer too much from these details it could, nonetheless, be suggested that when Charlie put the small hat in his mouth, removed it and immediately took up his mother's ruler, he was indicating that he had taken in something of his mother's authority and her concerned function of safeguarding him from swallowing something which could harm him. He immediately took up an object which might be said to represent this authority of which, in this sequence, he seemed not only to be aware, but also, momentarily, to be able to exercise on his own behalf. (This is in stark contrast to a rather older and very disturbed child who, in his therapy sessions, would characteristically brandish a ruler above his head shouting "I am the ruler", apparently believing himself actually to be so.)

Frank, already predisposed to put down his little brother ("naughty baby"), dealt with his own sense of exclusion from the mother/baby relationship by becoming the helpful, rescuing, big-boy-for-mummy (perhaps even daddy-for-mummy); at the ready in case of danger. Sensitively his mother realized that Frank's big-boy-self needed confirmation in this instance, and she supported his bid for status. One can see how, if Frank's little-boy-self had had to yield too consistently to his brother's baby demands, this uniform-wearing, slightly grandiose version of Frank-the-rescuer could become a fixed and defensive role, one that might protect his more needy self from exclusion or marginalization, but at a cost. It could also be that enough confirmation of his big-boy-self would enable him to acquire a sense of self-respect, rather than of superiority. One can see the danger in Frank's case that, if too often his sense of self required him to be big, when, in fact, he needed to be little, his real and fragile experience of who he was could become subsumed under the outer trappings of status and superiority. Here we can clearly see the subtle, moment by moment, shifts in the brothers' negotiation of their infant/adult selves as they responded to the ever-changing experience of intimacy and exclusion.

The difference between traits or roles, and functions is the difference between an infantile search for the "secrets" of being a "grown-up", in relation to external descriptive categories or characteristics, and the mysterious process of identifying with inner functions. This latter process belongs to the realm of psychic reality. It establishes the basis of character. The relationship between "secrets" and "mysteries" and their associated meanings has long preoccupied artists and creative writers. As a mode of denying anxiety and of avoiding painful experience, the desire to discover secrets rather than to seek out, to explore and endure the mysteries is a fundamental aspect of human nature.[3]

Such questions become more insistent than ever in adulthood. Now that the individual is technically "grown-up" the issue of what being a "man" or a "woman" really means has to be confronted. It is an issue which is as pressing for adults as the problem of sexual identity is for adolescents. There may, for example, be pseudo-mature identifications with masculine or feminine traits without any notion of what genuine manliness or womanliness might feel like or mean; or, indeed, without any notion of what all the possible positions between the two, or which combine the two, might mean.

The gender aspect of a sense of identity is particularly hard to determine with any precision since it is so often obscured by the various armours of social code and stereotype which denote gender difference in line with obvious physiological distinctions. A further confusion occurs when the terms "masculinity" or "femininity" are invoked with any certainty. Freud (1933) was in no doubt about the hazards of such an approach. His view was that "what constitutes masculinity and femininity is an unknown characteristic which anatomy cannot lay hold of" (p. 114).

Any stereotype will clearly run counter to a person's efforts to be himself or herself. Although conventional stereotypes are slowly being dismantled to the point where it is possible to speak of "nurturing fathers" or "career mothers", an air of judgement from one source or another is seldom far away, whether based on ignorance, insecurity, or, perhaps, envy. Contemporary elaborations of Klein's theories of splitting and projective identification, together with Bick's notion of second-skin functioning, enable us to have considerable understanding of the ways in which someone may get locked within a personality which is based on pseudo-mature identifications with adult patterns of life, at the expense of the courage to withstand counterfeit emotions and to hold out for the difference between imitation and reality, between seeming to be and actually being. This is often particularly the case where there are anxieties about gender identity.

As we have seen (Chapter 4), the kind of adhesive identification which gives rise to a second-skin, or "as-if", way of functioning tends to select the social appearance of things as a focus of cohesion and integration. A person is drawn towards attitudes which are based on the imitation of surface attributes and behaviour. He is in danger of becoming a slave to fashion rather than a servant of principle. These identifications are caught up with primarily narcissistic concerns. They are very different, as we have seen, from the kind of identification in which the functional capacities of the loved one are taken in and assimilated as valued and trusted resources, ones which can be made use of by the growing personality. In adulthood a clear and unconfused sense of gender identity may be regarded as the foundation of a properly separated capacity to love and to work. It is this link between a coherent sense of a sexual self and the nature of introjective processes that must now be considered at some length.[4]

It is impossible to separate the findings of psychoanalytic research into the individual mind from the cultural context in which the structure of the personality arises. When we speak of masculinity and femininity we are using terms which are largely a matter of sociological interest. In describing something as typically "male" or "female" we are adopting the language of cultural stereotypes, of externally visible qualities—a kind of armour of convention, to be associated primarily with defensive character formation.

When it comes to the concepts male:female, or masculine: feminine it is, as Meltzer (1973) suggests, necessary to clear the field of a certain type of semantic debris:

> We must set aside all historic, cultural or personal bias that would wish to appropriate specific traits of character or qualities of mind and fasten them preferentially to one or the other side of this dichotomy. Maleness and femaleness are highly complex concepts, differently faceted in meaning for different individuals and not to be bound to statistical ideas of normality, acculturation or adaptation. The meaning in the mind of each person is far more personal ...
> [p. 115]

Individual concepts of maleness and femaleness will inevitably be inflected by social experience. Yet there remains a fundamental distinction between external traits and internal functions. An adult sense of identity is manifest in a person's capacity to understand and perform those internal functions. A strong sense of identity grows out of such a capacity, and a false or confused sense grows out of a narcissistic identification with roles rather than with genuine qualities. The uncertainty does not relate to issues of whether something seems to be predominantly male or female. It is not about bisexuality or ambisexuality. It stems, rather, from the danger of having recourse to simulating behaviour which is based merely in the superficial attributes of, for example, motherliness and femininity, or of fatherliness and masculinity; in the secrets to be plundered; the romance of princes and princesses; the myth of "happy ever after". This kind of behaviour, orientated as it is to the external world, contrasts with a person's struggle towards what may be called gender capacities. These capacities develop through the complicated process of a particular aspect of introjective identification, one which has its foundations in the infant's relationship with the internal figures who perform genuine parental functions for him.

An extended example may help to clarify the complex relationships between these different kinds of identification as they bear on the distinction between role and function in the case of one young woman, Laura. Beginning therapy was a particularly courageous decision for her. It was an unusual thing to do for someone from her social background and she had constantly to fight against the lure towards social and familial conformity, which was felt to offer so much calmer a life. When first referred for treatment Laura was thirty-four, a teacher of children with severe learning disabilities. She came from a working-class, immigrant background in Scotland. She was seeking help for states of confusion, for an inability to think, for depression and general unhappiness. She had been married to her second husband for six years and longed for a baby, but had been unable to conceive. She was distressed and preoccupied by this fact, though it was not the main reason for seeking help.

Laura was the first child of hard-working and ambitious parents. They had started a shop, working night and day while Laura was an infant. They had, it seemed, had little time for their baby. Laura had memories of being, as she described it, put in a box underneath the counter. She had felt neglected and unhappy as a child. She remembered often being looked after by neighbours; feeling wretched at school; suffering a sense of persecution over fears of her own wickedness. She hated her teachers and always came bottom of the class. One year she had a teacher whom she liked and by whom she felt understood. She came top. Far from the praise for which she had so earnestly hoped, she was cruelly berated: why did she not always achieve, since she was clearly so capable?

She described her mother as elegant and bejewelled, but rather cold and distant; her father as temperamental and erratic, affectionate but liable to sexual intrusiveness. Laura's dreams were generally persecutory, often taking the form of animals, devils or malign spirits breaking into her flat/house/room and terrifying her. Her main devil was a figure called Mr Business. He had originated in childhood and continued to "visit" her as some kind of terrifying presence. Her mother's second baby, a boy, was born when Laura was five. He was an asthmatic and bronchitic child who "got all the care". Laura recalled a memory, dating from this period, of cutting all images of herself from family photographs. She could not bear to be "seen" in the projected images of "happy-family" groups when she had never felt "seen" as an individual in the lived-experience of her actual family.

Soon after the birth of her mother's third child, Laura, herself then aged fifteen, became pregnant. She was sent to London, alone, for an abortion. When she was eighteen she left home to work abroad for several years. On return, she trained as a teacher and married a fellow student. The marriage failed after only a few months. Several years later she married again, this time to a young man, John, whom she had known as a child. The relationship was, on the whole, harmonious, but Laura was often critical of it, feeling that it was "not very grown-up". She thought of herself as excessively "clingy", aware that what slight adult capacities the two of them had tended to collapse under the more infantile pressure between them to compete for being the baby—particularly in the area of financial incompetence. Laura and John's potential for any joint capacities for undertaking properly parental functions and responsibilities remained a sensitive and unproven area.

In the therapy setting it rapidly became clear that as soon as she became anxious, Laura would lose her capacity to think, to remember, or to dream. She tended to develop florid psychosomatic symptoms—excema, bronchitis, gastric troubles. She would have minor car accidents. Her bag would be stolen. She would become caught up in a variety of self-destructive acts which caused havoc in her emotional life, in her professional world and in her practical economy. Striking discrepancies would arise between her role as a competent "professional" woman, and a baby-self which often felt lost in a welter of confusion and unmet need. It was these discrepancies which brought her into therapy. She sought to relinquish her tendency to try to "act the part" of a grown woman, desiring instead genuinely to become one. In the course of therapy a shift began to occur from her attachment to the external, descriptive categories of womanliness and motherliness, to an understanding of the internal meaning of being a woman and being a mother.

Though dissimilar in many ways, Laura reminded her therapist of Dorothea at the beginning of *Middlemarch*—dedicated to good works, childlike in her "when I grow up I want to be good" attitude to life, and finding, in her intimate relationships, mainly "vague, labyrinthine extensions of herself". The changes that slowly took place were not wholly unlike the central developmental thrust of the novel. For Laura, like Dorothea, began to recognize and endure the pain of genuine separateness. The internal shift that was required was that from a narcissistic identification with an idealized internal aspect of herself to a more separated and other-related way of experiencing intimacy, with all the anguish that that entailed.

The following account draws on one thread only of the multi-layered fabric of the therapeutic work with Laura—a thread which offered much insight into the complex area under discussion. An early dream revealed a profoundly damaged internal world, and provided a clue to Laura's personal and professional problems of identity, to her impulse to care "in role" for the mutilated and disintegrated parts of herself, a role which seemed, at that time, to hold little hope for creative capacities from which something more genuine and lively could emerge.

This early dream described Laura

> walking into a dark tunnel in a local hospital, the walls of which were red and moist. She was leading a mentally and physically disabled child by the hand. They entered the innermost chamber which was filled with mutilated bodies—mainly of babies and children; parts of bodies, piled in unspecified heaps.

The images reminded her of the Holocaust. The dream represented for Laura a chamber of her own mind in which untold harm had been wreaked, leaving a legacy of guilt about damage done and a certainty of reciprocal damage to be visited upon her and on the inside of her body in particular. This state of mind seemed, by association, to link closely to the psychic reality of the abortion nearly twenty years earlier. It also linked to the emotional determinants of that first pregnancy, lodged as they seem to have been, in envious rage at her mother's continuing fertility, in jealousy at the arrival of a baby sibling, and in a desire to compete and to triumph.

In the months which followed this early dream there were a number of others which confirmed this picture of a putrid, festering internal space, dreams in which pregnancy turned out to be simulated—the abdominal swelling being faeces rather than foetus. In one dream,

> worms were breaking through the membrane of her skin, wriggling out of minute orifices in her shoulders or chest.

In another,

> apples were being dissected to reveal a mass of rotting seeds, from which fled the grim Reaper of Death.

Two-dimensional images would appear of menacing and caricatured puppet figures.

Common-sense tells us that early abortion may be followed by infertility and that that infertility does not appear to have an organic or physiological basis. What these dreams seem to illustrate is something of what the internal meaning of the abortion may have been for Laura and why, as a consequence, she may not have been able to conceive. Certainly she felt herself to be responsible for being "barren", a sense of responsibility that was based in very early anxieties about sin and about her own intrinsic "badness". What is of interest here is the emotional meaning for her of this sense of badness and its impact upon her, both physically and psychically.

The faeces/foetus dream was associated, in content, with a married couple, friends of Laura and John, for whom abundant fertility seemed linked to the capacity to nurture and to provide, both financially and emotionally. This couple were thought to be able to offer parental resources of a kind which Laura still felt unable to find in herself or in her relationship with John. She felt childish and inadequate when with them, tending to slip into what she described as a "babyish" stance whenever they were around. This sense of incapacity was again suggested in a dream which followed a few weeks later, one in which, for the first time,

> Laura actually gave birth to a baby. But the baby had no eyes, just yellow sockets with long, grey lashes. She showed the baby to her mother, insisting that she be allowed to keep it this time, despite the damage. She then went through a painful process of delivering the afterbirth. This turned out to consist of a series of contraceptive

devices and, finally, of the baby's liver and kidneys which Laura wrapped in cling-film and threw away.

The evidence of Laura's continued unreadiness, in her inner world, to bear and suckle a baby was clear. Internally, the adult structure of her personality was still very shaky. But there was a striking indication of the potential for change. At the end of this particular session Laura realized that the baby's eyelashes in the dream were identical with those of her husband. For the first time, the existence of a partner/father was introduced into her dream world. In response, she also felt able to tell her therapist of two miscarriages which had occurred soon after her abortion. She thus imparted to a now trusted person evidence of promiscuous behaviour which she had never revealed before. In so doing she took steps towards the possibility of depending on a mother/therapist who could understand and tolerate these profoundly contradictory and destructive aspects of herself. There were still internal "contraceptive devices" which opposed her more conscious desire for motherhood.

Many subsequent dreams, and much of the transference relationship, focused on the central importance of Laura's trying to find ways of being a "grown-up" lady, of her searching for the secrets. The sense seemed to be, "maybe it's the clothes? the make-up? the nails? the eyes?" As she dwelt, in her sessions, on her dull, dreary and confused self-conception, it was possible to observe, again and again, how these projections and imitations let her down and misled her; how the romance dissolved into the monotony of her daily struggles, into the pain of her monthly disappointments.

As long as her notion of being a grown-up woman depended on these kinds of identification, Laura herself was stuck. The therapy also felt stuck. Two painful external occurrences combined to alter things. Partly as a consequence of a change in her relationship with John, Laura did, in fact, become pregnant. But she lost the baby after a few weeks. She was told by the consultant that the foetus was dreadfully deformed and could not possibly have survived (a horrible confirmation of her worst fears). The second event was that it became necessary for her to move abroad because of John's employment. As a consequence she had to terminate her therapy prematurely.

The miscarriage brought in its wake a series of dreams which were quite different from previous ones. They were dreams which centred on a variety of sexual relationships both with men and with women. The dreams seemed to represent a new kind of struggle, one which involved an effort to try to sort out the internal qualities of the different figures with whom she was identified, rather than to settle for their superficial attributes. Gender became a question not so much of male/female, passive/active, strong/weak, hard/soft, intellectual/intuitive, as of the capacities for feeling which these various identifications carried, and of the ways in which they genuinely served Laura in those bitter days.

The final weeks of therapy were characterized by a leap of insight and an heroic effort to change in the midst of the turbulence of loss. They demonstrated the kind of thrust for development which may often occur in the context of painful separation. Hints of a growing ability to sustain genuine and shared parental concern had already begun to appear. In the penultimate week Laura described a dream which seemed to recapitulate the shifts, from one mental state to another, which had taken place in the course of her therapy. It was as if the dream offered a kind of guided tour of the different chambers of her mind, as she slowly developed and changed. In this "Pilgrim's Progress" dream there was no confusion or persecutory anxiety, but rather the representation of a distinct and unique journey from a destructive basement part of herself to the sunshine and clear air of a thinking-self—a self that could reflect how she *actually* was, her strengths and her limitations, and about how she could yet be.

> Laura was in a basement, one which she felt was somehow connected with her mother. The room flooded. Mutilated bits of body floated to the surface. She escaped into the hull of an old-fashioned sailing-ship and underwent a perilous, storm-tossed voyage over cresting waves and deep troughs, bravely charting a dangerous sea. The sea eventually became merged with a frozen, white landscape across which she landsailed. She eventually arrived at a grassy track which led her down between houses, past a place where people were coming and going about their daily business, and thence to a sunny landscape with fields on either side. Here she found a beautiful horse, apparently in need of a rider.

The last part of this long and detailed dream described the horse and rider being brought together and a suggestion of potential fertility. Laura's suffering over the imminent separation from her therapist not only re-evoked the stormy voyage of the therapy and of her past life, but also seemed to stir in her some hope of being able to be part of a parental couple (horse and rider) with capacities both to care and be cared for.

Here lay the essence of the shift in Laura: to be expressed again in further dreams of the same week. It seemed that, on some level, she had realized that in order genuinely to "feed" a baby one has to be cognizant of the baby parts of oneself, to know that, at times, that baby-self is more powerful than anything else. Becoming a mother, or parent, in the true sense of the word, begins with being able to be one's own independent self, while acknowledging continuing dependence on loved and respected internal resources.

A particularly clear juxtaposition of the unresolved, and yet hopeful, relationship between the different parts of herself occurred in a fragment of a dream remembered from the night before Laura's very last session.

> There were two aspects of herself, ones which were separate, and yet definitely parts of the whole. A line of three moles was positioned vertically above her left breast. These changed into mushrooms—a distasteful, indeed rather disgusting, phenomenon. But at the same time, on her fingers were many rings—beautiful, pale sapphires, almost aquamarine in hue, both blue like the sky and green like the sea.

It was not surprising that Laura's mother turned out to possess a beautiful sapphire ring which she had left to her daughter in her will. This was a legacy which, in dream-language, seemed to represent Laura's growing capacity to internalize, and to possess for herself, some qualities, though as yet pale ones, of genuine beauty and creativity. The presence of these qualities could be said to indicate the beginnings of a benign identification with her mother/ therapist, one based on a more positive appreciation of their actual strengths and less on her distorted versions of them. In the course of therapy it had become possible to recognize that Laura's wish to be like her mother, a wish that had been represented in her early dreams of strong, beautiful, accomplished, fertile women, was by no means based on the simple desire enviously to take over those qualities which she felt her mother to have. Nor was it based merely on the desire to "be" her therapist. Laura's wish was also based on love, and the guilt which she felt came from the attacks which she found herself making on this mother, the one whom she often hated, but to whom, she discovered, she was also devoted. What she had idealized in her mother were characteristics which, in all likelihood, did not belong to the actual person. But it was through that idealization (inseparably linked to hatred and destructiveness) that Laura reduced what good qualities her mother might really have had to offer her into quite superficial ones, ones which Laura had then sought to appropriate in their reduced form. Towards the end of her therapy she was able to begin to admire her mother and to experience her as someone in relation to whom she could feel genuine aspiration, rather than mere emulation of her superficial traits and characteristics.

This new experience was in marked contrast to her earlier preoccupations, with what she had felt to be the cruel, elegant and remote aspects of her mother. It was in contrast too with the presence of the three moles. These moles bore a double connotation. The intrusive getting-in-and-spying-on-the-secrets side of Laura was still there. Above the left breast were the unresolved, poisonous parts of herself which she wished to have "left" with her therapist. But these parts were also ones which she felt "left" with—the dark mushrooms which still threatened to poison and spoil any future beauty or procreativity. These fears of Laura's, as the dream clearly showed, were not yet wholly dispelled.

But there was now a distinctive recognition of those damaging aspects of herself which had become easier to see and could therefore be better thought about. The rings, far from being objects of superficial adornment as they had been in the past, carried with them a different quality of maternal identification, one that was culled from the anguish of loss and of premature separation. These experiences hurt Laura profoundly yet they also helped her towards a capacity for adult mourning, by contrast with the infantile dependency of earlier days. Over the period of the therapy she had become able to take in and to identify with qualities of genuine love and dependence. Laura was discovering in herself real strength and was able to become less reliant on the brittle and counterfeit resilience which stems from narcissistic identifications of the more projective or imitative kind.

The psychoanalytic approach to adulthood, and this central aspect of it, gender identity, resides essentially in the developmental mode of "exploring the mystery". Laura's many attempts at "solving the riddle", or "unearthing the secrets", simply produced more and more objects for identification, ones which ultimately let her down or misled her. In the course of her painful struggles in therapy her infantile search for secrets gave way to a more adult sense of the mysterious process of introjective identification. The "Pilgrim's Progress" dream summed up the way in which her pseudo-maturity, in place from early years, had yielded to a capacity to experience her "storm-tossed" self as the self, too, of a needy infant. This infant-Laura's frozen development, as she "sailed", or perhaps skated, across the surface of life, was eventually able to begin to thaw and, in the pain of her depressive anxiety, to emerge into the light and sunshine of possible future growth.

Notes

1. Coleridge, "Dejection: An Ode".
2. Roszika Parker, *Torn in Two, op. cit.*
3. I am drawing on the work of Meg Harris Williams who elaborates this distinction in the context of creative writers, "Knowing the mystery: against reductionism", *Encounter*, (1), June 1986.
4. The case material that follows is, in large part, drawn from an article of my own first published in 1989. "Gender identity fifty years on from Freud", *British Journal of Psychotherapy*, Vol. 5, No. 3, pp. 381–389.

CHAPTER THIRTEEN

"The later years"

"It is never too late to become the person you might have been"

George Eliot

George Eliot's optimistic words seem particularly fitting for the age group in question. "It is never too late ..." This concluding chapter will echo and reiterate the main themes of the book. The tune is essentially the same; only the key is different. Development, at whatever age, is founded in the capacity to go on engaging with the meaning of experience with imagination, courage and integrity. Freud's exhortation that "one must try to learn something from every experience" remains as true in the last part of life as it has ever been.[1]

These pages have traced the extraordinarily complex tangle of threads or forces, internal and external, which bear on one person's capacity to develop and grow psychologically, or bear on another's to put development into abeyance, either arresting creative potential or diverting it to purposes that will run counter to the best interests of the personality as a whole. Turning now to the later years, I want to pick up the same threads, to ravel them a little further, and then to weave them into a more complete picture which will take on its own distinctive shape and colouring.

By the age of fifty or so a person might be regarded, and be able to regard himself, as being "grown up". Yet it is often during the last decades of life that the capacity to sustain a mature state of mind is most severely tested. The question of whether or not it is possible to continue to develop remains as challenging as ever. But there is an essential difference between this period and the earlier phases of life. For the mental and emotional preoccupations related to physical decline, and to the fact that death itself is becoming more imminent, now have their own particular weighting. The extent to which these additional, and major, considerations spur, threaten or arrest emotional growth will very much depend on how securely an adult state of mind has been established in earlier decades. It will depend on the relative success or failure of previous struggles with separation and loss, in relation to mourning, absence, guilt or disappointment. It will depend, in other words, on a person's experience of bearing pain from the very first (see Chapter 4), and on the degree of integration already established between different parts of the self.

For at this point in life there may be many external losses to be faced: elderly parents may be ill or dying, and perhaps friends too. Children will be leaving home, or may already have left. For some redundancy can threaten. For others retirement will be in sight. But a fundamental psychic change, at once internal and also related to external circumstances, is beginning to occur: the contemplating of one's own death. Metaphorically, as literally, the prospect of death is the ultimate test of all efforts to come to terms with loss and to undergo the pain of experience—to suffer that experience rather than to evade it by defensive measures of conduct or of character. Here we are brought back full circle to the infant's early experience. The good, "thinking" breast can modulate the infant's primary fear that he is dying. It can modulate it if the infant feels sufficiently understood in the relationship with his mother/parents and, as a consequence, can take back into himself a tolerable and, as Bion put it, "growth-stimulating part of the personality" (1962b, p. 96). It is the "growth-stimulating" aspect of the experience which, if it is enjoyed sufficiently often, instils in the baby the sense of a self-that-can-endure-setbacks-and-loss. This is someone who is not afraid to advance psychically, to let redundant parts of the self go, to be separate as well as dependent, to have the courage to be different and to be honestly himself or herself.

A gratifying early experience with the mother stands the baby in good stead for negotiating the first major developmental hurdle, described by Klein (1935, 1945) as the depressive position. As we have seen (Chapters 1 and 5), Klein suggested that in this state of mind the well-supported infant, despite feelings of abandonment and rage, is able to begin to integrate his hitherto split and polarized view of the world. The excesses of love and hate can be modified. The capacity for ambivalence can be achieved. The person towards whom the loving feelings are directed, and the person towards whom the hating feelings are directed are no longer experienced in extreme terms as two different people, as the wicked witch and the fairy godmother, but as the same person, one who sometimes fulfils and sometimes frustrates. That person can be seen as a bit more ordinary. She can be felt to be in proportion. Thereafter this cluster of relationships, anxieties and defences is encountered in a myriad of ways. All pose the same basic question: can emotional experience be engaged with or does it have to be fended off?

Klein (1940, 1955) saw this alternative as a matter of psychic life or of psychic death. Elliott Jaques (1965) sums up her position:

> ... under conditions of prevailing love, the good and bad objects can in some measure be synthesised, the ego becomes more integrated, and hope for the re-establishment of the good object is experienced; the accompanying overcoming of grief and regaining of security is the infantile equivalent of having a notion of life.

> Under conditions of prevailing persecution, however, the working through of the depressive position will be to a greater or lesser extent, inhibited; reparation and synthesis fail; and the inner world is unconsciously felt to contain the persecuting and annihilating devoured and destroyed bad breast, the ego itself feeling in bits. The chaotic internal situation experienced is the infant's equivalent of the notion of death. [p. 507]

The capacity to develop is very much dependent, as we have seen, on the different degrees to which it is possible to tolerate frustration and absence. A person will be able to face up to, and undergo, middle and old age in-so-far as it has been possible, all along, to embrace the complexity of his experience and to integrate the painful with the pleasurable, rather than to seek to avoid, or to deny the hard bits and to clutch onto the "right to be happy". "The right to be happy" echoes, faintly, the American Declaration of Independence, but it also expresses something very specific to the pressures of contemporary culture. Such pressures tend to militate against endurance and to encourage indulgence in its place, thus making it all the harder to struggle with the challenges of this period of life.

If a person lacks an internal container of feeling, one that is sturdy enough to withstand new or renewed challenges to his peace of mind and sense of self, he may have recourse to earlier patterns of functioning, ones mobilized in the service of avoiding pain. The pain may now be that of actual bereavement and loneliness, or it may be associated with the many losses that will, at this later stage, shadow normal life: loss of opportunities, for example, or of health and vigour, of political and professional ideals, of procreativity, sexual potency, marriage, physical prowess and appearance, the presence and support of parents, the presence and support of children.

In the face of these difficulties it is to be expected that people will seek ways of protecting themselves from the immediacy of the impact. They will take defensive measures in order to lessen their psychic and physical discomfort. Some will revert to behaviour which seems typically infantile or adolescent, altering their attitudes and activities in order to try to alleviate internal stresses and conflicts which are felt to be intolerable. Others will adopt modes of cautious withdrawal, or lapse into obsessional tendencies, apparently settling back into a state of mind more characteristic of the latency years than of adulthood, in the attempt to avoid further struggle. Under the new pressures of the particular problems of later life, a person may go back and take up permanent residence in one of these earlier states. Equally, he may move between one such state and the state which is more appropriate to his age. But there is one other possibility. He may be able to resist the pull of these earlier modes of functioning and find himself able to bear the emotional burdens and thus progress into some new, and perhaps as yet little-experienced, adult state of mind.

At this stage, as in earlier years, there is an intimate relationship between the particular practical and emotional tasks which people are facing and the states of mind in which those tasks are being undertaken. Although, even now, the development of the personality is not in any simple way bound to chronology, there are, nonetheless, likely to be certain areas of responsibility which specifically belong to these years and which require a sustained capacity to maintain an adult view of the world, despite contending pressures. In the care of others, elderly parents may have started to take the place of young children. But the young children may simply have become old "children", and also still need care, especially when employment is hard to find and housing is limited. Or these children may now have their own children and look to grandparents for support. At the same time the work responsibilities of someone in these later years are likely to be especially arduous. These demands may mount even as social and family duties and ties become more exacting. All this is being undertaken as energy is beginning to diminish, enthusiasm possibly to wane, or illness to threaten.

Yet now, as ever, for those who have the capacity to learn, the passing of years certainly grants more time further to integrate their life experiences. For those who have not found it easy to let their experience teach them, the many regressive possibilities may beckon. Wordsworth's poem, "We Are Seven", contrasts the "wisdom" of the young child with the bewilderment of the adult:

> A simple child, dear brother Jim,
> That lightly draws its breath,
> And feels its life in every limb,
> What should it know of death? [ll. 1–4]

The source of wisdom in the eight-year-old cottage girl is expressed through a touching simplicity of language and rhyme in the few stanzas of the narrative. She is quite unlike her literal-minded interlocutor, who cannot understand how this child can maintain that she is still one of seven siblings, despite the deaths of her other six brothers and sisters. He cannot comprehend her capacity to keep these little friends alive in her mind, as internal presences to whom she sings and with whom she holds conversation. She keeps the lost figures alive internally as continuing sources of strength and comfort:

> "But they are dead; those two are dead!
> Their spirits are in heaven!"
> Twas throwing words away; for still
> The little Maid would have her will,
> And said, "Nay, we are seven!" [ll. 65–69]

The Wordsworth character, stuck in a pedantic, quantifying state of mind, was neither able to grasp the nature of psychic reality, nor to open himself to the unfamiliar nature of another's internal experience: in this case, what, to him, might have been the unthinkable grief of the kinds of losses which this little girl had already sustained. And yet the very writing of the poem is an expression of an acknowledgement of intimations and aspirations towards a way of being and understanding becoming available to the poet/self.

By this stage the various individual ways of evading pain which have been adopted in the past will, with the passing of time, have taken on the appearance of character. It may become tempting to describe a person, in broad terms as, for example, shallowing-out, or as giving-up, or giving-in; as trying to bypass the ageing process, or even to deny it. Each of these responses may give sad testimony to how much more has been learnt from the forces which impede development than from those which promote it. They may point to a predominantly passive and depressed mood in some people, one of feeling that life has let them down, or has disappointed them; that circumstances have defeated them. Yet these same responses may also describe something else, something which is clear in the examples which follow: that is, that early unresolved experiences of loss may have cast a long shadow over the development of the personality. The sense of failure, or the fear of failure, may stretch far across the years, but the underlying anxieties and inhibitions can, with courage, still become available to be thought about. The fear of suffering may be worse than the suffering itself. If sadness and loss overwhelm, the older personality finds its own ways of managing. They may, perhaps, be different ways from those of earlier years, but nonetheless be ones that are related to the same psychic choice, namely, whether the pain is to be evaded, or whether it can be modified, or modulated; whether the primary impulse is to try to get rid of the pain and avoid engaging with it, or to hold it mentally and to try to process it internally.

*   *   *

Two brief examples clarify the links between early difficulties and the very diverse ways in which they may be engaged with many years later. Mr Smith and Mrs Crawford both came for psychotherapy in their sixties. The reasons for referral were superficially very different but there turned out to be some important features in common, relating to early bereavement. Mr Smith was feeling guilty and demoralized. As he approached retirement, he was finding himself to be uncharacteristically irascible, indecisive, anxious and, to him more worrying, sexually interested in younger women. For the first time, he found himself preoccupied by his own fitness and physical appearance. He had spent a not very successful working life in middle-management and had always felt a "bit of a failure". He had left school with few qualifications, having always found it hard, as he put it, to "take anything in". He had joined a gang of "bad boys" and had been drawn into delinquent activities (mainly minor arson and car theft) and had wasted many hours of study-time in slot-machine arcades. His work life, too, had involved a series of minor deceits and "scams", but he had managed not to be found out.

It is not unusual for retirement to raise a degree of depressive anxiety, and with it a risk of character deterioration as if, without the routine of work to provide some kind of external, holding structure, internal integration is threatened. For those who lack their own internal sources of creative and imaginative activity, the pattern of the work-world may long have provided a serviceable carapace. But when well-established habits have to be broken, and the companionship of fellow-workers is not available, the absence of any other direction or meaning may become painfully evident.

The measures taken to evade the unwanted feelings, whether ones of demoralization, failure, emptiness, pointlessness, envy, or meaninglessness, are also familiar. In a culture where the young and beautiful are so highly valued and the old are accorded so little interest or respect, many, like Mr Smith, succumb to the impulse to join the race against time, seeking to beat the ageing body by trying to remain young and vigorous.

But the particularity of any single experience is in danger of getting lost in these generalizations. In Mr Smith, for example, there seemed to be an area of pain beyond the recognizable ones of ageing, a pain which was very hard to reach. His therapist at times glimpsed a quality of intensity and passion which stood out from his more usual flat and somewhat clichéd presentation of himself and of his life. There was a sense, which began to gather definition especially in his dreams, that somehow his personality had "thinned out", as if, early in life, he had settled for a safe and rather dull way of being, perhaps in order to avoid something that might otherwise have been experienced as too disruptive, something which could not be integrated into his personality as he knew it.

When Mr Smith was a child his father had died in an accident and he, the son, could remember very little about him. However, he conveyed a feeling to his therapist of something akin to irreparable loss. As time went on and Mr Smith established an increasingly trusting relationship with his therapist, he began to remember more details of his childhood. His father had been a garage mechanic and, as a boy of seven or eight, Mr Smith used to go to watch him mend the cars. He also spoke of an old shed in his parents' garden at home, a shed full of tools and old bits of engine, where he and his father used to potter together at weekends for hours on end. There were two other intensely shared joys: lighting and stoking bonfires, and playing on the old slot-machines which were collected in his father's attic. As more details emerged and the accounts acquired texture, colour and specificity, the sense of the passion of this shared intimacy between father and son was very palpable. Mr Smith's demeanour changed, and his language took on life and vigour as he remembered more and more of these happy times, a sort of Garden of Eden, from which he had found himself forever banished.

One day a piece of heavy lifting-equipment had failed and his father had been crushed. A few weeks later his mother had married his father's partner from the garage, and a few months after that a baby sister was born. It was many years before Mr Smith allowed himself to take in the possibility that his mother might have been having an affair with his father's partner before the death. With that marriage everything changed. The garden shed was locked and pronounced "out of bounds", as was the attic. The bonfire site was turfed over. Mr Smith was not taken to the funeral nor was he allowed to speak of his father thereafter. Not surprisingly, it was then that trouble started at school. His main memory of his mother at that time, was of being nagged about his poor performance, of being told that he used to be such a bright little boy, top of the class; why didn't he try anymore? Why had he gone so stupid?

Though extreme, Mr Smith's suffering is on a continuum with that of many children whose experiences of loss or bereavement, whether apparently trivial or obviously catastrophic, have not been properly registered or, worse, have been denied or ignored. The inability to attend to her son's pain by Mr Smith's mother may well have been rooted in her own, unspoken, unhappiness. But it also suggests that there may have been little opportunity, even before the accident, for him to share, and, in the process, to understand, the reality of his own emotional life, at least in relation to his mother.

It seemed that the intensity of his grief at his father's death, and of his rage at his mother and the new family, had necessitated his turning away from life, suspending his feeling and receptive self, and giving up on the robust and lively little boy. He remembered overhearing his mother saying to a neighbour that her son had "got over the death quite well". The only obvious and eloquent clues to the contrary were manifest in the particularity of his delinquent enterprises: arson, car theft and the near-addiction to slot-machines. Later he had settled into an unimaginative, hum-drum routine which passed for a life: getting through the years with no particular intimacy, joy or interest; on the whole disengaged. He had supported a wife and children but they seemed to have afforded him little real pleasure. It was family "life" only in the most empty and conventional sense.

What now began to emerge was the extent of his guilt: both irrational guilt about his father's actual death ("I used to think, 'If I'd been there I might have saved him'"), and also intense remorse about having allowed his father's memory to have been excised quite so swiftly and comprehensively from the family narrative, and, albeit more slowly, from his own mind and heart. Why had he colluded with the deceit and denial on which the new marriage had seemed to be based? He even began to wonder about whether the "accident" was more sinister than it had appeared. A further source of guilt also emerged: that his hunger for his father's time might have separated his parents, thereby bringing about what he was convinced was the "extra-marital affair" in the first place.

It became clear that the prospect of retirement, and all the attendant losses, was again stirring these old, unresolved issues. It was confronting Mr Smith not only with the reality of his own death, but also with some of the hating and destructive feelings which, hitherto, he had hardly recognized in himself. This crisis required emotional capacities which he had never had the opportunity to develop. He had spent his life making sure that he did not encounter the rage, despair and chaos within. Mentally and emotionally he had hardly developed beyond the latency boy he was when his father had died. As the "amnesia" slowly lifted and some of these feelings were thought about and engaged with in the sessions, Mr Smith, with enormous pain, embarked on a major, and long-postponed, task.

Jaques (1965) described such a task as "Working through again the infantile experience of loss and of grief [which] gives an increase in confidence in one's capacity to love and mourn what has been lost and what is past, rather than to hate and feel persecuted about it. We can begin to mourn our own eventual death" (p. 512). In so doing, one may truly establish a capacity to tolerate one's shortcomings and destructiveness. In Mrs Crawford's early childhood there was a not dissimilar tragedy, although she had found very different ways to manage it. She had always been aware that her life had been fundamentally affected by the death of her older brother, when she herself was eight. This brother had, apparently, been a golden boy, the sort of child whom Wordsworth describes in the poem "Michael" as one who,

> more than other gifts,
> Brings hope with it, and forward-looking thoughts. [ll. 54–55]

This child died under anaesthetic in the course of a minor operation. His parents' grief was irrecoverable. The father became alcoholic and the mother manic and brittle, forever preoccupied with minor and imagined illnesses, suffering constant migraines and filling her life with meaningless tasks. Mrs Crawford, the only remaining child, felt that despite being doomed to fail, she must somehow try to live up to her brother's memory. The parents had removed all traces of their son's existence from the house, and never spoke of him. Their experience had been, literally, unbearable.

As so often in families where a child has died, as a little girl Mrs Crawford's response to her sense of her parents' grief was to try to fulfil what she took to be their wishes. Ever aware of her brother's "ghost", she had vainly sought to measure up to what she imagined he was in her parents' minds. Subsequently, as an adult, she had quite consciously become as successful as she could possibly be. She had supported her husband and run "a very nice and efficient home", as she put it. She had brought up four children while working as a ward-sister in a busy local hospital. She conducted an extremely full and committed life, constantly "on the go", and preoccupied with a number of "lame ducks", as well as charitable works which extended well beyond her professional role. She had little time for reflection and none for any more challenging concern about her life's predicament. It was her hypochondria which finally prompted her doctor to suggest that she seek psychotherapeutic help. The recurrent bouts of acute fear of life-threatening disease (usually cancer) were of many years standing. At sixty she found herself unhappily married, increasingly anxious and suffering from a number of quite worrying symptoms, none of which turned out to have any organic foundation. If anything, she was now busier than ever and it was hard for her to contemplate making the time for the psychotherapy sessions which were suggested to her.

To begin with, in the therapy sessions, her manner was very matter-of-fact, brusque, a little hard and rather superficial. But as time went on what emerged, with unexpected ferocity, was the extent of her rage with a mother who had not been able to cope with her son's death. With that calamity Mrs Crawford felt that she herself had lost not only her brother, but her parents too. She described how insidiously her mother's incapacity to recover from the death had also infected her, as a little girl, indeed how it had blighted her whole life. The hypochondria had become her problem too. Without the opportunity to engage, at the time, with what this actual death had meant, she had busied herself with "managing" illness and death elsewhere, defensively, in order to avoid engaging with the impossible task that needed to be undertaken within.

In one session she recounted a childhood fear, dating from around the age of eight, when she had seen the film *King Kong*. She had long after remained terrified lest King Kong come and take her in his grip and carry her away. On one level this memory would seem to describe anxieties, unmodified by parental understanding, about being "carried away" like her brother. But in the session it immediately evoked a recent dream:

she was employed in the hospital, not as a nurse, but as some kind of engineer whose job it was to manage the gas leaks. One day there seemed to be a danger of a terrible explosion taking place. She was very worried that such an explosion would ruin the paintwork.

In discussion of the dream it became clear that Mrs Crawford felt that her "life's job" had been one of "managing the leaks", keeping the lid on everything lest any real (that is potentially destructive) emotion escape, or be recognized for what it really was. It was as if a rather tyrannical and controlling part of herself had gripped her more vulnerable "victim" self (King Kong's fair maiden, perhaps) and made off with it, leaving her personality bereft of any capacity to take in grief, terror and rage, and to understand their magnitude and their sources. In the dream she did not register the actual danger of mayhem nor of the mutilation of others. She was preoccupied by her concern with the superficialities—"the paintwork". The consequence was that the real impact of catastrophe, in terms of loss of life (dreamt or real) could not be metabolized. Instead, attention to, and concern about, the surfaces—"getting-on", respectability, good-deedishness—had prevailed.

As she began to take in the extent to which, by occupying the role of the perfect wife, worker and mother, she had removed herself from really engaging with the world, Mrs Crawford began to suffer deeply, both in relation to her own life and to her mother's. She allowed herself to be more understanding of her mother's early difficulties and to begin to realize that she could love as well as hate her; that she could appreciate her mother for what she had managed to do, rather than feel constantly aggrieved about what she had not managed to do. What she had not been able to bear in her mother, not surprisingly, were precisely those aspects of herself which she had been trying so hard not to recognize: constant somatic complaints, unnecessary busyness, do-gooding, and the general avoidance of genuine emotional contact. In recognizing some of these characteristics as being part of her own personality, Mrs Crawford was able to develop feelings of sympathy and warmth for her mother and an intense wish to repair their relationship, a wish which she said she could never previously have imagined could be possible.

In each of these two cases an actual bereavement had occurred, one which, in not having been emotionally digested at the time, had left a dark legacy, stretching far into the lives of the individuals concerned. The suggestion is not that therapy would always necessarily be required to gather up such hidden and unaddressed thoughts and feelings; but more that these cases exemplify the possibility of personality development continuing, or even beginning, in an emotionally containing environment, however late in life. The hardenings and softenings of age may become distinct, but, as these examples show, they are not necessarily irreversible.

A third case, drawing on a single session in the analysis of a sixty-year-old man, offers a more detailed account of how, even in later years, it may be possible for someone to be enabled to begin experiencing himself, and his life, in more meaningful and imaginative ways. Mr Williamson had come to analysis late in life, with a long and successful legal career behind him. He was deliberate in air and, to start with, somewhat formal in thought and bearing. He had always had difficulty in knowing what he felt. He described an emotionally deprived childhood. There seemed to have been little genuine family contact or warmth, rather a series of nannies followed by boarding school at seven. There were only sparse memories of this unhappy time. Mr Williamson's sense of his mother was very vague. There were few recollections of his childhood relationship with her, or of her early decline and death. "I think she just faded out." Nothing seemed to link up. Thoughts did not open the usual doors. Interpretations led nowhere. Lines of enquiry tended to be truncated. Everything, at this point, felt rather stuck.

In the early days of the analysis Mr Williamson struggled to find some point of contact. For a long time he could remember no dreams. But eventually he brought the first of what came to be referred to as "fragment" dreams. They constituted single images, visually vivid and sometimes with a clear "feeling" or "tone" attached. Yet they were puzzling and frustrating for they yielded few associations or reflections.

After many such dreams he brought one particular "fragment" which characteristically constituted a very simple visual statement.

There were a number of pillars of bricks, each about four foot high and very neatly stacked.

The precision of the stacking was the only point of focus or emphasis in the dream. The bricks were of no special *use* like that, it seemed, but so it was—they were arranged in separate piles, very *methodically*; carefully and perfectly stacked. He mentioned the fact that some landscape gardening was in progress at his home at the time, and that there were bricks lying around the garden to build walls which had been designed to "frame" the house. The purpose, he said, was aesthetic rather than practical.

These associative details, albeit very slight, made it possible to reflect on the "fragment" dream in the following way. The brick-stacks could be thought of as over-rigid aspects of mental processes which were not, in that form, available for any lively emotional or practical purpose. As it stood the arrangement was one of apparently pointless precision. The remoteness of the bricks from any useful or aesthetic function was reproduced in the dream-form's remoteness from any linkage to meaningful thought. Something was missing—the bricks could not, in their present shape and position, be employed in the service of construction—the construction of meaning.

The dream situation perfectly described Mr Williamson's personal predicament at the time. The brick/thoughts needed to be brought to the analyst in their detached and fragmented form in order for some preliminary shaping to occur so that they could be used for their proper task: a framing of the house/mind such that it could be better "seen". The sense was that the aesthetic and the functional aspects of the construction of those walls needed to be established as a different *kind* of creative process, before the house itself could be framed, observed, and therefore analytically thought about.

The very fragmentariness of the dream described the process of which it was a part. It initiated the dismantling of the rather rigid and "proper" thought/pillars which had hitherto been useless for any creative linking between the split-off parts of Mr Williamson's personality. This kind of dismantling made the real difficulties more available for thought. In order to engage with the meaning of the symbolic representations (those of the house/mind) a prior process had to have occurred. That is, a much more rudimentary ordering was necessary on the part of a mind (his analyst's) which was able to gather up the piecemeal bits, to hold them, and to think about them in such a way that the bricks were no longer statically fixed in their existing structures. As a result of being internally processed in this way, the bricks could begin to be used for building something useful, of a kind which could become a container of meaning; something which could then become *built into* the structure of his developing personality.

The quality of containment which the analytic process made available to Mr Williamson arose from the unconscious processes underlying the analyst's capacity to understand his rather fragmentary and formal communications. It is difficult to describe such processes in conceptual language but one way of putting it would be that the dream, and the interpretation of it, occurred within a therapeutic relationship in which hitherto unthinkable aspects of Mr Williamson's experience had begun to be shaped. In this session, his unconscious experience having been worked upon in the analyst's mind, he was provided with the wherewithal to "think about" that experience, first of all in the unconscious symbols of the dream thoughts, and then in the more conscious verbalization of those thoughts. As time went on his formality began to slacken, his hard emotional surfaces to soften, and genuine interest, humour and warmth began to come into the sessions and into his life.

In this same way the baby who has had an experience, enough of the time, of a mother who has the internal resources to contain his feelings in this active way, not only has the sense of being integrated and understood, but slowly himself acquires this very capacity to hold, albeit at first temporarily, his own mental state. The exchange between Mr Williamson and his analyst offers a description of what Bion refers to as "container/contained" taking place within the analytic space. It is an example of the mysterious process of symbol-formation, or alpha-function, as it occurs between patient and analyst, and the way in which that process may be re-evoked whatever the chronological age may be. Such processes are those very ones described in the earliest mother/baby encounters.

As a person moves into the later years of his life he may become softer, more forgiving, less envious, more appreciative, better able to accept life, children, job, for what it is, or they are, rather than what they "should", or "could", or even "might have been". "If onlys ..." can be let go. But he may, by contrast, become increasingly exacting, pompous, ruthless, aggrieved, intellectually dishonest.

These characteristics may all start out as defensive measures, possibly against pangs of envy, or against fear of loss. But they can also present themselves as increasingly unmodifiable and deeply ingrained habits of mind, ones which circumscribe or constrain the likelihood of any further emotional growth. The mechanisms that sustain these respective states of mind remain those which have been discussed all along, projection and introjection. Depending on the balance in any single person between these two tendencies, on their respective strength and intensity in earlier years, and on the nature of past and current pressures, each individual will approach this last part of life very differently equipped to encounter both the inevitable losses involved, and a conception of life to be lived in the setting of approaching death. Some will tend to close themselves off from unfamiliar ways of seeing things, others will embrace new experiences with a willingness to go on learning.

After a long conversation about the importance for children of being helped to mourn the loss of a sibling, one grandmother, speaking on behalf of her recently bereaved little grand-daughter, said, "Well, I still don't think she should be involved in the funeral." The other grandmother responded "Is that what is thought to be best? Tell me more about it." Simple though this latter remark may be, it represents a continuing curiosity, an ongoing quest for knowledge and understanding. Such qualities are powerfully embodied in the poetry of W. B. Yeats's middle and later years. "The Spur", a poem in his last collection, *The Winding Stair*, states the source of the lasting energy in his writing.

> You think it horrible that lust and rage
> Should dance attendance upon my old age,
> They were not such a plague when I was young:
> What else have I to spur me into song?

For some the "lust and rage" of youth become quiescent, as if a kind of middle-aged "latency" period has set in. But for others, as for Yeats, the ongoing vitality of the personality seems to reside in being able to continue, with honesty and with zest, to acknowledge and address more basic passions, in however different a key. For some, whether it is felt to be infantile or adult, necessary or unseemly, the potential for engagement with such emotions and impulses remains available and contributes further to a still developing sense of self.

In writing of the relationship between poetry and the poet in old age, T. S. Eliot quotes "The Spur" and describes with great clarity a more general distinction between the "man who's capable of experience", and the man who lacks the exceptional "honesty and courage" to be, or to become so. He notes the consequences of that distinction as determining whether a person is able, or unable, to sustain a creative old age. He stresses the importance of continuity between youth and age: if growth is to carry on, experiences of youth have to remain alive. Of certain other poems in *The Winding Stair* Eliot writes that in them

> one feels that the most lively and desirable emotions of youth have been preserved to receive their full and due expression in retrospect. For the interesting feelings of age are not just different feelings; they are feelings into which the feelings of youth are integrated. [pp. 258–259]

Eliot has a very acute sense of the hazards, for the creative individual, of growing old. His picture is a stark one. But the dangers he describes—of slipping away from sincerity and into mere respectability, or worse, dishonesty—are ones which are recognizable to many, indeed to anyone who is struggling to preserve his ordinarily creative self:

> For a man who is capable of experience finds himself in a different world in every decade of his life; as he sees it with different eyes, the material of his art is continually renewed. But in fact, very few poets have shown this capacity of adaptation to the years. It requires, indeed, an exceptional honesty and courage to face the change. Most men either cling to the experiences of youth, so that their writing becomes an insincere mimicry of their earlier work, or they leave their passion behind, and write only from the head, with a hollow and wasted virtuosity. There is another and even worse temptation: that of becoming dignified, of becoming public figures with only a public existence—coat-racks hung with decorations and distinctions, doing, saying, and even thinking and feeling what they believe the public expects of them. Yeats was not that kind of poet ... For the young can see him as a poet who in his work remained in the best sense always young, who even in one sense became young as he aged. But the old, unless they are stirred to something of the honesty with oneself expressed in the poetry, will be shocked by the

> revelation of what man really is and remains. They will refuse to
> believe that *they* are like that. [p. 257]

Here, as everywhere in this book, the emphasis is on the capacity,
and on the opportunity, to be honest with oneself. In thinking about
the later years, the focus has been on whether or not a person can
face death as an external fact and destructiveness as an internal one.
The reality of actual death throws into sharp perspective the different
ways in which someone may have "really" grown up, or may only
look as if he has done so. For death also stands as a metaphor for all
the other losses in life, ones which may have been feared as seeming
too final or too catastrophic and, as a consequence, have been
insistently shied away from. (Freud spoke of Life losing "in interest,
when the highest stake in the game, life itself, may not be risked".[2])
Properly engaging with life involves a readiness to face not only
mortality itself but the reality of death-dealing blows, both those
internal to the self and those which threaten from the external
"world of Circumstances", "the Misery and Heartbreak, Pain,
Sickness and oppression" which Keats described (*Letters*, p. 95). The
kind of thinking which contributes to someone becoming a person
who is "capable of experience", is mind-building. The process
involves a struggle between the forces in the self which promote life
and hope, ones which enable the personality to find its own shape
and to develop and grow, and those forces which pull the self back,
out of fear of pain and of the unknown. Even late in life some will
still be pushing further open the doorways to new experience;
others will be easing those doors shut.

The wonder and infinite complexity of the interlocking of a
person's internal and external lives is captured by Keats in the
image of the spider's web, and the exquisite ordinariness of the
spider spinning:

> Now it appears to me that almost any Man may like the Spider spin
> from his own inwards his own airy Citadel—the points of leaves or
> twigs on which the Spider begins her work are few and she fills the
> Air with a beautiful circuiting: man should be content with as few
> points to tip with the fine Webb of his Soul and weave a tapestry
> empyrean. [*Letters*, p. 66]

Keats's image lends metaphorical expression to a number of
thoughts—those underlying the ideas which have traced their

way through these pages. The image evokes the sense of freedom and open-mindedness, the capacity not to be bound to the "fine-points" of things but to build on them from inner resources. For each person carries within the potential to develop a personality of richness and depth, the potential to draw from his own experience the essential elements for further growth. Anyone can be distracted from his authentic self. Anyone, too, can construct a unique personal structure of great beauty.

This book has been about the rewards of understanding the meaning of one's experience and about the difficulties of so doing; the difficulties of developing a mind of one's own, of becoming oneself. The process of finding one's own place in the world from one generation to the next needs constant mental and emotional work, from the earliest struggles of the unborn child to those of the final years of life. It involves learning from others without merely becoming like them, and imparting to others without seeking to bind them. It involves conflict, but also opens limitless possibilities. For life need not be a vale of tears but rather is a vale of Soul-making, the process on which is founded the growth of the mind, the development of the personality.

Notes

1. There has been so little published from a psychoanalytic point of view on these later years, that it seems important to point out a few significant texts:

    Cohen, N. A. (1982) "On loneliness and the ageing process", *International Journal of Psychoanalysis*, 63: 149–155.
    Davenhill, R. (1989) "Working psychotherapeutically with older people", in *Clinical Psychology Forum*, 27–30.
    Hildebrand, P. (1982) "Psychotherapy with older patients", *British Journal of Medical Psychology*, 55: 19–28.
    King, P. H. M. (1980) "The life cycle as indicated by the nature of the transference in the psychoanalysis of the middle-aged and elderly", *International Journal of Psychoanalysis*, 61: 153–160.
    Limentani, A. (1995) "Creativity and the third age", *International Journal of Psychoanalysis*, 76: (4) 825–883.
    Murray-Parkes, C. (1972) *Bereavement*, London: Tavistock Press.

Segal, H. (1986) *Delusion and Artistic Creativity and Other Psychoanalytic Essays*, London: Free Association Books.

Settlage, C. (1996) "Transcending old age: Creativity, development and psychoanalysis in the life of a centenarian", *International Journal of Psychoanalysis*, 77: (3) 549–564.

2.   Quoted, Elliott Jaques (1965), p. 512.

CHAPTER FOURTEEN

The last years

"We shall not cease from exploration
And the end of all our exploring
Will be to arrive where we started
And know the place for the first time"

T. S. Eliot

Last scene of all,
That ends this strange eventful history,
Is second childishness and mere oblivion,
Sans teeth, sans eyes, sans taste, sans everything. [II, vii, 163–166]

T hese are the final words of Jacques's disquisition on the Seven Ages of Man in *As You Like It*. His reflections are prompted by an (off-stage) encounter with Touchstone (Duke Senior's clown), a meeting which is described at the beginning of the same scene. Jacques is exceedingly taken with Touchstone. He delightedly reports to Duke Senior and the outlawed court the "motley fool['s] 'pronouncements on how the world wags'."

And so, from hour to hour, we ripe and ripe,
And then, from hour to hour, we rot and rot;
And thereby hangs a tale. [II, vii, 26–28]

The "tale" is the most significant of all tales—it is that of the human condition. A central theme in this play, as in many of the comedies, relates to the necessity of incorporating the reality of endings (i.e. of loss, relinquishment, and ultimately of death) into the spirit of beginnings, and of potential beginning into the sense of an ending.

The "tale" that Shakespeare so often re-tells, explicitly and implicitly, is, at its barest, that of the importance of encompassing debility and death in any story of renewal. The straightforward statement is that "second childishness and mere oblivion" are facts of life which, at every stage and age, must be recognized and understood, not sequestered and denied, if any genuine development or understanding is to occur.

The inextricable relationship between beginnings and endings is one that I shall be tracing in quite literal terms now, in order to link together the ways in which psychoanalytic theories, clinical experience and observational work with early "childishness" may contribute very immediately, even practically, both to an understanding of "second childishness" and to how to engage with impaired and enfeebled states of mind. As *As You Like It* makes so clear, ripening and rotting are, in one sense, a straightforward matter of time, of chronological time, and although time is absolute—the next hour follows the last (Touchstone's assertion which Jacques is so taken by)—yet, as life in the Forest of Arden reveals, the important issue is what is *done* with those hours. In terms of development, as the foregoing chapters have shown, we need always to be aware that at every age the chief significance is what the hours *mean*, and how they are spent, in relation to the possibility of furthering and prolonging psychic growth or of limiting and foreclosing it. In this sense time is *not* absolute, for the extent to which we "ripe and ripe", only to "rot and rot", is dependent on the indissoluble relationship between physiological/neurological and psychological factors—between body/brain and mind. As a person physically deteriorates, early problematic psychological constellations, if unresolved, are likely to be re-played; infantile defences, if underlying anxieties remain unmodified, to be re-erected; childlike needs, if unmet, re-surface. These difficulties tend to occur the more as coping abilities fall away and raw, even abject, dependency asserts itself.

It is a full century since Freud established that a person could become mentally even physically sick for emotional and not just for organic reasons—an idea which prompted a furious response from the medical establishment—to be met by Freud's famous statement "From then on I realized that I was one who would disturb the sleep of the world".

A hundred years later we are nowhere near as far as we should be in understanding the emotional component in what are considered the organic origins of psychiatric, developmental and behavioural disturbances. In many areas the draw of the organic, medical explanation for such states still remains strong, and, of course, with the very elderly the actual deterioration is real and has to be taken centrally into account. But latterly neuroscience is itself coming up with evidence which strongly supports the research and intuitions of the so-called "folk psychologists", those of us who have long recognized the complex intimacy of the links between cognitive and emotional deficit, between organic impairment and affective disorders, between the functioning of the brain and of the mind. The issue is not only that the brain affects the mind, but that the mind affects the brain.

With some important exceptions, little psychoanalytic work has been done towards a greater understanding of the predicament of the very elderly—work of a kind which might harvest the insights of those most skilled in understanding the mind's capacity to grow and develop, and also its propensity to become stuck, deformed or fragmented. Clinicians who have engaged with the more severely disturbed adult patient, or who have been involved with the disordered and arrested development of young children, will be drawing on clinical and observational skills which are centrally relevant to the present problems.

The psychoanalytic picture of mid- and late-life stresses the ways in which a person's ability to face loss of all kinds, ultimately death, is rooted in very early capacities to bear psychic reality (see Chapter 13). At this stage there is still hope, as George Eliot put it, that "It is never too late to become the person you might have been". The present Chapter addresses that time in life when it *is* too late, in any obvious sense, and yet when the quality of mental and emotional life may still, if only very temporarily, be rendered a lot more bearable, meaningful and even enjoyable than is often recognized. Those same ways of thinking about early infantile and childlike states which have contributed to an understanding of the "later years" are particularly pertinent to the last years, those of "second childishness"—especially in relation to the joinings and fracturings involved in organic impairment, whether as a result of cortical vascular trauma (strokes) or of Alzheimer's disease, or of senile confusional states more generally (a distinction between any or all of these different states being very hard to make).

In Chapter 1, I recounted an exchange between eighty-nine-year-old Mrs Brown and her husband Eric. Basing my thoughts on detailed descriptive observations by their family, I shall now trace their lives further as, over the following two years, Mrs Brown steadily lost her lively, creative and enquiring mind to the depradations of Alzheimer's. The emphasis in this vignette was on how swiftly Mrs Brown became beset by a persecuted certainty of betrayal and abandonment by her husband, despite his many years of faithful devotion. At this point, the source of Mrs Brown's anxiety was fairly clear to any sensitive and attentive observer. She could still be reassured and given some peace of mind. Her ability, even then, to take an interest, albeit selective, in "the way the world wags" to a large extent remained. At times she would talk about death and recommend that her children be preserved from what she referred to as a *"too* ripe old age" (implicitly drawing an interesting contrast with what she clearly considered to be a reasonably positive "ripeness" in a *degree* of old age) and be allowed to rot a bit earlier than she herself, for she hated what she called "dying bit by bit".

Two years later, however, ordinary communication had ceased to be possible for Mrs Brown and the central issue became the struggle with an ever-recurring collapse of the characteristics of depressive position thinking back into a much more paranoid–schizoid state. Unlike earlier times, when Mrs Brown could swiftly re-emerge from a persecutory state, she was now in danger of remaining cut off from those about her by the seemingly impossible road-blocks of extreme old age—road-blocks to memory, recognition or shared meaning. Not only was she becoming cut off from others, but also from herself.

This is a poignant picture, and yet it may be that even *these* states are much less impenetrable than they seem. There is increasing evidence that the anxieties and mental disturbance even of the last years are often quite specifically linked to the nature of early emotional struggles. In Mrs Brown's case, as that early vignette suggests, there seem to have been underlying oedipal difficulties which had never been resolved, despite many decades of steadfast marriage and familial devotion. Following Bion, Segal, Britton, and others, the psychoanalytically-minded are especially alive to the ways in which the very early capacity to form symbols (and therefore independently to think) is rooted in the ability to bear separation, to cope with the loss of the phantasy of sole possession of the care-giver, and to tolerate being, at times, excluded from the primary pair. These are tasks of early infancy and childhood. Such capacities for "triangular" relationships—capacities which begin to develop in the first year of life—are, in turn, dependent on the relative security and mutual understanding of the primary dyadic relationship between infant and care-giver—usually the mother.

The very early managing of triangularity has much to do with later ways of negotiating oedipal constellations of whatever kind (see Chapter 5). If these earliest interactions are too disturbed, the development of thinking can itself be impaired, as well as emotional and social capacities, and a person may, for ever after, be struggling with the pains of love and loss, with fears of rejection and exclusion..

Many aspects of so-called "senility" offer close resemblances to early disturbances of thinking, relating and communicating. As we have seen in earlier Chapters, in the first or the ninety-first year, or any year in between, cognitive and emotional growth in the individual depends on the quality of emotional exchange between self and other. Whether in extreme youth or extreme age, a person has the impulse, one might even say necessity, to project feelings from the self into the other—whether in order to communicate those emotions, or to get rid of them. Much depends on whether the person acting as "container" can tolerate the disturbing projections and still go on thinking about the meaning of the experience.

It is when verbal communication is not yet developed on the one hand, or is all but lost on the other, or is put in abeyance by psychological catastrophe, that a care-giver's capacity to render meaningful the raw data, or sensa, of experience can determine the difference between "ripening" and "rotting". Following Bion's model, it is the mother's mental and emotional capacity to render the raw elements of the bodily and feeling states of her infant manageable, bearable, and thus comprehensible to the infant, that enables him or her mentally and emotionally to develop (see Chapter 7). The emotional intensity about which the baby is unable to think is projected into the feeding, nurturing, caring aspect of the mother—the "breast". The taking back in of that passionate, disturbed emotionality, now, because it is unconsciously understood, rendered amenable to meaning, forms the basis in the personality not only of a sense that emotional states have a shape and a form—and are not some long, utterly bewildered, terrifying internal or external scream—but also of a sense that the function (originally the mother's of bringing about that transformation) can itself become part of the developing personality. As we have seen, a later carer too can provide a setting and a mental attentiveness that renders him, or her, available as a thinking, containing presence whose functions can be internalized.

To return to Mrs Brown: what little her family knew of her childhood was that she suffered (like Bion himself) the emotional deprivation of being born in India during British Colonial rule, to be raised by others, albeit initially lovingly by her ayah, and sent off to school in that unthinkably distant place, "England". She scarcely knew her mentally disturbed, sadistic mother (for so she was described), nor her adored but remote, and often absent, father. Her childhood fate was to be constantly uprooted, relocated, re-disrupted and denied any consistent care or attention. During her youth and adulthood she had drawn on the resources of class and education to find ways of socially accommodating to what was expected. Yet she had never felt personally secure.

Mrs Brown had once confided to one of her daughters the painful details of her own mother's fierce, almost delusory, jealousy of, and competition with, what she felt was too close a relationship between her husband and daughter from very early days. Soon after her husband's early death, she seduced her daughter's young lover. Mrs Brown felt forever scarred by this betrayal and by the loss of the man to whom she was, at that time, so deeply devoted. She described herself as constantly having struggled to conceal her terrors over exclusion and her tendency towards "relegation", as she would put it, to the league of those who "service" rather than of those who "exercise power".

It is certainly true that fear of abandonment and inability to bear separateness are characteristic of dementia sufferers and that these persecutory states of mind increase with organic impairment. It is nonetheless striking that, in Mrs Brown's case, it was precisely the complexity of triangularity, and the assaults of jealous rage and anxiety that caused her particular distress. The horror of being pushed out and replaced had undermined her confidence since early childhood and had never quite been laid to rest. In advanced years, as she lost her acquired social skills, it was these old infantile insecurities that began to reassert themselves with an intensity that was scarcely imaginable. There follow some brief descriptions of simple situations in which her relatives' capacities for containment enabled them to render inchoate, or apparently random fragments of communication, not only meaningful, but also of evident support in maintaining contact, and even in re-forging old links, thus momentarily re-igniting the embers of a former self. The situations describe Mrs Brown in her ninety-first year. She had lost the capacity to remember or to think in any sustained or obviously recognizable way. She was becoming averse to anything new, and often to life itself. She had long been losing words, except for the most formal of learned, habitual responses. These were the last to go—the relatively mindless attention to proper enquiry and concern: "You must be so tired". "Did it take you long to get here?"—a lifetime of practice in "how-very-kind-of yous"—the *mores* of polite society. She could still take her cues for response from details of her companions' expression and intonation, based on her exceptional sight and hearing which remained blessedly unimpaired. This ability of hers often obscured how little she was, in fact, understanding.

As has long been established in the context of infants and children, changes of surrounding or of care-giver began to cause Mrs Brown acute anxiety. The insight and understanding accorded to the very young over matters of separation from the loved and dependable one, or from the familiar setting has, as yet, had little impact on the care of the very elderly. For them, too, searing and de-stabilizing "homesickness" for the site of psychic security can set in within an instant of any alteration of context. One of Mrs Brown's much-loved daughters unexpectedly arrived to stay for the weekend. The setting was immediately different. Mrs Brown looked at her husband, Eric, with intense anxiety: "Are we still at home Eric?"

At some point later that day, Eric got up to leave the room. In his turn challenged by his own increasing forgetfulness, he paused half way to the door and clasped his hands behind his back, indicating self-irony as much as frustration—his characteristic pose when having lost track of *his* original purpose. Mrs Brown pointed to his hands and gazed at her daughter with what was later described as "almost youthful delight". Insistently she pointed again at Eric's posture, her finger crooked for emphasis. Her daughter said, smilingly, "Yes, good old Dad, he's forgotten something". Mrs Brown laughed. Eric collected himself again and left the room, shutting the door behind him. Mrs Brown looked suddenly terrified: "When is he coming back? where has he gone?" "I think he's remembered something he wants in the kitchen. He'll be back in a moment." Mrs Brown remained anxious. Her daughter wondered aloud, "Would it help if he told you what he was doing, and where he was going, so that you would know?" Her mother nodded.

In this simple set of interactions, one can trace the almost moment-by-moment shifts in states of mind so characteristic of the infant or young child. The shared, humorous understanding between mother and daughter of the meaning of Eric's gesture of uncertainty occurred within an assured sense of available and communicable meaning. The daughter was able rightly to interpret her mother's mood, gesture and gaze and to articulate it—much as a sensitive therapist might speak to a wordless child, or a parent to a baby. It was clear, however, that when the door shut, Eric's unexplained absence made his wife feel utterly cut off from her base, and as terrified as any infant registering loss of the needed presence and feeling, as a consequence, overwhelming abandonment and dread—"He's gone"; "He's never coming back"; "I'm all alone in the world" etc. What was required, and what, as a result of her daughter's observation, subsequently became a habit in the household, was some simple explanation of the kind that a mother might offer a young child: "I'm just going to do X, I'll be back in a minute". Mrs Brown's emotional state could be described as shifting from depressive to paranoid–schizoid and back to depressive again in a way that was exquisitely related to the psychically disturbing experience of being, at one moment, safely held within a shared triangular psychic structure (husband–daughter–self) and at the next, feeling severed from her source of safety and, as a result, in some kind of emotional free fall.

Mrs Brown's unresolved oedipal anxieties and the associated guilt, fear and longing had, despite impressive social accommodation, nonetheless persisted throughout her adult life. As her social defences, and more importantly her memory, fell away and actual mental impairment compounded the underlying emotional difficulties, she became anguishingly prey to her tormenting jealousy, and increasingly incapable of negotiating the hazards of relating to more than one other.

Her son recounted an occasion on which, just before lunch, his mother was sitting by the fire with a glass of wine beside her, but not, as yet, her customary, once daily, cigarette. Son and husband were holding an animated conversation. As usual, they included her, but only by eye contact. Her son observed his mother agitatedly reaching for a matchbox. As she struck successive matches with her right hand, her left hand moved, scarcely perceptibly, towards her mouth. She would glance at the "couple" with apparent irritation, shake the match to extinguish it, and cast it into the fire. This occurred many times over. Her son, who was observing these details while yet discoursing with his father, came over to her smiling: "Is it that by lighting a match, you think that the cigarette you are hoping for will somehow materialize?" Mrs Brown looked uncertain, smiled, and then nodded as if in affirmation. (What he did not register was the likelihood of his mother's unconscious wish to extinguish or burn up one or other of her rivals.)

These examples bring to mind a recent study of the significance of "joint attention skills" and of "gaze monitoring", which is effectively what was going on between Mrs Brown and her daughter and son. Child psychotherapist, Anna Burhouse (1999) brings together concepts from cognitive psychology, child development research and psychoanalysis, with her own observations of young infants. She focuses, in particular, on impairments in the formation of triangular mental space with special reference to the severe difficulties in relating characteristic of the autistic spectrum. Many aspects of this research have an important bearing on the understanding of the kinds of problems associated with the very elderly, as the following examples indicate.

Lost for words, Mrs Brown would characteristically point to a focus of stimulation and interest and then look to a secure companion, as if sometimes anticipating a shared response. At other times, more anxiously, she would look for confirmation or enlightenment. When she encountered an emotional presence of mind which could appreciate and engage with the substance of her communication, or could find a meaning where as yet, for her, there was none, she was able to make something of it—to enjoy the fact that something had been understood. This was particularly the case when she seemed to be wishing to articulate her sense of beauty— the sky, birds and flowers were among her few remaining sources of interest and pleasure. As if holding a wand, she would gently and wordlessly waft a hand in the direction of some object which attracted her. This would be followed by an intense and often quizzical look at her companion, and back again to the bird or flower, and then, in turn, back to her companion. When the sensed meaning of her gestures was articulated in simple terms—"Isn't that evening sky absolutely lovely"—Mrs Brown would break into a smile of serene pleasure.

These were indeed moments of intense communication between herself and one other. But when a third factor was involved, things were different. The following incident occurred on a day when Mrs Brown's jealousy and anxiety about exclusion had already been aroused. The occasion of this disturbance was a card addressed to Eric, from an elderly widow, wishing him a swift recovery following a recent medical problem. Mrs Brown was to be observed staring at the card, opening and shutting it for quite long periods of time and repeatedly muttering to herself, "Love from Lily"—the words written in the card. She seemed to become irritable at Eric's temporary, unusual debility and was herself more physically dependent than usual. At one point she limped across the room, leaning heavily on her frame. Eric was observing her. He looked stricken and sad, but was unable to help. When he said to her, "Mind the carpet" (meaning "don't trip over it") she crossly commented to her son "All he can think about is the carpet". She proceeded on her way, looking back every few steps to scrutinize her husband's face, half mocking and, it almost seemed, half jeering. Was this change of mood related to trying, as a defense against her anxiety, to gang up with her son on her unusually fragile husband? Was she seeking to make Eric feel useless (*"he* can't help"), to crow, for once, over *his* helplessness?

The next day, the three of them were in the kitchen. Mrs Brown was sitting holding a yellow, checked washing-up cloth. There was a bit of rubbish lying in front of her on the table. She pointed to it questioningly, as if to say, "Where does this go?" and looked at Eric. Misunderstanding her "question", and thinking that she was referring to the rubbish, Eric replied, slightly impatiently, "Over there", nodding towards the bin. His wife stared at him uncomprehendingly—seeming to know that something was wrong but not being able to work out what it could be. She demurred. Fleetingly she glanced down at the cloth and then at herself: "That's a terrible thing to say" she muttered. Ignoring this comment (Mrs Brown clearly thinking that he had meant that she herself was a piece of rubbish) Eric insisted irritably, "In there, in the proper place". She looked unhappy and continued to dither, arousing further irritation in her husband who quite suddenly left the room. Her son put the rubbish in the bin and also left the room, without, on this occasion, the emotional resources to pause and try to understand what the problem really was. Later Eric found the yellow, checked cloth carefully folded and placed on top of the bin. Recalling the incident he described himself as feeling very guilty: his wife had so wanted to be obedient, and to do the right thing, but had been unable to sort out her muddle between the rubbish, herself and the cloth. She had tried to follow instructions but was mystified by her residual sense that the yellow checked cloth was *not* something that should be put in the bin, and nor, indeed, was she herself—although her life-long tendency to feel like rubbish had temporarily taken on a confused but all too concrete reality for her.

The following morning, Eric had to go into hospital for the day for a further check. Despite having been carefully prepared for his departure, Mrs Brown was intensely anxious, repeating angrily "He didn't say he was going. He didn't tell me". There was an exceptionally strong wind blowing that day and Mrs Brown stared into the garden, distraught at the swaying, cracking branches of the nearby trees. She turned to her daughter with an air of a terrified child, and said, pleadingly, falteringly, "Home [long pause] ... where's home? [another pause]. Take me home ... *please*". Instead of swiftly reassuring her ("You *are* at home, mum. Look, here are the flowers I brought this morning"—or some such thing), her daughter tried to understand something of her mother's state of terror. She talked to her quietly about the crashing and banging. She remembered that on the night of the mighty 1989 storm her mother had also been terrified, telling her afterwards that she had thought it was war-time again. She now suggested that her mother might be feeling that she was back in London, that the war was on and that "home" meant the Old Brompton Road flat. Mrs Brown looked momentarily puzzled and then murmured "Yes. [pause] But I can't see anyone with guns out there." As her daughter drew the curtains and talked to her mother about why the high wind in the trees was so distressing, the old lady's anxiety began to subside. It was as if the room became itself again and not an alien place where she was stranded and desolate.

In their different ways, these examples show how glimmers of light can be thrown on the nature of impaired and confusional states. One facet of the picture which these glimmers reveal is the fact that, whether in infancy or in old age, development runs unevenly; that the situation is not quite as Touchstone had described it—a steady process of ripening followed by a steady process of rotting.

From the incidents described it is possible to see how helpful to an understanding of the opaque mental states of old age might be the skills of those who work with similarly opaque mental and emotional states in childhood. Such professionals have a very particular experience of the power of infantile transference; of the way in which a mother's unconscious registering, reflecting and thinking, gives *meaning* to the infant's world—a meaning which is communicated in her responsive care; or of how, in the language of developmental psychology, "gaze monitoring" may yield insight into an infant's needs and intentions. By the mechanism of projective identification the baby/child/old person who cannot understand, think or talk about his or her fragmentary, or fragmenting experience, may nonetheless be able to engender in the care-giver some version of that basic experience. If, as we have seen, the care-giver can offer a mentally receptive state of mind, conscious or unconscious, the communication can be received, modified, if it is one of pain and rage, appreciated if one of love and pleasure, and re-communicated, whether in more manageable, or in reciprocal mode. The care-giver's mind functions as a container for, and a sorter of, the projected emotional fragments which, as a consequence, become "the contained". Care of the very elderly, those so often lacking the capacity to speak, yet so intensely riven by extreme emotional states, requires a painful reversal of the original pattern of container/contained (the young now struggling to offer states of reverie to the old).

We are familiar with observing how the behaviour of the baby is fostered by its relationship with its primary sources of love and care, but the foregoing describes the same sort of value of receptiveness to elderly as to infantile emotional experience. The turbulence of feeling, whether of joy, frustration, helplessness, rage, fear, pleasure, persecution, is quite as intense in the old as in the young and test the care-taker in equivalently extreme ways. In these situations the carers too have much to learn and may themselves be enriched. As Margaret Rustin (1991) says: "The capacity to contain and observe emotionally powerful psychic phenomena is the basis for knowledge of oneself, and for that contact with psychic reality which is at the core of an authentic personality" (p. 244).

Mrs Brown was fortunate to have, in Eric, a loving, sensitive and deeply patient husband who had an unusual "untrained" capacity to bear his wife's states of mind. She was also fortunate to have children who were, in their different ways, experienced in the so-called "caring" professions. They were "good enough" at knowing when her insistent pointing to an object indicated, for example, a request, or a plea for enlightenment, or whether it asserted a demand or, by contrast, was a communication of feeling in a situation of shared intimacy. At such times of inwardness with her specific state of mind it was possible to observe a distinctive renewal of cognitive capacities in Mrs Brown's now very limited range. That is, despite in all obvious respects "rotting", Mrs Brown was still able, however briefly, to "ripen"—to a point that could, at times, even feel like a momentary late flowering.

Each time this occurred it was as if mental pathways which had seemed to be totally overgrown, or mysteriously to diverge where once there had been a single track, had for a moment, cleared, or miraculously re-joined. For her, as we have seen, the times of greatest anxiety were those of being unable to tolerate feeling at the lonely point of the Oedipal triangle, fearing that two others could come together only if one, usually herself, were excluded. Unable to speak or to think clearly at such times, Mrs Brown would seek, as in the cigarette incident, primitive reassurance (as if from breast or dummy). At other times she would become angry, and, on occasions, abusive. Mentally to hold these latter states required immense emotional resources of her carers. They had to bear their own impatience, anger and at times even hatred as part of their love.

The kinds of interaction described above became rarer and rarer as Mrs Brown's Alzheimer's made ever more destructive claims on her mental capacities. She physically deteriorated, became wholly dependent and increasingly silent. Eventually this protracted "second childishness" yielded to "mere oblivion". By the time that point was reached, the "mere" of Jacques's account seemed less stark and challenging, and more appropriate than first reading suggests. For after so long a struggle in life, Mrs Brown's death seemed, to her loved ones, and almost certainly to herself, to be a matter of lesser importance, a comparatively easy thing. She had had enough. She had lived out Jacques's "last scene of all".

This book has been about the rewards of understanding the meaning of one's experience and about the difficulties of so doing; the difficulties of developing a mind of one's own, of becoming oneself. The process of finding one's own place in the world from one generation to the next needs constant mental and emotional work, from the earliest struggles of the unborn child to those of the final years of life. It involves learning from others without merely becoming like them, and imparting to others without seeking to bind them. It involves conflict, but also opens limitless possibilities. For life need not be a vale of tears but rather is a vale of Soul-making, the process on which is founded the growth of the mind, the development of the personality.

Notes

There is very little written about the area addressed in this Chapter. I include a few helpful references.

Davenhill, R., & Rustin, M. (1999). Age. In: D. Taylor (Ed.), *Talking Cure: Mind and Method of the Tavistock Clinic*. London: Duckworth.

King, P. (1999). In the end is my beginning. In: D. Bell (Ed.), *Psychoanalysis and Culture: A Kleinian Perspective*. London: Duckworth.

Kitwood, T. (1987). Dementia and its pathology: in brain, mind or society? *Free Associations, 8*.

Kitwood, T. (1987). Explaining senile dementia: the limits of neuropathological research', *Free Associations, 10*.

McKenzie-Smith, S. (1992). A psychoanalytical observational study of the elderly. *Free Associations, 3/3(27)*.

Schore, A. (1997). A century after Freud's project—is a rapprochement between psychoanalysis and neurobiology at hand? *Journal of the American Psychoanalytic Association, 45*.

Sinason, V. (1992). The man who was losing his brain. In: *Mental Handicap and the Human Condition: New Approaches from the Tavistock*. London: Free Association Books.

Appendix

There are certain complex ideas which are fundamental to the story of development at whatever age or stage. They are somewhat opaque, even to those who are already familiar with them, and quite mystifying to those less well-versed in psychoanalytic theory. They are, in particular, the mechanisms of projective and introjective identification, and the concept of the Oedipus Complex. These notions continue to be much discussed, and still do not readily lend themselves to definition. In the course of the book, as different versions of them appear and re-appear, they gradually acquire further shape and meaning. But they need to be described in their most simple form.

The psychological mechanisms of projection and introjection have their analogy in the physical processes of expelling and of taking in. They are basic modes of establishing and conducting relationships; as basic as nourishment and elimination. Projection and introjection are the channels for the traffic of conscious and unconscious feeling between self and other. In the development of the personality, much depends on the force, the quality, the intensity, the fluidity or the intransigence of these mechanisms.

The baby initially relates to the world, and takes it in, via his experience of his mother. Because she is his whole world, he is exquisitely sensitive to her moods. Her laugh will make him smile; her sadness will make him frown. When a baby is angry he is totally angry. With his whole being he perceives his mother as the source of his pain and anger. He feels bad. He wants to get rid of this feeling. He thrusts it back into its supposed source, namely his mother. In his eyes his mother herself then becomes bad. And so he takes in the sense of having a bad mother. He has a bad mother within him. When she comforts and feeds him, and he has a good feeling, his mother again becomes good. He "projects" his bad feeling and identifies her with it. He "introjects" his experience of her as calm, satisfying and good, and he himself acquires a good feeling within. He feels himself to *be* "good".

If, on the other hand, he continually experiences a mother who rejects his communications, and who seems to be impervious to his feelings, repeatedly meeting them with an emotional "blank wall", then the baby introjects something which is unresponsive to the communication of feeling, and he himself may also become so. That is, he feels himself to be some version of the qualities and characteristics which he experiences first as belonging to his mother, and then as belonging to him himself.

The texture of a person's experience is made up by a constant interplay between these projective and introjective mechanisms. Each term is confusing, because psychoanalytic theory draws on each of these mechanisms to understand so many different ideas and functions. Together, in effect, "projection" and "introjection" characterize the nature and meaning of one person's communication with another. The terms comprehend a range of motives on the part of the self (coming from different degrees of need, anxiety or security), and a range of responses on the part of the other.

When Klein first formulated the mechanism of projective identification, she described it as having different emphases and intensities. She pointed to the projection of good feelings as being the basis of empathy. She also suggested that the infant needed to get rid of, or to disown his bad feelings because they were too much for him to bear. Later, other psychoanalysts hypothesized further motives: that the baby might be seeking to feel indissolubly linked to his mother, for example, or to be the same as her, or in control of her, or, indeed, simply in communication with her. In relation to this last, Bion drew attention to the fact that these projective processes, even those which seemed to be mainly for the purpose of the evacuation of bad feelings, also contained, almost always, a germ of communication. As the infant begins to realize that his crying elicits a particular response, more and more does that crying become an attempt to communicate—to communicate to his mother the fact that he is in pain, or in distress.

As far as the response on the part of the mother is concerned, the term "projective identification" describes the phantasy on the baby's part that his mother herself feels whatever it is that he is directing towards her or is seeking to "put into" her. He feels that his mother has become the embodiment of those feelings. The mother then becomes the hated and hating self. But the term can also describe the reality of her *actually* being affected, if the original emotion or impulse is a particularly strong one, and the force behind it is powerful and relentless. For a terrified baby can instil fear in his mother. She may begin to feel his feelings of fear in *reality*. She may even *act* on these feelings. Here "projective identification" involves something being put into, or pushed into, somebody else. Psychoanalytic theory concerns itself with why it is so put, or pushed; and what then happens to it.

Where an infant's cry or smile goes without any answering echo in the mother, there will be no opportunity for the baby to take back in, or to introject an experience of having painful feelings understood and held by a mind, or by an emotional presence, that is felt to have the care and capacity to make things bearable for him. The bad "something" that is felt will be taken back in; it will be a "something" which is experienced as not fitting, or as a "foreign body", or as a persecutory feeling inside. In order for the baby to achieve or maintain any kind of peace of mind, this "something" will have to be got rid of again, to be re-projected.

In this book, because the main focus is on development rather than on pathology, our chief concern with the introjective process is a positive one. We have not dwelt very much on sequences such as this last, where there is immediate projection–introjection-and-re-projection. Nor have we dwelt very much on those longer-term processes, where there is introjection in the course of which the baby builds up a sense of himself as somehow the same as, or engulfed by, a non-responding, cold or distracted mother, and he comes to feel *himself* to be just such a person. We have not dwelt on those sequences, although they do make their appearance in some of the case-histories reported.

Returning to the simpler case of introjection, the experience of a sensitive, responsive mother increasingly allows the baby to feel himself also to be sensitive and responsive. He takes in an experience (the pleasure of being fed or of being thought about) which he stores within—a picture of loving eyes, or an impression of being physically and emotionally contained. This is felt as if it is an *actual* taking-in of the mother's capacities (of the holding and of the loving capacities), as if these capacities were concrete objects. Through this process being repeated, the infant begins to feel the containing, loving mother as a definite presence within himself, as part of himself. Thus he himself gradually develops the capacity also to be containing and loving.

Introjective identification of this more positive kind leads to the strengthening of the personality, in-so-far as the baby has been able slowly to absorb good experiences, experiences which have modified infantile fears and anxieties. There is less and less necessity for the insistent or forceful projection–introjection–re-projection of the rather desperate kind which characterizes early persecutory states. Simple introjection encourages the capacity to be separate, and with separateness goes the increasing capacity to think for oneself and to be oneself.

Projection and introjection can be described in this sort of way, by reference to their simplest forms. An observer, armed with ideas about them, can make sense of all sorts of human interrelations in this way. By further observation and hypothesis we learn more about them. They cannot lend themselves to outright definitions. As Martha Harris (1978) said:

> Introjection remains a mysterious process: how do involvement and reliance upon objects in the external world which are apprehended by the senses (and, Wilfred Bion has pointed out, described in a language which has been evolved to deal with external reality), become assimilated in the mind into what he calls the "psycho-nalytic object" which can contribute to the growth of the sonality; this is a process about which we have almost every-ᶾ to learn. [p. 168]

ᴎ and introjection, like so many other processes, are

inherently problematic notions. They are constantly relied upon and further elaborated in the course of the book. This Appendix is intended to enable the reader to start where our account of these things starts.

The Oedipus Complex is something that we often return to in relation to different ages and stages of development. Although Freud himself drew on the drama that Sophocles based upon the myth, the brief account of the myth itself in the *The Oxford Companion to Classical Literature* (1937), ed. Harvey, offers many sources of interest and resonance, which may be kept in mind as bearing on the immensely important influences, in developmental terms, of family legacies, both conscious and unconscious, from one generation to the next.

Oedipus (OIDIPOUS), in Greek mythology, the son of Laius, the King of Thebes. When Amphion and Zethus gained possession of Thebes, Laius had taken refuge with Pelops, but had ill-requited his kindness by kidnapping his son, Chrysippus, thereby bringing a curse on his own family. Laius recovered his kingdom after the death of Amphion and Zethus, and married Jocasta, but was warned by Apollo that their son would kill him. Accordingly, when Oedipus was born, a spike was driven through his feet and he was exposed on Mount Cithaeron. There a shepherd found him and he was taken to Polybus, King of Corinth, and Merope, his queen, who brought him up as her own son. Later, being taunted with being no true son of Polybus, Oedipus enquired of the Delphic Oracle concerning his parentage, but was only told that he would slay his father and wed his mother. Thinking this referred to Polybus and Merope, he determined never to see Corinth again. At a place where three roads met, he encountered Laius (whom he did not know) and was ordered to make way. A quarrel followed in which Oedipus slew Laius. He went on to Thebes, which was at that time plagued by a Sphinx, a monster which asked people riddles and killed those who could not answer them. Creon, brother of Jocasta, the Regent of Thebes, offered the kingdom of Thebes to whoever should rid the country of this pest. Oedipus solved the riddle of the Sphinx, which thereupon killed itself. [Oedipus] became King of Thebes and married Jocasta. They had two sons, Eteocles and Polynices, and two daughters, Ismene and Antigone. At last, in a time of death and pestilence, the oracle announced that these disasters would be averted if the slayer of Laius was expelled from the city. Oedipus thereupon set about discovering who had killed Laius. The result was to establish that he himself was Laius's son and his murderer. On this discovery Jocasta hanged herself and Oedipus blinded himself. Oedipus was deposed and banished. He wandered, attended by Antigone, to Colonus in Attica where he was protected by Theseus and died. [p. 292]

Select bibliography

Abrams, M. H. (1953). Changing metaphors of the mind. In: *The Mirror and the Lamp: Romantic Theory and the Critical Tradition*. Oxford: O.U.P.

Anderson, R., & Dartington, A. (Eds) (1998). *Facing it Out: Clinical Perspectives on Adolescent Disturbance*. London: Duckworth.

Austen, J. (1816). *Emma*. Harmondsworth: Penguin [reprint Blythe, R., 1973].

Barrie, J. M. (1911). *Peter Pan*. London: Everyman.

Bick, E. (1968). The experience of the skin in early object relations. *International Journal of Psycho-Analysis*, 49: 484–486 [reprint in: Harris, M., & Bick, E. (1987). *Collected Papers of Martha Harris and Esther Bick*. Strath Tay, Perthshire: Clunie Press].

Bion, W. R. (1959). Attacks on linking. *International Journal of Psycho-Analysis*, 40: 308–315 [reprint in: Bion, W. R. (1967). *Second Thoughts*. London: Heinemann].

Bion, W. R. (1961). *Experiences in Groups*. London: Tavistock Publications [reprint London: Routledge].

Bion, W. R. (1962a). A theory of thinking. *International Journal of Psycho-Analysis*, 43: 306–310 [reprint in: Bion, W. R. (1967) Second Thoughts. London: Heinemann].

Bion, W. R. (1962b). *Learning from Experience*. London: Heinemann.

Bion, W. R. (1963). *Elements of Psycho-Analysis*. London: Heinemann.

Bion, W. R. (1970). *Attention and Interpretation*. London: Tavistock Publications.

Blythe, R. (1966). *Emma* [Introduction], Austen, J. Harmondsworth: Penguin.

Bowlby, J., & Winnicott, D. W. (1939). Letter: "Evacuation of small children". *British Medical Journal*, 16th December: 1202–1203.

Bowlby, J., Miller, E., & Winnicott, D. (1939). *British Medical Journal*, 16th December, 1202–1203.

Britton, R. (1992). The oedipus situation and the depressive position. In: R. Anderson (Ed.), *Clinical Lectures on Klein and Bion*. London: Routledge.

Britton, R. (1998). Subjectivity, objectivity and triangular space. In: *Belief and Imagination*. London: Routledge.

Brontë, C. *Jane Eyre*. Harmondsworth: Penguin.

Burhouse, A. (1999). *Me, You and It*: Conversations about the significance of joint attention skills from cognitive psychology, child development research and psychoanalysis. MA Diss (unpubl.).

Coote, S. (1995). *John Keats: A Life*. London: Hodder and Stoughton.

Copley, B. (1993). *The World of Adolescence: Literature, Society and Psychoanalytic Psychotherapy*. London: Free Association Books.

Deutsch, H. (1934). Ueber einen typus der pseudoaftektivitaet ("als ob"). *Zeitschrift fuer Psychoanalyse*, 20: 323–335.

Eliot, G. (1859). *Adam Bede*, reprint Harmondsworth: Penguin, 1985.

Eliot, G. (1872). *Middlemarch*, reprint Harmondsworth: Penguin, 1985.

Eliot, G. (1876). *Daniel Deronda*, reprint Harmondsworth: Penguin, 1986.

Eliot, T. S. (1957). *On Poetry and Poets*. London: Faber and Faber.

Fox, P. (1989). *A Likely Place*. New York: Houghton Mifflin Co.

Freud, A. (1958). Adolescence. *Psychoanalytic Study of the Child*, 13: 255–278.

Freud, S. (1905). Three Essays on the Theory of Sexuality. In: *The Standard Edition of the Complete Psychological Works of Sigmund Freud, Vol. 20*. London: Hogarth Press, 1955.

Freud, S. (1911). Formulations on the Two Principles of Mental Functioning. *S.E., 12*.

Freud, S. (1925). Inhibitions, Symptoms and Anxiety. *S.E., 20*.

Freud, S. (1933). The Dissection of the Psychical Personality. *S.E., 22*.

Freud, S. (1933). Femininity. *S.E., 22*.

Harris, M. (1970). Some notes on maternal containment in 'good-enough' mothering. In: *The Collected Papers of Martha Harris and Esther Bick*. Strath Tay, Perthshire: Clunie Press, 1987.

Harris, M. (1975). *Thinking About Infants and Young Children*. Strath Tay, Perthshire: Clunie Press.

Harris, M., & Meltzer, D. (1977). Family patterns and educability. In: D. Meltzer (Ed.), *Studies in Extended Metapsychology*. Strath Tay, Perthshire, Clunie Press, 1986.

Harris, M. (1978). Towards learning from experience in infancy and childhood. In: *The Collected Papers of Martha Harris and Esther Bick*. Strath Tay, Perthshire: Clunie Press, 1987.

Harris, M. (1981). The individual in the group: on learning to work with the psychoanalytical method. In: *The Collected Papers of Martha Harris and Esther Bick*. Strath Tay, Perthshire: Clunie Press, 1987.

Heaney, S. (1966). *Death of a Naturalist*. London: Faber and Faber.

Hinshelwood, R. D. (1989). *A Dictionary of Kleinian Thought*. London: Free Association Books.

Hodgson Burnett, F. (1905). *The Little Princess*. Harmondsworth: Puffin.

Hodgson Burnett, F. (1911). *The Secret Garden*. Harmondsworth: Puffin.

Isaacs, S. (1948). *Childhood and After*. London: Routledge and Kegan Paul.

Jaques, E. (1965). Death and the mid-life crisis. *International Journal of Psycho-Analysis*, 46: 502–514.

Jones, E. (1922). Some problems of adolescence. *British Journal of Psychology*, 13: 31–47.

Joseph, B. (1997). *Psychic Structure and Psychic Change: Therapeutic Factors in Psychoanalysis*. Paper given at University College London, February, 1997.

Keats, J. *Letters of John Keats*, R. Gittings (Ed.). Oxford: O.U.P., 1987

Keats, J. *John Keats, The Complete Poems*. Harmondsworth: Penguin Classics, 1988

Klein, M. (1921). The development of a child. *International Journal of Psycho-Analysis*, 4: 419–474.

Klein, M. (1923). The role of the school in the libidinal development of the child. In: M. Klein (Ed.), *Love, Guilt and Reparation and Other Works, 1921–1945*. London: Hogarth, 1985.

Klein, M. (1923b). The role of the school in the libidinal development of the child. *International Journal of Psycho-Analysis*, 5: 312–331.

Klein, M. (1928). Early stages of the oedipus complex. In: M. Klein (Ed.), *Love, Guilt and Reparation and Other Works, 1921–1945*. London: Hogarth, 1985.

Klein, M. (1929). Personification in the play of children. *International Journal of Psycho-Analysis*, 9: 193–204.

Klein, M. (1931). A contribution to the theory of intellectual inhibition.

In: M. Klein (Ed.), *Love, Guilt and Reparation and Other Works, 1921–1945*. London: Hogarth, 1985.

Klein, M. (1935). A contribution to the psychogenesis of manic-depressive states. *International Journal of Psycho-Analysis, 16*: 145–174 [reprint in *Contributions to Psychoanalysis 1921–1945*. London: Hogarth, 1973].

Klein, M. (1940). Mourning and its relation to manic-depressive states. In: *International Journal of Psycho-Analysis 1921–1945*. London: Hogarth, 1973.

Klein, M. (1940). Mourning and its relation to manic–depressive states. In: M. Klein (Ed.), *Love, Guilt and Reparation and Other Works, 1921–1945*. London: Hogarth, 1985.

Klein, M. (1946). Notes on some schizoid mechanisms. In: M. Klein (Ed.), *Envy, Gratitude and Other Works, 1946–1963*. London: Hogarth, 1975.

Klein, M. (1952). Some theoretical conclusions regarding the emotional life of the infant. In: M. Klein (Ed.), *Envy, Gratitude and Other Works, 1946–1963*. London: Hogarth, 1975.

Klein, M. (1955). On identification. In: M. Klein (Ed.), *Envy, Gratitude and Other Works, 1946–1963*. London: Hogarth, 1975.

Klein, M. (1957). Envy and gratitude. In: M. Klein (Ed.), *Envy and Gratitude and Other Works, 1946–1963*. London: Hogarth, 1987.

Klein, M. (1958). On the development of mental functioning. In: M. Klein (Ed.), *Envy, Gratitude and Other Works, 1946–1963*. London: Hogarth, 1975.

Klein, M. (1959). Our adult world and its roots in infancy. In: M. Klein (Ed.), *Envy, Gratitude and Other Works, 1946–1963*. London: Hogarth, 1975.

Meltzer, D. (1967). *The Psycho-Analytic Process*. London: Heinemann.

Meltzer, D. (1973). *Sexual States of Mind*. Strath Tay, Perthshire: Clunie Press.

Meltzer, D. (1978). A note on introjective processes. In: A. Hahn (Ed.), (1994) *Sincerity and Other Works: Collected Papers of Donald Meltzer*. London: Karnac, 1994.

Meltzer, D. (1988). *The Apprehension of Beauty*. Strath Tay, Perthshire: Clunie Press.

O'Shaughnessy, E. (1964), The absent object. *Journal of Child Psychotherapy, 1*(2): 134–143.

Piontelli, A. (1992). *From Foetus to Child: An Observational and Psychoanalytic Study*. London: Routledge.

Parker, R. (1995). *Torn in Two: The Experience of Maternal Ambivalence*. London: Virago.

Rivière, J. (1937). Hate, greed and aggression. In: J. Rivière (Ed.), *Love, Hate and Reparation*. New York: Norton.

Rivière, J. (1952). The unconscious phantasy of an inner world reflected in examples from English literature. *International Journal of Psycho-Analysis, 33*: 160–172 [reprint in: M. Klein, P. Heimann & R. Money-Kyrle (Eds), (1955) *New Directions in Psycho-Analysis* (pp. 346–369). London: Tavistock Publications].

Rustin, M., & Rustin, M. (1987). *Narratives of Love and Loss. Studies in Modern Children's Fiction*. London: Verso.

Rustin, M., & Trowell, J. (1991). Developing the internal observer in professionals in training. *Infant Mental Health Journal, 12*(3).

Segal, H. (1957). Notes on symbol formation. *International Journal of Psycho-Analysis, 38*: 391–397 [reprint in: E. B. Spillius (Ed.), (1988) *Melanie Klein Today, Vol. I: Mainly Theory*. London: Routledge].

Segal, H. (1994). Salman Rushdie and the sea of stories: a not-so-simple fable about creativity. *International Journal of Psycho-Analysis, 75*: 611–618 [reprint in: J. Steiner (Ed.), (1997) *Psychoanalysis, Literature and War*. London: Routledge].

Shakespeare, W. *A Midsummer Night's Dream*. The Arden Shakespeare ed. London: Routledge, 1991; *As You Like It*. The Arden Shakespeare ed. London: Routledge, 19??.

Shuttleworth, J. (1989). Psychoanalytic theory and infant development. In: L. Miller *et al.* (Eds), *Closely Observed Infants* (pp. 22–51). London: Duckworth.

Spillius, E. (1992). [Preface to Piontelli, A. (1992)] *From Fetus to Child: An Observational and Psychoanalytical Study*. London: Routledge.

Spillius, E. B. (1994). Developments in Kleinian thought: overview and personal view. *Psycho-Analytic Inquiry, 14*:(13), 324–364.

Steiner, J. (1996). The aim of psychoanalysis in theory and in practice. *International Journal of Psycho-Analysis, 77*:(6) 1073–1083.

Tanner, T. (1986). *Jane Austen*. London: Macmillan.

Thomson, M. (1989). *On Art and Therapy: an exploration*. London: Virago [reprint London: Free Association Books, 1997].

Wilde, O. (1892). *Lady Windermere's Fan*. London: Ernest Benn.

Williams, G. (1997). Some reflections on some dynamics of eating disorders: 'No Entry' defences and foreign bodies. *International Journal of Psycho-Analysis, 78*:(5) 927–941.

Williams, G. (1998). *Internal Landscapes and Foreign Bodies: Eating Disorders and Other Pathologies*. London: Duckworth.

Williams, M. H. (1986). Knowing the mystery: against reductionism.

Encounter, 67(1).

Williams, M. H., & Waddell, M. (1991). *The Chamber of Maiden Thought: Literary Origins of the Psychoanalytic Model of the Mind*. London: Routledge.

Winnicott, D. W. (1958). *Through Paediatrics to Psycho-Analysis*. London: Hogarth.

Winnicott, D. W. (1965). *The Maturational Process and the Facilitating Environment*. London: Hogarth.

Wordsworth, W. *William Wordsworth*, S. Gill (Ed.). Oxford: O.U.P., 1984.

Yeats, W. B. (1933). *Collected Poems*. London: Macmillan.

Index